ENGLISH Essentials

THE LANGAN SERIES

Essay-Level

College Writing Skills, Eighth Edition
ISBN: 0-07-337-165-0 (Copyright © 2011)

College Writing Skills with Readings, Eighth Edition
ISBN: 0 07 337166-1 (Copyright © 2011)

Paragraph-Level

English Skills, Tenth Edition
ISBN: 0-07-353330-0 (Copyright © 2012)

English Skills with Readings, Eighth Edition
ISBN: 0-07-337168-8 (Copyright © 2012)

Reading

Reading and Study Skills, Tenth Edition
ISBN: 0-07-353331-9 (Copyright © 2013)

Sentence-Level

Sentence Skills: A Workbook for Writers, Form A, Ninth Edition
ISBN: 0-07-337169-6 (Copyright © 2011)

Sentence Skills: A Workbook for Writers, Form B, Eighth Edition
ISBN: 0-07-353327-0 (Copyright © 2009)

Sentence Skills with Readings, Fourth Edition
ISBN: 0-07-353326-2 (Copyright © 2010)

Grammar Review

English Brushup, Fifth Edition
ISBN: 0-07-337163-7 (Copyright © 2011)

Sentence-to-Paragraph

Exploring Writing: Sentences and Paragraphs, Second Edition
ISBN: 0-07-337186-6 (Copyright © 2010)

Paragraph-to-Essay

Exploring Writing: Paragraphs and Essays, Second Edition
ISBN: 0-07-337185-8 (Copyright © 2010)

ENGLISH Essentials

What Every College Student Needs to Know about Grammar, Punctuation, and Usage

THIRD EDITION

John Langan

ATLANTIC CAPE COMMUNITY COLLEGE

Beth Johnson

The McGraw-Hill Companies

ENGLISH ESSENTIALS, THIRD EDITION

Published by McGraw-Hill, a business unit of The McGraw-Hill Companies, Inc., 1221 Avenue of the Americas, New York, NY 10020.

Some ancillaries, including electronic and print components, may not be available to customers outside the United States.

 This book is printed on recycled, acid-free paper.

1 2 3 4 5 6 7 8 9 0 QDB/QDB 1 0 9 8 7 6 5 4 3 2

ISBN: 978-0-07-353332-2
MHID: 0-07-353332-7 (Student's Edition)
ISBN: 978-0-07-745302-2
MHID: 0-07-745302-6 (Instructor's Edition)

Vice President & Editor-in-Chief: *Michael Ryan*
Vice President & Director Specialized Publishing: *Janice M. Roerig-Blong*
Publisher: *David Patterson*
Sponsoring Editor: *Jessica Cannavo*
Marketing Manager: *Jaclyn Elkins*
Senior Project Manager: *Lisa A. Bruflodt*
Design Coordinator: *Margarite Reynolds*
Buyer: *Laura Fuller*
Media Project Manager: *Sridevi Palani*
Cover Designer: *Mary-Presley Adams*
Production Service: *Aptara®, Inc.*
Composition: *12/14 Adobe Garamond by Aptara®, Inc.*
Printing: *45# Pub Era Matte by Quad/Graphics.*

Cover image credits: *Clockwise from top left, ColorBlind Images/Blend Images/Corbis; BananaStock/Jupiterimages; Image Source/Jupiterimages; Image Source/Getty Images; Dave & Les Jacobs/Getty Images*

Credits: Insert: p. 2, Onoky/Getty Images; p. 3, left: © Lars Niki; right: Photodisc/Getty Images; p. 4, Image Source/ Getty Images; p. 5, Royalty-Free/CORBIS; p. 6, © Thinkstock; p. 7, top: © Javier Pierini/Getty Images; bottom: ColorBlind Images/Blend Images/Corbis; p. 8, ColorBlind Images/Blend Images LLC; p. 9, © Digital Vision

Main text: p. 40, © Ingram Publishing/AGE Fotostock; p. 42, Image Source/Getty Images; p. 82, top: Jose Luis Pelaez Inc/Blend Images LLC; bottom: © Helen King/Corbis; p. 83, Hoby Finn/Getty Images; p. 85, top: Image Source/ Jupiterimages; bottom: Goodshoot/Corbis; p. 114, © Stockbyte/PunchStock; p. 115, © Stockbyte/PunchStock; p. 135, top: Ingram Publishing; bottom: © Digital Vision/Getty Images; p. 137, PhotoAlto/Veer; p. 156, top: Getty Images/Stockbyte; bottom: C. Borland/PhotoLink/Getty Images; p. 157, BananaStock/Jupiterimages

Library of Congress Cataloging-in-Publication Data

Langan, John, 1942–
English essentials : what every college student needs to know about grammar, punctuation, and usage / John Langan, Beth Johnson.—3rd ed., Instructor annotated ed.
p. cm.—(The Langan series)
Includes index.
ISBN 978-0-07-353332-2 (alk. paper)
1. English language—Grammar—Problems, exercises, etc. 2. English language—Punctuation—Problems, exercises, etc. 3. English language—Usage—Problems, exercises, etc. I. Johnson, Beth. II. Title.
PE1112.L26 2012
428.2—dc23 2011038515

www.mhhe.com

Contents

Preface to the Instructor

"What's the catch?" you might be asking. "What are people's photographs doing in this textbook? And just how will they help me teach *English Essentials: What Everyone Needs to Know about Grammar, Punctuation, and Usage*?"

We think the student-pleasing photographs are just one of a number of features that distinguish this book from other grammar texts on the market:

1 **Personal photos and stories.** All too often, grammar books are dry, dull affairs, about as interesting as a study of rock dust on the planet Mars. As teachers, we sometimes felt we were leading our students on a death march when we moved them through a traditional grammar text. So we have added a strong human dimension to this book by illustrating the grammar skills with photos and stories of interesting people from all walks of life. The stories describe not only their personal lives but also their involvement with reading and writing. More photos appear in a newly revised full-color section of writing assignments.

2 **Ease of use.** All of the following make the book easy for students to understand and use:

- The essentials are presented in a highly accessible way. Take a look at any of the one-page reviews that open each of the skill chapters in Part One—the first such review is on page 38. Just the basics of each skill are presented on this page, which students can read and understand fairly quickly. Once they have grasped this basic material, they can go on to learn additional information about the skill and practice applying the skill.

  It is better to learn a step at a time than to risk confusion by trying to learn everything at once. For example, dependent-word fragments are the subject of one chapter; other common fragments appear in a second chapter. The most common homonyms are covered in Part One; other homonyms follow in the chapter "More about Homonyms" in Part Two.
- The chapters are self-contained, so that students can work on just those skills they need.
- Explanations are written in simple, familiar language, with a real emphasis on clarity and a minimum of grammatical terminology.
- An inviting two-color design has been used throughout, with headings and other design elements chosen to make the content as clear as possible.
- Finally, the book is written in a friendly and helpful tone of voice—one that never condescends to students, but instead treats them as adults.

3 **Abundant practice.** The book is based on the assumption that students learn best when clear explanations are followed by abundant practice. For each chapter in Part One, there are three full-page activities and five full-page tests. The last two tests are designed

to resemble standardized tests and permit easy grading, including the use of Scantron sheets. We've also added even more accessible student-friendly writing prompts.

4 **Engaging materials.** In addition to the photos and true stories, lively and engaging examples and practice materials will help maintain student interest throughout the book.

5 **Inclusiveness.** The Introduction includes a brief guide to writing and a series of writing assignments to help students practice the grammar, punctuation, and usage skills that appear in the rest of the book. A combined forty years of teaching experience has taught us that applying the skills in actual writing situations helps students truly master them. Part One consists of primary information about fifteen key skills. Part Two presents secondary information about these skills and also covers topics not discussed in Part One. Part Three offers guidance and practice in the crucial skill of proofreading. And Part Four deals with areas that some other grammar texts neglect: spelling improvement and dictionary use. Within the covers of *English Essentials,* then, are all the basic writing materials that instructors and students are likely to need.

6 **Superior supplements.** The following supplements are available at no charge to instructors adopting the book:

- An Instructor's Edition that is identical to the student text except that it includes answers to all the practices and tests.
- A combined Instructor's Manual and Test Bank that includes teaching hints, diagnostic and achievement tests, a full answer key, and a bank of additional mastery tests.
- A Student Answer Key consisting of answers for all the activities in Part One and to the practices and tests in the rest of the book.

New to the Third Edition

The third edition of *English Essentials* continues along the path of previous editions with ease of use, abundant practice and examples, and an engaging tone and writing style. The new edition also includes:

A thoroughly revised section of color photographs and writing prompts that engage students in the writing process through the use of thought-provoking visuals

New and revised examples, exercises, and tests based on the everyday issues and topics students encounter most

A revised Online Learning Center that includes a wealth of learning resources for students and useful teaching tools for instructors.

In short, *English Essentials* is designed as a core worktext that will both engage the interest of today's students and help them truly master the skills they need for writing well.

John Langan **Beth Johnson**

About the Book

"What is this?" you might ask as you page through this book and notice the photographs within it. "Who are these people, and what do they have to do with English essentials? And what are English essentials, anyway?"

The answers to those questions go hand in hand. As you know, "essentials" means things that are basic, necessary, and useful. We've designed *English Essentials* to help you quickly master practical English skills that you need every day. How quickly? Glance at one of the one-page reviews that open each of the chapters in Part One of the book. Chances are that you will be able to read that page in perhaps no more than a minute or two. That page will contain basic information about a particular skill. Once you understand the basics, you can turn to the pages that follow to practice that skill. You can also turn to Part Two to learn anything else you may need to know about the skill.

One advantage of *English Essentials*, then, is that it makes grammar skills easy to master. Basic information is presented in a very clear way on the first page of each chapter; the pages that follow reinforce that information with activities and tests. You will be learning in the best possible way: through doing.

And why the photographs? They provide a second benefit of the book by showing real people—men and women, boys and girls, young and not so young, current and former students—who use essential English skills in their daily lives. Their photographs add a human dimension to a subject that people often find dry and unappealing. At the same time you are learning a given skill, you will share in the real lives of interesting people.

A third advantage of the book is that it provides a full treatment of the essential English skills you need to know. Here is what is covered in the four parts of the book:

INTRODUCTION. This opening overview of the book is followed by a section titled "Becoming a Better Writer," which presents the writing process in a nutshell. Then a section titled "Writing Assignments" provides writing topics you can use to practice the rules of grammar, punctuation, and usage presented in the rest of the book.

PART ONE: Fifteen Basic Skills. Look at the table of contents on page 26 for a list of the fifteen basic grammar and punctuation skills presented in Part One. Then turn to the first page of one of the first skills, "Subjects and Verbs." You will notice that the basic information about subjects and verbs is presented on one page. Ideally, in a minute or so you should be able to review the basic information about subjects and verbs.

- Now turn to the second page of the chapter, page 39. Write down the two headings on this page:

  ____

  ____

On the second page of this chapter and all the other chapters in Part One, you are given examples of the skill in question, along with a chance to check your understanding of that skill. You are also introduced, in photos and in the text, to the person or persons featured in the chapter.

- Turn to the third, fourth, and fifth pages of the chapter (pages 40, 41, and 42). How many activities are included on those pages? ____________

  It is through repeated and varied practice in the skill that you best learn it.

- Turn to the last five pages in the chapter (pages 43–47). How many tests are included on those pages? ____________

Note that the last two tests are designed to resemble standardized tests, and you or your teacher can easily grade them.

PART TWO: Extending the Skills. Look again at the table of contents on page 186.

- Part Two presents some topics not included in Part One. For example, what is the first topic, on page 187? ____________________
- Part Two also includes additional information about many of the topics presented in Part One. For example, what is the first "More about" section? ____________ ____

PART THREE: Proofreading. An important part of becoming a good writer is learning to proofread—to carefully check the next-to-final draft of a paper for grammar, punctuation, and other mistakes. This chapter provides you with the hints and practice you need to improve your proofreading skills.

- How many proofreading tests appear at the end of the chapter? ____________

  You'll see there are ten tests in all.

PART FOUR: Related Matters. These chapters include two areas that may be part of English courses: spelling tips and rules and dictionary use.

A FINAL WORD

English Essentials has been designed to benefit you as much as possible. Its format is inviting, its explanations are clear, and its many activities, practices, tests, and assignments will help you learn through doing. It is a book that has been created to reward effort, and if you provide that effort, you can make yourself a competent and confident writer. We wish you luck.

John Langan **Beth Johnson**

Becoming a Better Writer

What, in a nutshell, do you need to become a better writer? You need to know the basic goals in writing and to understand the writing process—as explained on the pages that follow.

TWO BASIC GOALS IN WRITING

When you write a paper, your two basic goals should be (1) to make a point and (2) to support that point. Look for a moment at the following cartoon:

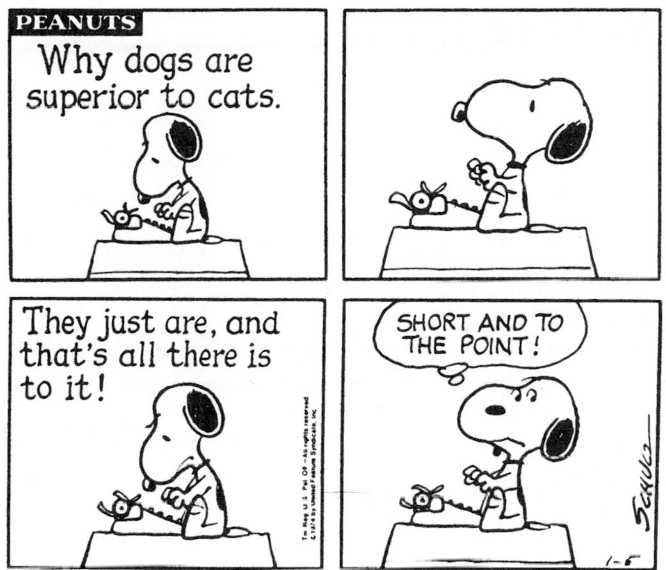

PEANUTS © 1974 Peanuts Worldwide LLC. Dist. By UNIVERSAL UCLICK. Reprinted with permission. All rights reserved.

See if you can answer the following questions:

- What is Snoopy's point in his paper?

  Your answer: His point is that ______________________________

- What is his support for his point?

  Your answer: ______________________________

Explanation Snoopy's point, of course, is that dogs are superior to cats. But he offers no support whatsoever to back up his point! There are two jokes here. First, he is a dog and so is naturally going to believe that dogs are superior. The other joke is that his evidence ("They just are, and that's all there is to it!") is a lot of empty words. His somewhat guilty look in the last panel suggests that he knows he has not proved his point. To write effectively, you must provide real support for your points and opinions.

WRITING PARAGRAPHS

A paragraph is a series of sentences about one main idea, or point. A paragraph typically starts with a point (also called the *topic sentence*), and the rest of the paragraph provides specific details to support and develop that point.

Look at the following paragraph, written by a student named Carla.

Three Kinds of Bullies

There are three kinds of bullies in schools. First of all, there are the physical bullies. They are the bigger or meaner kids who try to hurt kids who are smaller or unsure of themselves. They'll push other kids off swings, trip them in the halls, or knock books out of their hands. They'll also wait for kids after school and slap them or yank their hair or pull out their shirts or throw them to the ground. They do their best to frighten kids and make them cry. Another kind of bully is the verbal bully. This kind tries to hurt with words rather than fists. Nursery-school kids may call each other "dummy" or "weirdo" or "fatty," and as kids get older, their words carry even more sting. "You are such a loser," those bullies will tell their victim, making sure there is a crowd nearby to hear. "Where did you get that sweater—a trash bin?" The worst kind of bully is the social bully. Social bullies realize that they can make themselves feel powerful by making others feel unwanted. Bullies choose their victims and then do all they can to isolate them. They roll their eyes and turn away in disgust if those people try to talk to them. They move away if a victim sits near them at lunch. They make sure the unwanted ones know about the games and parties they aren't invited to. Physical, verbal, and social bullies all have the same ugly goal: to hurt and humiliate others.

- What is the point of the above paragraph? ______________________________

____

- What are the three kinds of evidence that Carla has provided to back up her point?

1. ______________________________

2. ______________________________

3. ______________________________

The above paragraph, like many effective paragraphs, starts by stating a main idea, or point. In this case, the clear point is that there are three kinds of bullies in schools. An effective paragraph must not only make a point but also support it with specific evidence—reasons, examples, and other details. Such specifics help prove to readers that the point is a reasonable one. Even if readers do not agree with the writer, at least they have the writer's evidence in front of them. Readers are like juries: they want to see the evidence for themselves so that they can make their own judgments.

As you have seen, the author of the paragraph provides plenty of examples to support the idea that there are physical, verbal, and social bullies. To write an effective paragraph, always aim to do what the author has done: begin by making a point, and then go on to back up that point with strong specific evidence.

WRITING ESSAYS

Like a paragraph, an essay starts with a point and then goes on to provide specific details to support and develop that point. However, a paragraph is a series of sentences about one main idea or point, while an essay is a series of paragraphs about one main idea or point—called the central point or thesis. Since an essay is much longer than one paragraph, it allows a writer to develop a topic in more detail.

Look at the following essay, written by Carla after she was asked to develop more fully her paragraph on bullies.

A Hateful Activity: Bullying

Introductory Paragraph

Eric, a new boy at school, was shy and physically small. He quickly became a victim of bullies. Kids would wait after school, pull out his shirt, and punch and shove him around. He was called such names as "Mouse Boy" and "Jerk Boy." When he sat down during lunch hour, others would leave his table. In gym games he was never thrown the ball, as if he didn't exist. Then one day he came to school with a gun. When the police were called, he told them he just couldn't take it anymore. Bullying had hurt him badly, just as it hurts so many other students. As Eric's experience shows, there are three hateful forms of bullying in schools: physical, verbal, and social.

First Supporting Paragraph

First of all, there is physical bullying. Bigger or meaner kids try to hurt kids who are smaller or unsure of themselves. They'll push kids into their lockers, knock books out of their hands, or shoulder them out of the cafeteria line. In gym class, a popular bully move is to kick someone's legs out from under him while he is running. In the classroom, bullies might kick the back of the chair or step on the foot of the kids they want to intimidate. Another classic bully move is to corner a kid in a bathroom. There the victim will be slapped around, will have his or her clothes half pulled off, and might even be shoved into a trash can. Bullies will also wait for kids after school and bump or wrestle them around, often while others are looking on. The goal is to frighten kids as much as possible and try to make them cry. The victims are left bruised, hurting, and feeling emotional pain.

Second Supporting Paragraph

Perhaps even worse than physical attack is verbal bullying, which uses words, rather than hands or fists, as weapons. We may be told that "sticks and stones may break my bones, but names can never harm me," but few of us are immune to the pain of a verbal attack. Like physical bullies, verbal bullies tend to single out certain targets. From that moment on, the victim is subjected to a hail of insults and put-downs. These are usually delivered in public, so the victim's humiliation will be greatest: "Oh, no; here comes the nerd!" "Why don't you lose some weight, blubber boy?" "You smell as bad as you look!" "Weirdo." "Fairy." "Creep." "Dork." "Slut." "Loser." Meanwhile, the victim retreats into a painful shell, hoping to escape further notice.

Third Supporting Paragraph

As bad as verbal bullying is, perhaps the most painful type of bullying is social bullying. Many students have a strong need for the comfort of being part of a group. For social bullies, the pleasure of belonging to a group is increased by the sight of someone who is refused entry into that group. So, like wolves targeting the weakest sheep in a herd, the bullies lead the pack in isolating people who they decide are different. They roll their eyes and turn away in disgust if those people try to talk to them. They move away if a victim sits near them at lunch or stands near them in a school hallway or at a bus stop. No one volunteers to work with these victims on class activities, and they are the ones that no one wants as part of gym teams. The bullies make sure the unwanted ones know about the games and parties they aren't invited to. As the victims sink into isolation and depression, the social bullies feel all the more puffed up by their own popularity.

Concluding Paragraph

Whether bullying is physical, verbal, or social, it can leave deep and lasting scars. If parents, teachers, and other adults were more aware of the types of bullying, they might help by stepping in before the situation becomes too extreme. If students were more aware of the terrible pain that bullying causes, they might think twice about being bullies themselves.

- Which sentence in the introductory paragraph expresses the central point of the essay?

  ____

- How many supporting paragraphs are provided to back up the central point? ______

THE PARTS OF AN ESSAY

Each of the parts of an essay is explained below.

Introductory Paragraph

A well-written introductory paragraph will normally do the following:

- Gain the reader's interest by using one of several common methods of introduction.
- Present the thesis statement. The thesis statement expresses the central point of an essay, just as a topic sentence states the main idea of a paragraph. The central idea in Carla's essay is expressed in the last sentence of the introductory paragraph.

Four Common Methods of Introduction

Four common methods of introduction are (1) telling a brief story, (2) asking one or more questions, (3) shifting to the opposite, or (4) going from the broad to the narrow. Following are examples of all four.

1 **Telling a brief story.** An interesting anecdote is hard for a reader to resist. In an introduction, a story should be no more than a few sentences, and it should relate meaningfully to the central idea. The story can be an experience of your own, of someone you know, or of someone you have read about. Carla uses this method of introduction for her essay on bullying:

> Eric, a new boy at school, was shy and physically small. He quickly became a victim of bullies. Kids would wait after school, pull out his shirt, and punch and shove him around. He was called such names as "Mouse Boy" and "Jerk Boy." When he sat down during lunch hour, others would leave his table. In gym games he was never thrown the ball, as if he didn't exist. Then one day he came to school with a gun. When the police were called, he told them he just couldn't take it anymore. Bullying had hurt him badly, just as it hurts so many other students. Every member of a school community should be aware of bullying and the three hateful forms that it takes: physical, verbal, and social bullying.

2 **Asking one or more questions.** These questions may be ones that you intend to answer in your essay, or they may indicate that your topic is relevant to readers—it is something

they care about. If Carla had used this approach, here is how her introductory paragraph might have looked:

> When you were a kid, were you ever pushed around by bigger children? Were you shoved aside in hallways or knocked out of your seat in classrooms? Were you ever called hurtful names like fatso, worm, dogface, or retard? Or were you coldly ignored by other students? Did they turn their backs on you, pretending you didn't exist? If the answer to any of these questions is "yes," then you were a victim of one of three forms of bullying: physical, verbal, or social.

3 **Shifting to the opposite.** Another way to gain the reader's interest is to first present an idea that is the opposite of what will be written about. Using this approach, Carla could have begun her essay like this:

> For many children, school is a happy experience. They like their teachers, they see their friends on a daily basis, and they feel comfortable and welcome. But for the victims of bullies, school is a nightmare. Every day they must face someone bigger or meaner than they are and endure humiliation in a variety of forms—physical, verbal, and social.

4 **Going from the broad to the narrow.** Broad, general observations can capture your reader's interest; they can also introduce your general topic and provide helpful background information. If Carla had used this method of introduction, she might have written first about typical problems in growing up and then narrowed her focus down to one problem: bullying.

> Many unpleasant parts of growing up seem unavoidable. Pimples happen, voices crack, and students worry all the time about their looks and their changing bodies. In time, the pimples disappear, the voices deepen, and the worries recede. But one all-too-common aspect of growing up, bullying, can have lasting negative results. Young people should not have to put up with bullying in any of its forms—physical, verbal, or social.

Supporting Paragraphs

The traditional school essay has three supporting paragraphs. But some essays will have two supporting paragraphs, and others will have four or more. Each supporting paragraph should have its own topic sentence stating the point to be developed in that paragraph.

Notice that the essay on bullying has clear topic sentences for each of the three supporting paragraphs.

Transitional Sentences

In a paragraph, transitional words like *First, Another, Also, In addition,* and *Finally* are used to help connect supporting ideas. In an essay, transitional sentences are used to help tie the supporting paragraphs together. Such transitional sentences often occur at the beginning of a supporting paragraph.

- Look at the topic sentences for the second and third supporting paragraphs in the essay on bullying. Explain how those sentences are also transitional sentences.

____

____

Concluding Paragraph

The concluding paragraph often summarizes the essay by briefly restating the thesis and, at times, the main supporting points. It may also provide a closing thought or two as a way of bringing the paper to a natural and graceful end.

- Look again at the concluding paragraph of the essay on bullies. Which sentence summarizes the essay? ________________ Which sentences provide closing thoughts? ________________ How many closing thoughts are there? ________________

A NOTE ON A THIRD GOAL IN WRITING

A third important goal in writing (see page 3 for the first two goals) is to organize the supporting material in a paper. Perhaps the most common way to do so is to use a **listing order**. In other words, provide a list of three or more reasons, examples, or other details. Use signal words such as *First of all*, *Another*, *Secondly*, *Also*, and *Finally* to mark the items in your list. Signal words, better known as transitions, let your reader know that you are providing a list of items.

- Turn back to page 4 and look again at the paragraph on bullies. What signal words does Carla use to mark each of the three kinds of bullies?

  ________________ ________________ ________________

You'll note that she uses "First of all" to introduce the first kind of bully, "Another" to introduce the second kind of bully, and "worst" to introduce the last kind of bully.

Activity: Using a Listing Order

Read the paragraph below and answer the questions that follow.

Drunk Drivers

People caught driving while drunk—even first offenders—should be jailed. For one thing, drunk driving is more dangerous than carrying a loaded gun. Drunk drivers are in charge of three-thousand-pound weapons at a time when they have little coordination or judgment. Instead of getting off with a license suspension, the drunk driver should be treated as seriously as someone who walks into a crowded building with a ticking time bomb. In addition, views on drunk driving have changed. We are no longer willing to make jokes about "funny" drunk drivers, to see drunk driving as a typical adolescent stunt, or to overlook repeat offenders who have been lucky enough not to hurt anybody—so far. Last of all, a jail penalty might encourage solutions to the problem of drinking and driving. People who go out for an evening that includes drinking would be more likely to select another person as the driver. That person would stay completely sober. Bars might promote more tasty and trendy nonalcoholic drinks such as fruit daiquiris and "virgin" piña coladas. And perhaps beer and alcohol advertising would be regulated so that young people would not learn to associate alcohol consumption with adulthood. By taking drunk driving seriously enough to require a jail sentence, we would surely save lives.

- What is the writer's point in this paragraph? ________________________________
  ____
- What transition introduces the first supporting reason for the point? ________________

- What transition introduces the second supporting reason? ______________________
- What transition introduces the third supporting reason? ______________________

The author's list of reasons and use of transitions—"For one thing," "In addition," and "Last of all"—both help the author organize the supporting material and help the reader clearly and easily understand the supporting material.

Another common way to organize supporting details is to use a **time order**. In time order, supporting details are presented in the order in which they occurred. *First* this happened; *next,* this; *after* that, this; *then* this; and so on. The events that make up a story are organized in time order.

Activity: Using a Time Order

Read the paragraph below, which is organized in a time order. In the spaces provided, write appropriate transitions showing time relationships. Use each of the following transitions once: *Before, Then, When, As, After.*

An Upsetting Incident

An incident happened yesterday that made me very angry. I got off the bus and started walking the four blocks to my friend's house. ______________ I walked along, I noticed a group of boys gathered on the sidewalk about a block ahead of me. ______________ they saw me, they stopped talking. A bit nervous, I thought about crossing the street to avoid them. But as I came nearer and they began to whistle, a different feeling came over me. Instead of being afraid, I was suddenly angry. Why should I have to worry about being hassled just because I was a woman? I stared straight at the boys and continued walking. ______________ one of them said, "Oooh, baby. Looking fine today." ______________ I knew what I was doing, I turned on him. "Do you have a mother? Or any sisters?" I demanded. He looked astonished and didn't answer me. I went on. "Is it OK with you if men speak to them like that? Shouldn't they be able to walk down the street without some creeps bothering them?" ______________ I spoke, he and the other boys looked guilty and backed away. I held my head up high and walked by them. An hour later, I was still angry.

The writer makes the main point of the paragraph in her first sentence: "An incident happened yesterday that made me very angry." She then supports her point with a specific account of just what happened. Time words that could be used to help connect her details include the following: "As I walked along," "When they saw me," "Then one of them said," "Before I knew," "After I spoke."

THE WRITING PROCESS

Even professional writers do not sit down and write a paper in a single draft. Instead, they have to work on it one step at a time. Writing a paper is a process that can be divided into the following five steps:

STEP 1 **Getting Started through Prewriting**
STEP 2 **Preparing a Scratch Outline**
STEP 3 **Writing the First Draft**
STEP 4 **Revising**
STEP 5 **Editing**

STEP 1 Getting Started through Prewriting

What you need to learn, first, are methods that you can use to start working on a writing assignment. These techniques will help you think on paper. They'll help you figure out both the point you want to make and the support you need for that point. Here are three helpful prewriting techniques:

- Freewriting
- Questioning
- List making

Freewriting

Freewriting is just sitting down and writing whatever comes into your mind about a topic. Do this for ten minutes or so. Write without stopping and without worrying in the slightest about spelling, grammar, and the like. Simply get down on paper all the information that occurs to you about the topic.

Below is part of the freewriting done by Carla for her paragraph about bullies. Carla had been given the assignment "Write about the types of bullying that go on in school." She began prewriting as a way to explore her topic and generate details about it.

Example of Freewriting

Bullying is part of school most of the time teachers dont have a clue. I really never thought about it and was just glad I wasn't part of it. At least for the most part. I'd see some phisikal stuff now and then but kind of turned my head not wanting to look at it. The worst thing with girls was words, they meant more than phisikal stuff. I rember once being called a name and it stung me so bad and it bothered me for weeks. . . .

Notice that there are lots of problems with spelling, grammar, and punctuation in Carla's freewriting. Carla is not worried about such matters, nor should she be—at this stage. She is just concentrating on getting ideas and details down on paper. She knows that it is best to focus on one thing at a time. At this point, she just wants to write out thoughts as they come to her, to do some thinking on paper.

You should take the same approach when freewriting: explore your topic without worrying at all about writing "correctly." Figuring out what you want to say should have all your attention in this early stage of the writing process.

Activity: Freewriting

On a sheet of paper, freewrite for at least ten minutes on the best or worst job or chore you ever had. Don't worry about grammar, punctuation, or spelling. Try to write—without stopping—about whatever comes into your head concerning your best or worst job or chore.

Questioning

Questioning means that you generate details about your topic by writing down a series of questions and answers about it. Your questions can start with words like *what, when, where, why,* and *how.*

Here are just some of the questions that Carla might have asked while developing her paper:

Example of Questioning

- Who was bullied?
- Who were the bullies?
- When did bullying take place?
- Where did it happen?
- Were there different kinds of bullying?
- Why were some kids teased and bullied?

Activity: Questioning

On a sheet of paper, answer the following questions about your best or worst job or chore.

- When did you have the job (or chore)?
- Where did you work?
- What did you do?
- Whom did you work for?
- Why did you like or dislike the job? (Give one reason and some details that support that reason.)
- What is another reason you liked or disliked the job? What are some details that support the second reason?
- Can you think of a third reason you liked or did not like the job? What are some details that support the third reason?

List Making

In list making (also known as brainstorming), you make a list of ideas and details that could go into your paper. Simply pile these items up, one after another, without worrying about putting them in any special order. Try to accumulate as many details as you can think of.

After Carla did her freewriting about bullies, she made up a list of details, part of which is shown below.

Example of List Making

some bullies were phisikal
boys would push kids around
kids would be tripped in hallways
some kids would cry
names would be used
"dummy" or "creep" or "fairy"
no one would sit near some kids
some kids never chosen for games
. . . .

One detail led to another as Carla expanded her list. Slowly but surely, more supporting material emerged that she could use in developing her paper. By the time she had finished her list, she was ready to plan an outline of her paragraph and to write her first draft.

Activity: List Making

On a separate piece of paper, make a list of details about the job (or chore). Don't worry about putting them in a certain order. Just get down as many details about the job as occur to you. The list can include specific reasons you liked or did not like the job and specific details supporting those reasons.

STEP 2 Preparing a Scratch Outline

A scratch outline is a brief plan for a paragraph. It shows at a glance the point of the paragraph and the support for that point. It is the logical framework on which the paper is built.

This rough outline often follows freewriting, questioning, list making, or all three. Or it may gradually emerge in the midst of these strategies. In fact, trying to outline is a good way to see if you need to do more prewriting. If a solid outline does not emerge, then you know you need to do more prewriting to clarify your main point or its support. And once you have a workable outline, you may realize, for instance, that you want to do more list making to develop one of the supporting details in the outline.

In Carla's case, as she was working on her list of details, she suddenly discovered what the plan of her paragraph could be. She realized that she could describe in turn each of three different kinds of bullies.

Example of a scratch outline

There are three kinds of bullies.

1. Physical
2. Verbal
3. Social

After all her preliminary writing, Carla sat back pleased. She knew she had a promising paper—one with a clear point and solid support. Carla was now ready to write the first draft of her paper, using her outline as a guide.

Activity: Scratch Outline

Using the list you have prepared, see if you can prepare a scratch outline made up of the three main reasons you liked or did not like the job.

________________________________ was the best (or worst) job (or chore) I ever had.

Reason 1: ________________________________

Reason 2: ________________________________

Reason 3: ________________________________

STEP 3 Writing the First Draft

When you do a first draft, be prepared to put in additional thoughts and details that didn't emerge in your prewriting. And don't worry if you hit a snag. Just leave a blank space or add a comment such as "Do later" and press on to finish the paper. Also, don't worry yet about grammar, punctuation, or spelling. You don't want to take time correcting words or sentences that you may decide to remove later. Instead, make it your goal to develop the content of your paper with plenty of specific details.

Here are a few lines of Carla's first draft:

First Draft

There are different kinds of bullies that can be seen in schools. One kind of bullying that goes on is done by phisikal bullies. You see kids who will get pushed around on the playground. You see kids getting shoved into lockers and that kind of stuff. There was a girl I knew who was a real bully and a bit crazy because of a really bad home life. She would shove gum into another girl's hair and would also pull her hair. Other bullying went on with words and the calling of names. There were awful names that kids would use with each other, words included "creep" and "weirdo" and names that I don't even want to write here. . . .

Activity: First Draft

Now write a first draft of your paper. Begin with your topic sentence stating that a certain job (or chore) was the best or worst one you ever had. Then state the first reason why it was the best or the worst, followed by specific details supporting that reason. Use a transition such as *First of all* to introduce the first reason. Next, state the second reason, followed by specific details supporting that reason. Use a transition such as *Secondly* to introduce the second reason. Last, state the third reason, followed with support. Use a transition such as *Finally* to introduce the last reason.

Don't worry about grammar, punctuation, or spelling. Just concentrate on getting down on paper the details about the job.

STEP 4 Revising

Revising is as much a stage in the writing process as prewriting, outlining, and doing the first draft. *Revising* means that you rewrite a paper, building upon what has been done, to make it stronger and better. One writer has said about revision, "It's like cleaning house—getting rid of all the junk and putting things in the right order." A typical revision means writing at least one or two more drafts, adding and omitting details, organizing more clearly, and beginning to correct spelling and grammar.

Here are a few lines of Carla's second draft.

Second Draft

There are three kinds of bullies in schools. First of all, there are the physical bullies. They are the bigger kids who try to hurt smaller kids. They'll push kids off of swings in the playground or shove them into lockers. Other examples are knocking books out of the hands of kids or waiting for them after school and slapping them around or yanking their hair. Another kind of bullying is by verbal bullies. The aim here is to hurt with words rather than with fists. A victim will be called a "creep" or "weirdo" or "fatty" or will be told "You are such a loser." . . .

Notice that in redoing the draft, Carla started by more concisely stating the point of her paragraph. Also, she inserted transitions ("First of all" and "Another") to clearly set off the kinds of bullies. She omitted the detail about the crazy girl she knew because it was not relevant to a paragraph focusing on bullies. She added more details so that she would have enough supporting examples for the types of bullies.

Carla then went on to revise the second draft. Since she was doing her paper on a computer, she was able to print it out quickly. She double-spaced the lines, allowing room for revisions, which she added in longhand as part of her third draft, and eventually the paragraph on page 4 resulted. (Note that if you are not using a computer, you may want to skip every other line when writing out each draft. Also, write on only one side of a page, so that you can see your entire paper at one time.)

Activity: Revising the Draft

Ideally, you will have a chance to put the paper aside for a while before doing later drafts. When you revise, try to do all of the following:

- Omit any details that do not truly support your topic sentence.
- Add more details as needed, making sure you have plenty of specific support for each of your three reasons.
- Be sure to include a final sentence that rounds off the paper, bringing it to a close.

STEP 5 Editing

Editing, the final stage in the writing process, means checking a paper carefully for spelling, grammar, punctuation, and other errors. You are ready for this stage when you are satisfied that your point is clear, your supporting details are good, and your paper is well organized.

At this stage, you must read your paper out loud. Hearing how your writing sounds is an excellent way to pick up grammar and punctuation problems in your writing. Chances are that you will find sentence mistakes at every spot where your paper does not read smoothly and clearly. This point is so important that it bears repeating: To find mistakes in your paper, read it out loud!

At this point in her work, Carla read her latest draft out loud. She looked closely at all the spots where her writing did not read easily. She used a grammar handbook to deal with the problems at those spots in her paper, and she made the corrections needed so that all her sentences read smoothly. She also used her dictionary to check on the spelling of every word she was unsure about. She even took a blank sheet of paper and used it to uncover her paper one line at a time, looking for any other mistakes that might be there.

Activity: Editing

When you have your almost-final draft of the paper, edit it in the following ways:

- Read the paper aloud, listening for awkward wordings and places where the meaning is unclear. Make the changes needed for the paper to read smoothly and clearly. In addition, see if you can get another person to read the draft aloud to you. The spots that this person has trouble reading are spots where you may have to do some revision and correct your grammar or punctuation mistakes.
- Using your dictionary (or a spell-check program if you have a computer), check any words that you think might be misspelled.
- Finally, take a sheet of paper and cover your paper so that you can expose and carefully proofread one line at a time. Use your handbook to check any other spots where you think there might be grammar or punctuation mistakes in your writing.

Final Thoughts

When you have a paper to write, here in a nutshell is what to do:

1 Write about what you know. If you don't know much about your topic, go on the Internet and use the helpful search engine Google. You can access it by typing this:

www.google.com

A screen will then appear with a box in which you can type one or more keywords. For example, if you were thinking about doing a paper on some other topic involving bullies, you could type in the keyword *bullies*. Within a second or so you will get a list of over 9 million hits on the Web about bullies!

You would then need to narrow your topic by adding other keywords. For instance, if you typed "bullies in schools," you would get a list of over 3 million items. If you narrowed your potential topic further by typing "how should schools handle cyberbullying?" you would get a list of 535,000 items. You could then click on the items that sound most promising to you. As you read and think about bullies, you will gradually get a sense of a topic you might be able to develop.

Keep in mind that you do not want to take other people's ideas or words—that would be stealing. The formal term is *plagiarizing*—using someone else's work and presenting it as your own. Rather, your goal is to use other people's information and thoughts as a springboard for your own words and ideas about a topic.

2 Use prewriting strategies to begin to write about your topic. Look for a point you can make, and make sure you have details to support it.

3 Write several drafts, aiming all the while for three goals in your writing: a clear point, strong support for that point, and well-organized support. Use transitions to help organize your support.

4 Then read your paper out loud. It should read smoothly and clearly. Look closely for grammar and punctuation problems at any rough spots. Check a grammar handbook or a dictionary as needed.

Writing Assignments

Writing is best done on topics about which you have information and in which you have interest. To ensure that you have a choice of topics, following are twelve groups of **two** writing assignments. Your instructor may ask you, for example, to write on your choice of one of the two topics in Group A. As the semester proceeds, he or she may ask you to write paragraphs on your choice of topics from additional groups as well. This section also includes eight additional writing prompts with accompanying visuals to jump-start your ideas.

GROUP A

1 **Hometown.** If a friend wrote to you asking whether your hometown would be a good place for him or her to move to, what would be your response? Write a one-paragraph letter to your friend explaining the advantages or disadvantages of living in your hometown. Begin your remarks with a specific recommendation to your friend; it will serve as the topic sentence of the paragraph. Cover such matters as employment, recreation, housing, schools, and safety. Be sure your details are as specific and descriptive as you can make them. To connect your ideas, use transitions such as *in addition*, *furthermore*, *on the other hand*, and *however*.

2 **Best or Worst Childhood Experience.** Some of our most vivid memories are of things that happened to us as children, and these memories don't ever seem to fade. In fact, many elderly people say that childhood memories are clearer to them than things that happened yesterday. Think back to one of the best or worst experiences you had as a child. Try to remember the details of the event—sights, sounds, smells, textures, tastes.

You might begin by freewriting for ten minutes or so about good or bad childhood experiences. That freewriting may suggest to you a topic you will want to develop.

After you have decided on a topic, try to write a clear sentence stating what the experience was and whether it was one of the best or worst of your childhood. For example, "The time I was beaten up coming home from my first day in fifth grade was one of my worst childhood moments."

You may then find it helpful to make a list in which you jot down as many details as you can remember about the experience. Stick with a single experience, and don't try to describe too much. If a week you spent at summer camp was an unpleasant experience, don't try to write about the entire week. Just describe one horrible moment or event.

When you write the paper, use a time order to organize details: first this happened, then this, next this, and so on.

As you write, imagine that someone is going to make a short film based on your paragraph. Try to provide vivid details, quotations, and pictures for the filmmaker to shoot.

GROUP B

1 **A Certain Song or Movie.** Is there a certain song or movie that is especially memorable to you? If so, mention the title of the song (the title should be in quotation marks) or movie (the title should be underlined or in italics), and write about the time when the song or movie became so meaningful to you. To be convincing, you will need to include numerous details and clear explanations.

2 **A Special Place or Object.** Write a paragraph describing either a place or an object you respond to with strong emotion, such as love, fear, warmth, dread, joy, or sadness. Specific details and vivid descriptions will need to be provided if your emotional reaction is to be understood.

GROUP C

1 **A Good or Bad Day in Your Life.** Write in detail about a recent good or bad day in your life—your activities, feelings, and experiences during the day. You might begin by making a list of things that you did, felt, saw, thought, heard, and said during that day. Your aim is to accumulate a great many details that you can draw upon later as you begin writing your paper. Making a long list is an excellent way to get started.

Then select and develop those details that best support the idea that the day was a good one or a bad one. Organize your paragraph using a time order—first this happened, then this, next this, and so on.

2 **Directions to a Place.** Write a set of specific directions on how to get from the English classroom to your house. Imagine you are giving these directions to a stranger who has just come into the room and who wants to deliver a million dollars to your home. You want, naturally, to give exact directions, including various landmarks that may guide the way, for the stranger does not know the area.

To help you write the paper, first make up a list of all the directions involved. Also, use words like *next*, *then*, and *after* to help the reader follow clearly as you move from one direction to the next.

GROUP D

1 **A Helpful Experience.** Write an account of an experience you have had that taught you something important. It might involve a mistake you made or an event that gave you insight into yourself or others. Perhaps you have had school problems that taught you to be a more effective student, or you have had a conflict with someone that you now understand could have been avoided. Whatever experience you choose to write about, be sure to tell how it has changed your way of thinking.

2 **Hindsight.** Occasionally, we call someone a "Monday-morning quarterback." By this we mean that it's easy to say what should have been done after an event (or game) is over. But while we're in the midst of our daily lives, it's hard to know which is the right decision to make or what is the right course of action. We've all looked back and thought, "I wish I'd done . . ." or "I wish I'd said . . ."

Think back to a year or two ago. What is the best advice someone could have given you then? Freewrite for ten minutes or so about how your life might have changed if you had been given that advice.

Then go on to write a paper that begins with a topic sentence something like this: "I wish someone had told me a year ago to cut back a little on my work hours while I'm in school."

GROUP E

1 **Parents and Children.** It has been said that the older we get, the more we see our parents in ourselves. Indeed, any of our habits (good and bad), beliefs, and temperaments can often be traced to one of our parents.

Write a paragraph in which you describe three characteristics you have "inherited" from a parent. You might want to think about your topic by asking yourself a series of questions: "How am I like my mother (or father)?" "When and where am I like her (or him)?" "Why am I like her (or him)?"

One student who did such a paper used as her topic sentence the following statement: "Although I hate to admit it, I know that in several ways I'm just like my mom." She then went on to describe how she works too hard, worries too much, and judges other people too harshly. Another student wrote, "I resemble my father in my love of TV sports, my habit of putting things off, and my reluctance to show my feelings." Be sure to include examples for each of the characteristics you mention.

2 **A Matter of Survival.** Someone has written, "There are times for each of us when simple survival becomes a deadly serious matter. We must then learn to persist—to struggle through each day." What has been your worst struggle? Write a paper describing the problem, what you had to do to deal with it, and how things worked out. You may also wish to comment on how you'd handle the problem today if you had to face it again.

As you work on the drafts for this paper, consider including the following to add interest and clarity:

- Exact quotations of what people said
- Descriptions of revealing behavior, actions, and physical characteristics
- Time transitions to clarify relationships between events

GROUP F

1 **Avoiding Responsibility.** M. Scott Peck, the author of several best-selling self-help books, has written, "The extent to which people will go psychologically to avoid assuming responsibility for personal problems, while always sad, is sometimes almost ludicrous." Think of times you have observed people blaming other people or circumstances for their own problems. Then write a paragraph that begins with the following topic sentence:

- I have seen someone refuse to take responsibility for his (or her) own problem.

Then go on to support that statement with an example. As you develop that example, be sure to explain what the person's problem was, how he had helped create it, and how he blamed other people or circumstances rather than accepting responsibility for it.

As you think of how to develop your paragraph, ask yourself questions such as these:

- Whom do I know who usually seems to be in one kind of trouble or another?
- Does that person always seem to blame others for his or her problems?
- What are some specific problems that person has in his or her life?
- How has he or she helped to create the problems?
- Whom or what does the person blame for those problems?

2 **Dealing with a Problem.** M. Scott Peck states that the only way to solve a problem is to solve it—in other words, to take responsibility for the problem and find a solution. When did you accept the responsibility for a problem in your own life and figure out a solution for it? Write about what happened. Be sure to answer the following questions:

- How was the problem affecting my life?
- When did I realize that I was (in part) responsible for the problem?
- What solution for the problem did I come up with?
- What happened after I put my solution to work?

In selecting a topic for this assignment, think about various kinds of problems you may have experienced: problems getting along with other people, money problems, relationship problems, problems completing work on time, difficulties in self-discipline, use of alcohol or other drugs, and so on. Then ask yourself which of these problems you have accepted responsibility for and solved. Once you have thought of a topic, you might begin with a statement like one of the following:

- This past year, I began to take responsibility for my continuing problems with my mother.
- I recently faced the fact that I have a self-discipline problem and have taken steps to deal with it.
- After years of spending my money on the wrong kinds of things, I've acted to deal with my money problems.

This statement could then be supported with one or more examples of the problem, a description of how and when you realized the problem, and a detailing of the steps you have taken to deal with the problem.

GROUP G

1 **A Key Experience in School.** Write a paragraph about one of your key experiences in grade school. Use concrete details—actions, comments, reactions, and so on—to help your readers picture what happened. To select an event to write about, try asking yourself the following questions:

- Which teachers or events in school influenced how I felt about myself?
- What specific incidents stand out in my mind as I think back to elementary school?

Once you know which experience you'll write about, use freewriting to help you remember and record the details. Here is one student's freewriting for this assignment:

> In second grade, Richard L. sat next to me, a really good artist. When he drew something, it looked just like what it was meant to be. He was so good at choosing colors, the use of crayons, watercolors. His pictures were always picked by teacher to be shown on bulletin board. I still remember his drawing of a circus. He drew acrobats, animals, and clowns. Many colors and details. I felt pretty bad in art, even though I loved it and couldn't wait for art in class. One day the teacher read story about a boy who looked at the mountains far away, wondering what was on the other side, mountains were huge, dark. After reading, it was art time. "Paint something from the story" teacher said. I painted those mountains, big purple brown mountains with watercolor dripping to show

the slopes and coloring of sunset. Also a thin slice of very blue sky at top. Next day I sat down at my desk in the morning. Then I saw my picture was on the bulletin board! Later teacher passed by me, bent down, put hand on my shoulder and whispered good job, lovely painting. Made me feel capable, proud. The feeling lasted a long time.

Once the details of the experience are on paper, you will be free to concentrate on a more carefully constructed version of the event. The author of the above freewriting, for instance, needed to think of a topic sentence. So when writing the first draft, she began with this sentence: "A seemingly small experience in elementary school encouraged me greatly." Writing drafts is also the time to add any persuasive details you may have missed at first. When working on her second draft, the author of the above added at the end: "I felt very proud, which gave me confidence to work harder in all my school subjects."

Before writing out your final version, remember to check for grammar, punctuation, and spelling errors.

2 Finding Time for Reading. A number of authors have described how a parent or teacher has helped them become regular readers—and how that habit of reading then led to enormous positive changes in their lives. Most of us, however, don't have someone around to insist that we do a certain amount of personal reading every week. In addition, many of us don't seem to have a great deal of free time for reading. How can adults find time to read more? Write a paragraph listing several ways adults can add more reading to their lives.

A good prewriting strategy for this assignment is list making. Simply write out as many ways as you can think of. Don't worry about putting them in any special order. You will select and organize the strategies you wish to include in your paper after accumulating as many ideas as you can. Here is an example of a prewriting list for this paper:

Ways adults can increase the amount of time they spend reading

— on the bus to and from work/school

— while eating breakfast

— instead of watching some TV

— by choosing motivating materials (articles, books about hobbies, problems, etc.)

Feel free to use items from the above list, but add at least one or two of your own points to include in your paper.

GROUP H

1 An Embarrassing Moment. In a paragraph, tell about a time you felt ashamed or embarrassed. Provide details that show clearly what happened. Explain what you and the other people involved said and did. Also, explain how you felt and why you were so uncomfortable.

For example, the paragraph might begin with a sentence like this:

- I was deeply ashamed when I was caught cheating on a spelling test in fifth grade.

The paragraph could continue by telling how the writer cheated and how he was caught; how the teacher and other students looked, spoke, and acted; what the writer did when he was caught; and what emotions and thoughts the writer experienced throughout the incident.

On the facing page are some other topic sentence possibilities. Develop one of them or a variation on one of them. Feel free as well to come up with and write about an entirely different idea.

- My first formal date was the occasion of an embarrassing moment in my life.
- To this day, I wince when I think of an incident that happened to me at a family party.
- I can still remember the shame I felt in my teenage body when I had to use the shower room at school.
- An event that occurred in high school makes my cheeks glow hot and red even today.

2 **A Fear of Looking Foolish.** Write a paragraph about how the fear of looking foolish affected your behavior in grade school or high school. Choose an example of a time you acted in a particular way because you were afraid of being ridiculed. Describe how you behaved, and be sure to explain just what kind of embarrassment you were trying to avoid.

Your paragraph might begin with a topic sentence like one of the following:

- Not wanting other students to turn on me, I joined them in making fun of a high school classmate who was very overweight.
- My mother's idea of how I should dress caused me a great deal of embarrassment in school.
- Because I didn't want to admit that I needed glasses, I had a lot of problems in fifth grade.

GROUP I

1 **A Special Person.** Who has helped you the most in your quest for an education? Write a paper explaining who this person is and how he or she has helped you. Here are some possible topic sentences for this paper:

- My best friend has helped me with my college education in several ways.
- If it weren't for my father, I wouldn't be in college today.
- It was my aunt who impressed upon me the importance of a college education.

To develop support for this paper, try listing the problems you faced and the ways this person has helped you deal with each problem. Alternatively, you could do some freewriting about the person you're writing about.

2 **Reaching a Goal.** Write a paragraph telling of something you wanted very badly but were afraid you would not be able to attain. Describe the struggles you had to overcome to get to your goal. How did you finally reach it? Include some details that communicate how strongly you wanted the goal and how difficult it was to reach. In thinking about a topic for this paper, you may wish to consider the following common goals:

- A certain job
- Enough money for college
- A passing grade
- Quitting smoking or drugs
- Overcoming an illness

Once you've decided on the goal you wish to write about, use it to write a topic sentence, such as any of the following:

- After several false starts, I finally quit smoking.
- After gradually changing my attitude about school, I have begun to get good grades.
- After two years of medical treatment and support, I feel I have learned to live with my illness.
- Following a careful budget, I was finally able to afford to …

To develop supporting material for your topic sentence, try freewriting. For example, here is part of one person's freewriting about the struggle to quit smoking:

> The first time I tried to quit, it lasted a short time. Only a month or less. I made the mistake of not getting rid of all the cigarettes in the house, I kept a few here and there for emergencies. But there should be no emergencies when you quit. Once I took a few puffs on a cigarette I found in the silverware drawer. It was all over—I ran out that day to buy a pack. I told myself I would smoke only one or two cigarettes a day until I was ready to really quit. That type of promise is always a lie because I can't really control myself once I start smoking. It's either all or nothing, and for me, even a puff or two isn't nothing. It wasn't long before I started thinking about quitting again. I was coughing a lot and several news stories were about people with lung cancer and the father of someone in my apartment building died of lung cancer. Also I read in a magazine that smoking causes wrinkles. Finally, about a year ago . . .

GROUP J

1 **A Bad Decision.** We all know someone who has made a bad decision. Write a paragraph describing a bad decision made by a family member or friend (or yourself) who usually knows better. You can start by introducing the person, and explaining why this particular decision or choice proved to be a poor one. A useful way to gather ideas for this paper is to combine two prewriting techniques: outlining and listing. Begin with an outline of the general areas you expect to cover. Your outline may look something like this:

- Introduce the person, explain relationship to you
- Describe the bad decision
- Discuss what he or she learned, or how it affected his or her life

Once you have a workable outline, then use list making to produce specific details for each point. Here is an example:

Person

- Lyle
- Best friend
- Usually smart with money
- Has a good job

Bad decision

- On vacation
- Went gambling for the first time
- Wouldn't leave the table
- Lost a lot of money

What he learned/how it affected his life

- Discovered he may have addictive personality
- Working to make sure he's more careful in the future

2 **A Time for Courage.** Write about a time when you had to have courage. Think of an action that frightened you, but that you felt you needed to take anyway. Perhaps you were afraid to ask someone out on a date, or to say no when someone asked you to do something you felt was wrong, or to perform a dangerous activity. In your paper, describe the frightening situation that faced you and how you made the decision to act with courage. Then tell what happened—the actions that you took, the responses of those around you, significant things people said, and how things turned out.

For example, you might begin with a statement like this:

- When I was in junior high, it required courage for me to resist the temptation to shoplift with my favorite cousin.

That passage would then continue with a description of what the cousin did and said, how you found the courage to say no to the idea, how the shoplifting cousin reacted, and how you felt throughout the whole process.

As you describe the incident, use time transition words to make the sequence of events clear, as in this example: "At *first* I didn't think I could do it. *Later,* however, I had an idea."

GROUP K

1 **Too Good to Be True.** We often see advertisements on TV, the Internet, or in newspapers that seem too good to be true; for example, a diet pill that promises near instant results without changing eating patterns or exercising. Or, perhaps you've seen an advertisement for a credit card that promises 0% interest, but after a few months, the interest rate jumps significantly. Write a paragraph describing a situation when you encountered something that seemed too good to be true. What specifically was the situation or offer? Did you participate? Why or why not?

2 **Reconnecting on the Internet.** Have you had the experience of finding an old friend or love interest on the Internet using such social media as Facebook or MySpace? Write a paragraph describing the overall experience of reconnecting on the Internet. Did you look up the person or did the person find you? Were you surprised by what you learned about your long-lost friend? Did you feel a desire to get involved with a former flame? Why? To get started, you could try freewriting about the feelings you had when you first saw your old friend/flame's photograph.

GROUP L

1 **Trying Something New.** Write a paragraph telling about a time you tried something that was completely new to you—for example, it could be a food, an activity, or a job. Explain the circumstances, why you had never tried it before, and how you reacted to the new experience. For example, the paragraph might begin with a sentence like this.

- I never imagined that I would try bungee jumping, but it turned out to be an amazing experience.

The paragraph could continue by telling what made the writer decide to try bungee jumping; his or her thoughts and feelings leading up to the jump; the experience of taking the jump; and whether the experience was as scary or exciting as what he or she expected. In your paragraph, using a time order may help organize your thoughts and narration.

2 **A Unique Recommendation.** Many people have unique or interesting taste in music, clothing, books, or sports that would seem completely foreign to those who haven't shared their experiences. Write a paragraph recommending something you enjoy that may not be widely known—it could be a suggestion for a fun activity, or a band not many people have heard of, or a book you think everyone should read. You might try explaining how you first acquired this taste, using concrete details to describe both the experience and why you think others would enjoy it.

The following eight writing assignments are paired with full-color images to help you get started.

Technology, such as laptops, iPads, and cell phones, along with social networking sites such as Facebook and Twitter, has made us more connected but also more distracted. Write a paragraph explaining how technology and/or social networking sites have had a positive or negative effect on your life. Be sure to use specific details and examples for support.

If you get stuck, examine this picture. What are some of the advantages to technology and social networking sites this picture might illustrate? What are some disadvantages?

Would you prefer to live in a rural area, an urban area, or somewhere in between? What kind of area did you live in growing up? Write a paragraph about someplace you've lived, describing what it was like to live there. Here are some questions you might ask yourself to prepare:

- Where did you live?
- Was it a rural, urban, or suburban environment, or a mixture?
- How long did you live there?
- What friends or relatives were living there at the same time?
- What did you like about it?
- What were some disadvantages to living there?

You can also use the two pictures above for inspiration. How might the daily lives of these two women differ?

We never know what experiences—good or bad—life has in store for us. In the blink of an eye, for example, an ordinary drive with friends can turn to disaster (as depicted in this photo). Write a paragraph telling about an unexpected experience in your life. It could be something that happened to you at home, work, or school. Try using strong, specific details to convey to the reader what the experience was like and why it was memorable.

What makes a job meaningful? Is it confronting danger on a daily basis, as illustrated in this photograph of a firefighter battling flames while several feet in the air? Can you make lots of money as a stockbroker, for example, and still find the work meaningful? Write a paragraph about a meaningful job you've held, describing what you did and what made it particularly enjoyable, interesting, or even terrifying. Alternatively, you could choose to write a paragraph about your dream job—what you would do if you could choose anything, and why. What is it about this job that would bring meaning to your life?

Is there a particular dish you could prepare in your sleep? Write a paragraph with a step-by-step explanation of how to cook something—or how to do something else, like how to throw a surprise party or how to prepare for a job interview. You might try using time order to make sure the steps are clear and easy to follow.

Write a paragraph describing what you think is happening in one of the two photographs above. Describe the setting you can see in the photograph, and feel free to invent other details about who the people are and what they're doing. Be sure to use specific details to make your paragraph vivid.

Have you ever dreamed of owning your own business? What type of business would it be? The woman in the above photograph realized her lifelong dream when she opened her own clothing store. Write a paragraph about the type of business you would like to start. Be sure to use specific details about the type of business it would be, why you think you would be good at such a business, and what you think the advantages and disadvantages would be of owning a business.

Write a paragraph about a situation where you felt like an outsider or were treated like an outsider. Or, write about a situation where you felt the most comfortable, such as having dinner with a close friend. Try freewriting about these feelings—of belonging, or of feeling out of place—to brainstorm ideas.

PART ONE Fifteen Basic Skills

PART ONE
Fifteen Basic Skills

PREVIEW

Part One presents basic information about fifteen key grammar, punctuation, and usage concepts.

1 Parts of Speech

Words—the building blocks of sentences—can be divided into eight parts of speech. **Parts of speech** are classifications of words according to their meaning and use in a sentence.

This chapter will explain the eight parts of speech:

nouns	**prepositions**	**conjunctions**
pronouns	**adjectives**	**interjections**
verbs	**adverbs**	

NOUNS

A **noun** is a word that is used to name something: a person, a place, an object, or an idea. Here are some examples of nouns:

woman	**city**	**pancake**	**freedom**
Alice Walker	**street**	**diamond**	**possibility**
Johnny Depp	**Chicago**	**Starbucks**	**mystery**

Most nouns begin with a lowercase letter and are known as **common nouns**. These nouns name general things. Some nouns, however, begin with a capital letter. They are called **proper nouns**. While a common noun refers to a person or thing in general, a proper noun names someone or somcthing spccific. For example, *woman* is a common noun—it doesn't name a particular woman. On the other hand, Alice Walker is a proper noun because it names a specific woman.

Parts of Speech: PRACTICE 1

Insert any appropriate noun into each of the following blanks.

1. Sally and Keisha brought ____________________ to the picnic.
2. ____________________ helped the old man cross the street.
3. Daryl and Emma hiked all the way to the top of the ____________________.
4. Alisha decided to write a story about ____________________.
5. Maria interviewed Warren for the ____________________.

Singular and Plural Nouns

Singular nouns name one person, place, object, or idea. **Plural nouns** refer to two or more persons, places, objects, or ideas. Most singular nouns can be made plural with the addition of an ***s.***

Some nouns, like *box*, have irregular plurals. You can check the plural of nouns you think may be irregular by looking up the singular form in a dictionary.

Singular	Plural
goat	goats
alley	alleys
friend	friends
truth	truths
box	boxes

For more information on nouns, see "Subjects and Verbs," pages 38–47.

Parts of Speech: PRACTICE 2

Underline the three nouns in each sentence. Some are singular, and some are plural.

1. Two bats swooped over the heads of the frightened children.

2. The artist has purple paint on her sleeve.

3. The lost dog has fleas and a broken leg.

4. Gwen does her homework in green ink.

5. Some farmers plant seeds by moonlight.

PRONOUNS

A **pronoun** is a word that stands for a noun. Pronouns eliminate the need for constant repetition. Look at the following sentences:

- The phone rang, and Bill answered the phone.
- Lisa met Lisa's friends at the movie theater. Lisa meets Lisa's friends there every Saturday.
- The waiter rushed over to the new customers. The new customers asked the waiter for menus and coffee.

Now look at how much clearer and smoother the sentences sound with pronouns.

- The phone rang, and Bill answered **it**.
  The pronoun *it* is used to replace the word *phone.*
- Lisa met **her** friends at the movie theater. **She** meets **them** there every Saturday.
  The pronoun *her* is used to replace the word *Lisa.* The pronoun *she* replaces *Lisa.* The pronoun *them* replaces the words *Lisa's friends.*

- The waiter rushed over to the new customers. **They** asked **him** for menus and coffee. The pronoun *they* is used to replace the words *the new customers.* The pronoun *him* replaces the words *the waiter.*

Following is a list of commonly used pronouns known as **personal pronouns**:

I	you	he	she	it	we	they
me	your	him	her	its	us	them
my	yours	his	hers		our	their

Parts of Speech: PRACTICE 3

Fill in each blank with the appropriate personal pronoun.

1. Andrew feeds his pet lizard every day before school. ____________________ also gives ____________________ flies in the afternoon.
2. The female reporter interviewed the striking workers. ____________________ told ____________________ about their demand for higher wages and affordable health care.
3. Students should save all returned tests. ____________________ should also keep ____________________ review sheets.
4. The pilot announced that we would fly through some air pockets. ____________________ said that we should be past ____________________ soon.
5. Randy returned the flash drive to Sheila last Friday. But Sheila insists ____________________ never got ____________________ back.

There are a number of types of pronouns. For convenient reference, they are described briefly in the box below.

Types of Pronouns

Personal pronouns can act in a sentence as subjects, objects, or possessives.

Singular I, me, my, mine, you, your, yours, he, him, his, she, her, hers, it, its

Plural we, us, our, ours, you, your, yours, they, them, their, theirs

Relative pronouns refer to someone or something already mentioned in the sentence.

who, whose, whom, which, that

Interrogative pronouns are used to ask questions.

who, whose, whom, which, what

Demonstrative pronouns are used to point out particular persons or things.

this, that, these, those

NOTE Do not use *them* (as in *them* shoes), *this here, that there, these here,* or *those there* to point out.

Reflexive pronouns are those that end in *-self* or *-selves.* A reflexive pronoun is used as the object of a verb (as in *Cary cut* ***herself***) or the object of a preposition (as in *Jack sent a birthday card to* ***himself***) when the subject of the verb is the same as the object.

Singular	myself, yourself, himself, herself, itself
Plural	ourselves, yourselves, themselves

Intensive pronouns have exactly the same forms as reflexive pronouns. The difference is in how they are used. Intensive pronouns are used to add emphasis. (*I* ***myself*** *will need to read the contract before I sign it.*)

Indefinite pronouns do not refer to a particular person or thing.

each, either, everyone, nothing, both, several, all, any, most, none

Reciprocal pronouns express shared actions or feelings.

each other, one another

For more information on pronouns, see "Pronoun Forms," pages 196–204, and "Pronoun Problems," pages 205–214.

VERBS

Every complete sentence must contain at least one verb. There are two types of verbs: **action verbs** and **linking verbs.**

Action Verbs

An **action verb** tells what is being done in a sentence. For example, look at the following sentences:

- Mr. Jensen **swatted** at the bee with his hand.
- Rainwater **poured** into the storm sewer.
- The children **chanted** the words to the song.

In these sentences, the verbs are *swatted, poured,* and *chanted.* These words are all action verbs; they tell what is happening in each sentence.

For more about action verbs, see "Subjects and Verbs," pages 38 and 248.

Parts of Speech: PRACTICE 4

Insert an appropriate word into each blank. That word will be an action verb; it will tell what is happening in the sentence.

1. The surgeon ____________________ through the first layer of skin.
2. The animals in the cage ____________________ all day.
3. An elderly woman on the street ____________________ me for directions.
4. A man in the restaurant ____________________ to the waitress.
5. Our instructor ____________________ our papers over the weekend.

Linking Verbs

Some verbs are **linking verbs**. These verbs link (or join) a noun to something that is said about it. For example, look at the following sentence:

- The clouds **are** steel gray.

In this sentence, *are* is a linking verb. It joins the noun *clouds* to words that describe it: *steel gray.* Other common linking verbs include *am, appear, become, feel, is, look, seem, sound, was,* and *were.*

For more about linking verbs, see "Subjects and Verbs," page 38 and "More about Subjects and Verbs," pages 249–250.

Parts of Speech: PRACTICE 5

Into each slot, insert one of the following linking verbs: *am, feel, is, look, were.* Use each linking verb once.

1. The secret documents ____________________ put in the shredder.
2. I ____________________ anxious about my date tonight.
3. The bananas ____________________ ripe.
4. The grocery store ____________________ open 24 hours.
5. Whenever I ____________________ angry, I go off by myself to calm down.

Helping Verbs

Sometimes the verb of a sentence consists of more than one word. In these cases, the main verb will be joined by one or more **helping verbs**. Look at the following sentence.

- The basketball team **will be leaving** for their game at six o'clock.
  In this sentence, the main verb is *leaving.* The helping verbs are *will* and *be.*

Other helping verbs include *can, could, do, has, have, may, must, should,* and *would.*

For more information about helping verbs, see "Subjects and Verbs," pages 38–47; "More about Subjects and Verbs," pages 251–252.

Parts of Speech: PRACTICE 6

Into each slot, insert one of the following helping verbs: *does, must, should, could,* and *has been.* Use each helping verb once.

1. Mario ________________ think about where to go on vacation.
2. The athlete ________________ jump higher than her competitor.
3. You ________________ go outside and enjoy this beautiful day!
4. My neighbor ________________ planting tomatoes in his garden.
5. I'm sure the train ________________ stop in that city.

PREPOSITIONS

A **preposition** is a word that connects a noun or a pronoun to another word in the sentence. For example, look at the following sentence:

- A man **in** the bus was snoring loudly.
  In is a preposition. It connects the noun *bus* to *man.*

Here is a list of common prepositions:

about	before	down	like	to
above	behind	during	of	toward
across	below	except	off	under
after	beneath	for	on	up
among	beside	from	over	with
around	between	in	since	without
at	by	into	through	

The noun or pronoun that a preposition connects to another word in the sentence is called the **object** of the preposition. A group of words that begins with a preposition and ends with its object is called a **prepositional phrase**. The words *in the bus,* for example, are a prepositional phrase.

Now read the following sentences and explanations.

- An ant was crawling **up the teacher's leg.**
  The noun *leg* is the object of the preposition *up. Up* connects *leg* with the word *crawling.* The prepositional phrase *up the teacher's leg* describes *crawling.* It tells just where the ant was crawling.
- The man **with the black mustache** left the restaurant quickly.
  The noun *mustache* is the object of the preposition *with.* The prepositional phrase *with the black mustache* describes the word *man.* It tells us exactly which man left the restaurant quickly.

- The plant **on the windowsill** was a present **from my mother**.

  The noun *windowsill* is the object of the preposition *on.* The prepositional phrase *on the windowsill* describes the word *plant.* It describes exactly which plant was a present.

  There is a second prepositional phrase in this sentence. The preposition is *from,* and its object is *mother.* The prepositional phrase *from my mother* explains *present.* It tells who gave the present.

For more about prepositions, see "Subjects and Verbs," page 38, "Subject-Verb Agreement," pages 60–69, and "More about Subjects and Verbs," page 246.

Parts of Speech: PRACTICE 7

Into each slot, insert one of the following prepositions: *of, by, with, in,* and *without.* Use each preposition once.

1. The letter from his girlfriend had been sprayed ____________________ perfume.
2. The weedkiller quickly killed the dandelions ____________________ our lawn.
3. ____________________ giving any notice, the tenant moved out of the expensive apartment.
4. Donald hungrily ate three scoops ____________________ ice cream and an order of French fries.
5. The crates ________________ the back door contain glass bottles and old newspapers.

ADJECTIVES

An **adjective** is a word that describes a noun (the name of a person, place, or thing). Look at the following sentence.

- The dog lay down on a mat in front of the fireplace.

Now look at this sentence when adjectives have been inserted.

- The **shaggy** dog lay down on a **worn** mat in front of the fireplace.

  The adjective *shaggy* describes the noun *dog*; the adjective *worn* describes the noun *mat.* Adjectives add spice to our writing. They also help us to identify particular people, places, or things.

Adjectives can be found in two places:

1 An adjective may come before the word it describes (a **damp** night, the **moldy** bread, a **striped** umbrella).

2 An adjective that describes the subject of a sentence may come after a linking verb. The linking verb may be a form of the verb *be* (he is **furious**, I am **exhausted**, they are **hungry**). Other linking verbs include *feel, look, sound, smell, taste, appear, seem,* and *become* (the soup tastes **salty**, your hands feel **dry**, the dog seems **lost**).

NOTE The words *a, an,* and *the* (called **articles**) are generally classified as adjectives.

For more information on adjectives, see "Adjectives and Adverbs," pages 215 and 218–221.

Parts of Speech: PRACTICE 8

Write any appropriate adjective in each slot.

1. The ____________________ pizza was eaten greedily by the ____________________ teenagers.
2. Melissa gave away the sofa because it was ____________________ and ____________________.
3. Although the alley is ____________________ and ____________________, Karen often takes it as a shortcut home.
4. The restaurant throws away lettuce that is ____________________ and tomatoes that are ____________________.
5. When I woke up in the morning, I had a(n) ____________________ fever and a(n) ____________________ throat.

ADVERBS

An **adverb** is a word that describes a verb, an adjective, or another adverb. Many adverbs end in the letters *ly*. Look at the following sentence:

- The canary sang in the pet-store window as the shoppers greeted each other.

Now look at this sentence after adverbs have been inserted.

- The canary sang **softly** in the pet-store window as the shoppers **loudly** greeted each other.

The adverbs add details to the sentence. They also allow the reader to contrast the singing of the canary to the noise the shoppers are making.

Look at the following sentences and the explanations of how adverbs are used in each case.

- The chef yelled **angrily** at the young waiter.
  The adverb *angrily* describes the verb *yelled.*
- My mother has an **extremely** busy schedule on Tuesdays.
  The adverb *extremely* describes the adjective *busy.*
- The sick man spoke **very** faintly to his loyal nurse.
  The adverb *very* describes the adverb *faintly.*

Some adverbs do not end in *-ly.* Examples include *very, often, never, always,* and *well.*

For more information on adverbs, see "Adjectives and Adverbs," pages 215–224, and "More about Subjects and Verbs," page 253.

Parts of Speech: PRACTICE 9

Write any appropriate adverb in each slot.

1. The water in the pot boiled ____________________.
2. Carla ____________________ drove the car through ____________________ moving traffic.
3. The 911 operator spoke ____________________ to the young child.
4. The game show contestant waved ____________________ to his family in the audience.
5. Wes ____________________ studies, so it's no surprise that he did ____________________ poorly on his finals.

CONJUNCTIONS

Conjunctions are words that connect. There are two types of conjunctions, coordinating and subordinating.

Coordinating Conjunctions (Joining Words)

Coordinating conjunctions join two equal ideas. Look at the following sentence:

- Kevin **and** Steve interviewed for the job, **but** their friend Anne got it.

  In this sentence, the coordinating conjunction *and* connects the proper nouns *Kevin* and *Steve.* The coordinating conjunction *but* connects the first part of the sentence, *Kevin and Steve interviewed for the job,* to the second part, *their friend Anne got it.*

Following is a list of all the coordinating conjunctions. In this book, they are simply called **joining words.**

and	for	or	yet
but	nor	so	

For more on coordinating conjunctions, see information on joining words in "Sentence Types," pages 70–80, and "Run-ons and Comma Splices I," pages 102–111.

Parts of Speech: PRACTICE 10

Write a coordinating conjunction in each slot. Choose from the following: *and, but, so, or,* and *nor.* Use each conjunction once.

1. Either Jerome ________________ Alex scored the winning touchdown.
2. I expected roses for my birthday, ________________ I received a vase of plastic tulips from the dollar store.
3. The cafeteria was serving liver and onions for lunch, ________________ I bought a sandwich at the corner deli.
4. Marian brought a pack of playing cards ________________ a pan of brownies to the company picnic.
5. Neither my sofa ________________ my armchair matches the rug in my living room.

Subordinating Conjunctions

When a **subordinating conjunction** is added to a word group, the words can no longer stand alone as an independent sentence. They are no longer a complete thought. For example, look at the following sentence:

- Karen fainted in class.

  The word group *Karen fainted in class* is a complete thought. It can stand alone as a sentence.

See what happens when a subordinating conjunction is added to a complete thought:

- **When** Karen fainted in class

Now the words cannot stand alone as a sentence. They are dependent on other words to complete the thought:

- **When** Karen fainted in class, we put her feet up on some books.

In this book, a word that begins a dependent word group is called a **dependent word**. Subordinating conjunctions are common dependent words.

Below are some subordinating conjunctions.

after	even if	unless	where
although	even though	until	wherever
as	if	when	whether
because	since	whenever	while
before	though		

Following are some more sentences with subordinating conjunctions:

- **After** she finished her last exam, Joanne said, "Now I can relax."

  After she finished her last exam is not a complete thought. It is dependent on the rest of the words to make up a complete sentence.

- Veejay listens to audio books **while** he drives to work.

  While he drives to work cannot stand by itself as a sentence. It depends on the rest of the sentence to make up a complete thought.

- **Since** apples were on sale, we decided to make an apple pie for dessert.

  Since apples were on sale is not a complete sentence. It depends on *we decided to make an apple pie for dessert* to complete the thought.

For more information on subordinating conjunctions, see information on dependent words in "Sentence Types," pages 70–80; "Fragments I," pages 81–90; and "Run-Ons and Comma Splices II," pages 112–121.

Parts of Speech: PRACTICE 11

Write a logical subordinating conjunction in each slot. Choose from the following: *even though*, *because*, *until*, *when*, and *before*. Use each conjunction once.

1. The bank was closed down by federal regulators ______________________ it lost more money than it earned.
2. ______________________ Paula wants to look mysterious, she wears dark sunglasses and a scarf.
3. ______________________ the restaurant was closing in fifteen minutes, customers sipped their coffee slowly and continued to talk.
4. ______________________ anyone else could answer it, Carl rushed to the phone and whispered, "It's me."
5. The waiter was instructed not to serve any food ______________________ the guests of honor arrived.

INTERJECTIONS

Interjections are words that can stand independently and are used to express emotion. Examples are *oh*, *wow*, *ouch*, and *oops*. These words are usually not found in formal writing:

- "**Hey**!" yelled Maggie. "That's my bike."
- **Oh**, we're late for class.

A Final Note

A word may function as more than one part of speech. For example, the word *dust* can be a verb or a noun, depending on its role in the sentence.

- I **dust** my bedroom once a month, whether it needs it or not. (verb)
- The top of my refrigerator is covered with an inch of **dust**. (noun)

2 Subjects and Verbs

Basics about Subjects and Verbs

Every complete sentence contains a **subject** and a **verb.**

SUBJECTS

The **subject** of a sentence is the person, place, thing, or idea that the sentence is about. The subject can be called the "who or what" word. To find the subject, ask yourself, "Who or what is this sentence about?" or "Who or what is doing something in this sentence?"
For example, look at the following two sentences:

- People applauded.
- Gloria wrote the answers on the board.

People is what the first sentence is about; they are the ones who applauded. So *people* is the subject of the first sentence. The second sentence answers the question, "Who is doing something in the sentence?" The answer is *Gloria.* She is the person who wrote the answers on the board. So *Gloria* is the subject of the second sentence.

A subject will always be either a noun or a pronoun. A **noun** is the name of a person, place, thing, or idea. A **pronoun** is a word—such as *I, you, he, she, it, we,* or *they*—that stands for a noun.

VERBS

Many **verbs** express action; they tell what the subject is doing. You can find an **action verb** by asking, "What does the subject do?" Look again at these sentences:

- People applauded.
- Gloria wrote the answers on the board.

You remember that *people* is the subject of the first sentence. What did they do? They *applauded. Applauded* is the verb in the first sentence. *Gloria* is the subject in the second sentence. What did Gloria do? She *wrote,* so *wrote* is the verb in the second sentence.

Some verbs do not show action; they are called **linking verbs**. Linking verbs like *is, are, was,* and *were* join (or link) the subject to something that is said about the subject. For example, in the sentence *Gloria is a teacher*, the linking verb *is* connects the subject *Gloria* with what is said about her—that she is a teacher.

NOTES

1 Some verbs consist of more than one word—a **helping verb** plus the main verb. Here are some examples of verbs containing more than one word:

- Gloria has written the answer on the board.
  The verb is *has written.*
- The balloons were drifting slowly to earth.
  The verb is *were drifting.*

2 The verb of a sentence never begins with *to.* For example:

- Gloria is going to write the answer on the board.
  The verb of the sentence is *is going.* It is not *write* or *to write.*
- The balloons seemed to hang in the air.
  The verb of the sentence is *seemed.* It is not *hang* or *to hang.*

Understanding Subjects and Verbs

In each sentence, underline the subject once and the verb twice. Then check your answers below.

[1]Daisy Russell lives in Missouri. [2]Her dog's name is Happy. [3]Daisy is happy now, too, after an unhappy past. [4]Daisy experienced a difficult childhood. [5]Her father beat her. [6]He called her worthless. [7]He even tried to sell her to another couple. [8]Her family moved constantly. [9]Unable to read, Daisy felt stupid and ashamed. [10]Now things are different. [11]Daisy has learned to read. [12]Moreover, she teaches other adults to read. [13]Today, Daisy has a lot to smile about.

ANSWERS

[1]Daisy Russell, lives; [2]name, is; [3]Daisy, is; [4]Daisy, experienced; [5]father, beat; [6]He, called; [7]He, tried; [8]family, moved; [9]Daisy, felt; [10]things, are; [11]Daisy, has learned; [12]she, teaches; [13]Daisy, has

Check Your Understanding

Underline each subject once and each verb twice.

[1]Daisy often baby-sits her grandchildren. [2]Their childhood is very different from hers. [3]She was often lonely and afraid. [4]They live without fear. [5]In the photo to the right, Daisy appears with her granddaughter Tiffany. [6]Daisy taught Tiffany to read. [7]The two visit the library in their town often. [8]Daisy's grandchildren both enjoy reading. [9]They have no need to feel ashamed. [10]Their grandmother feels great about that.

A Note on Prepositional Phrases

The subject of a sentence is never part of a prepositional phrase. A **prepositional phrase** is a group of words that begins with a preposition and ends with a noun. Common prepositions are *about, after, as, at, before, between, by, during, for, from, in, into, like, of, on, outside, over, through, to, toward, with,* and *without.* As you look for the subject of a sentence, it may help to cross out any prepositional phrases that you find. Here are examples:

The coffee ~~from the leaking pot~~ stained the carpet.

One ~~of my classmates~~ fell asleep ~~during class~~.

The woman ~~on that motorcycle~~ has no helmet.

The cracks and booms ~~during the thunderstorm~~ were terrifying.

Subjects and Verbs: PRACTICE 1

In each sentence below, cross out the prepositional phrases. Then underline the subject of each sentence once and the verb of each sentence twice.

1. Daisy is looking through her "brag book."
2. She keeps special papers in it.
3. One letter in the book is especially important to her.
4. She had entered a scholarship contest for college students.
5. Her entry was an essay about her life.
6. The letter from the contest officials awarded her first prize.
7. The eagle on the front of her brag book has a special meaning.
8. It tells her to "fly" over any obstacle to her success.
9. Daisy used the scholarship money for a computer.
10. On the computer she writes more essays, poems, and stories.
11. Daisy's life has changed a great deal during the last few years.
12. She learned to read as an adult.
13. She earned her high-school diploma at age 44.
14. She has told her life story on radio and TV.
15. Daisy truly has taken charge of her own life.

A Note on Helping Verbs

As already mentioned, many verbs consist of a main verb plus one or more helping verbs. Helping verbs are shown below:

Forms of *be*:	be, am, is, are, was, were, being, been
Forms of *have*:	have, has, had
Forms of *do*:	do, does, did
Special verbs:	can, could, may, might, must, ought (to), shall, should, will, would

Subjects and Verbs: PRACTICE 2

In each sentence below, cross out the prepositional phrases. Then underline the subject of each sentence once and the verb of each sentence twice.

1. Dogs at the animal shelter wait for a good home.
2. The frozen fish on the counter defrosted quickly.
3. My computer's screen went blank without warning.
4. The kitchen in my parents' house smells like vanilla and cinnamon.
5. A very large truck stalled on the bridge.
6. The orange in the refrigerator has purple spots.
7. Everyone cried at one point during the movie.
8. Several sad-looking puppies huddled in the small cage.
9. Two young boys from the neighborhood were playing catch in the alley.
10. By the end of the day, we had sold between 350 and 400 tickets.

Subjects and Verbs: PRACTICE 3

In each sentence below, cross out the prepositional phrases. Then underline the subject of each sentence once and the verb of each sentence twice.

1. Jolene's friends told her to try speed dating.
2. They decided to go together.
3. On Saturday night, a large group of men and women gathered at a local restaurant.
4. Jolene was a little nervous since it was her first time.
5. Men and women sit across from a new person every 5 minutes.
6. At the end of 5 minutes, everyone moves to a new table.
7. At the end of the evening, Jolene especially liked a man named Jeremy.
8. She wrote his name down on her speed dating form.
9. She was pleased to find out that Jeremy had written her name down too.
10. Jeremy called Jolene to invite her on a date.

Name ______________________ Section ____________ Date ____________

Score: (Number right) ________ x 10 = ____________ %

Subjects and Verbs: TEST 1

For each sentence, cross out any prepositional phrases. Then underline the subject once and the verb twice. Remember to include any helping verb(s).

NOTE To help in your review of subjects and verbs, explanations are given for three of the sentences.

1. A group of new students wandered aimlessly through the school bookstore.
   Of new students and *through the school bookstore* are prepositional phrases.
   The sentence is about a *group* {of students}; what they did was *wandered.*

2. Lucia hopes to compete in the next Special Olympics.
   Since *compete* has *to* in front of it, it cannot be the verb of the sentence.

3. Several part-time salespeople have been fired in the last week.
   Have been fired {*fired* plus the helping verbs *have been*} is what the sentence says the *salespeople* did.

4. The bucket of nails rested precariously on the ladder.

5. That wrench works best on very small pipes.

6. In spite of the weather, we lounged on the patio.

7. Our holiday abroad was filled with relaxing, sightseeing, and eating.

8. The man in the long line complained to the nearest employee about the wait.

9. The mountain lion in the cage lunged at the small child in the front row.

10. The forgetful teenager left his jacket in the movie theater.

Name ______________________ Section ____________ Date ____________

Score: (Number right) ______ x 10 = ________ %

Subjects and Verbs: TEST 2

For each sentence, cross out any prepositional phrases. Then underline the subject once and the verb twice. Remember to include any helping verb(s).

1. The candles on the table smell like vanilla.
2. The people in my family speak two languages.
3. Clean clothes on the line fluttered in the breeze.
4. Without a word, Hugh raced out of the house and into the front yard.
5. Teams of cheerleaders yelled on opposite sides of the gym.
6. Sofia's boyfriend is good with cars.
7. I work at the computer lab between classes.
8. Huge mounds of dirt surround the construction site.
9. The tiles on the bathroom floor look gray in the dim light.
10. Movies about vampires always seem popular with audiences.

Name ______________________ Section ____________ Date ____________

Score: (Number right) ______ x 10 = __________ %

Subjects and Verbs: TEST 3

In each sentence below, cross out the prepositional phrases. Then underline the subject of each sentence once and the verb of each sentence twice.

1. In 2004, Ivo Karp immigrated to the United States from Estonia.

2. In Estonian schools, English was and is now widely taught.

3. Few children, in theory, do not know some English.

4. Most, however, cannot understand enough English to communicate with non-Estonian speakers.

5. Ivo, in addition to having little English, did not have any friends or relatives in America.

6. In spite of this fact, he bravely sought employment by filling out an application at the bus company.

7. He struggled with the application for several days before filling it out with the help of his Estonian-English dictionary.

8. The bus company hired him with the stipulation that he take English-language classes immediately.

9. Ivo met an English teacher on one of his first bus runs.

10. She agreed to teach him English in the hope that she might learn about Estonia at the same time.

Name ______________________________ Section ____________ Date ____________

Score: (Number right) ______ x 10 = ________ %

Subjects and Verbs: TEST 4

Read the sentences below. Then, in the space provided, write the letter of the correct answer to each question.

● The movie audience shrieked in terror and glee at the sight of the seven-headed monster.

_____ **1.** In the sentence above, the subject is
a. audience. **b.** terror. **c.** monster.

_____ **2.** In the sentence above, the verb is
a. shrieked. **b.** glee. **c.** sight.

● A solution to the problem suddenly popped into my head.

_____ **3.** In the sentence above, the subject is
a. problem. **b.** head. **c.** solution.

_____ **4.** In the sentence above, the verb is
a. popped. **b.** suddenly. **c.** head.

● During the long bus trip from Baltimore to Florida, many passengers slept.

_____ **5.** In the sentence above, the subject is
a. bus. **b.** many. **c.** passengers.

_____ **6.** In the sentence above, the verb is
a. During. **b.** many. **c.** slept.

● For his birthday dinner, Will had a pizza with pepperoni, mushrooms, and onions.

_____ **7.** In the sentence above, the subject is
a. dinner. **b.** birthday. **c.** Will.

_____ **8.** In the sentence above, the verb is
a. dinner. **b.** had. **c.** with.

● After my final exam, I can forget about school for a week.

_____ **9.** In the sentence above, the subject is
a. exam. **b.** I. **c.** school.

_____ **10.** In the sentence above, the verb is
a. can. **b.** can forget. **c.** forget.

Name ______________________ Section ____________ Date ____________

Score: (Number right) ______ x 10 = ________ %

Subjects and Verbs: TEST 5

Read the sentences below. Then, in the space provided, write the letter of the correct answer to each question.

● During the hot, dry summer, the farmers worried about their crops.

_____ **1.** In the sentence above, the subject is
a. summer. **b.** crops. **c.** farmers.

_____ **2.** In the sentence above, the verb is
a. During. **b.** about. **c.** worried.

● Drops of icy rain began to fall on the basketball players.

_____ **3.** In the sentence above, the subject is
a. Drops. **b.** rain. **c.** players.

_____ **4.** In the sentence above, the verb is
a. icy. **b.** began. **c.** fall.

● As a result of my father's illness, my family in the past two months has lived a nightmare.

_____ **5.** In the sentence above, the subject is
a. illness. **b.** result. **c.** family.

_____ **6.** In the sentence above, the verb is
a. lived. **b.** has lived. **c.** has.

● To catch the bus to school, Stacy awakens before sunrise.

_____ **7.** In the sentence above, the subject is
a. Stacy. **b.** bus. **c.** sunrise.

_____ **8.** In the sentence above, the verb is
a. catch. **b.** to catch. **c.** awakens.

● Tracy has been sending romantic e-mails to her boyfriend during computer lab.

_____ **9.** In the sentence above, the subject is
a. Tracy. **b.** boyfriend. **c.** e-mails.

_____ **10.** In the sentence above, the verb is
a. has. **b.** has been sending. **c.** during.

3 Irregular Verbs

Basics about Irregular Verbs

Most English verbs are **regular**. That is, they form their past tense and past participle by adding *-ed* or *-d* to the basic form, as shown here:

Basic Form	Past Tense	Past Participle
ask	asked	asked
raise	raised	raised

Some English verbs are **irregular**. They do not form their past tense and past participle by adding *-ed* or *-d* to the basic form of the verb. Instead, their past tenses and past participles are formed in other ways. Here are some of the most common irregular verbs.

Basic Form	Past Tense	Past Participle	Basic Form	Past Tense	Past Participle
become	became	become	go	went	gone
begin	began	begun	grow	grew	grown
break	broke	broken	have	had	had
bring	brought	brought	hide	hid	hidden
catch	caught	caught	is	was	been
choose	chose	chosen	keep	kept	kept
come	came	come	know	knew	known
do	did	done	leave	left	left
drink	drank	drunk	read	read	read
drive	drove	driven	see	saw	seen
eat	ate	eaten	shake	shook	shaken
feel	felt	felt	spend	spent	spent
find	found	found	take	took	taken
forget	forgot	forgotten	tell	told	told
get	got	got, gotten	write	wrote	written
give	gave	given			

A word about helping verbs Sometimes the verb of a sentence consists of more than one word. In these cases, the main verb will be joined by one or more **helping verbs**. Look at the following sentence:

I **should have gone** to bed earlier last night.

In this sentence, the main verb is *gone.* The helping verbs are *should* and *have.* Other common helping verbs include *be, can, could, do, has, may, must, will,* and *would.*

When you use the above chart, keep these two points in mind:

1 If your sentence does **not** have a helping verb, choose the past tense form.
I **ate** a bacon, lettuce, and tomato sandwich.

2 If the sentence **does have** a helping verb, choose the past participle.
I **had eaten** a bacon, lettuce, and tomato sandwich.

NOTES

- If you think a verb is irregular, and it is not in the above list, look it up in your dictionary. If it is irregular, the principal parts will be listed. See "Dictionary Use," page 349.

Understanding Irregular Verbs

In the following passage about college student Zamil Ortiz, **five** mistakes in irregular verbs are underlined. The correct forms of the verbs are then shown in the spaces below.

[1]During her first semester at college, Zamil becomed discouraged. [2]The workload nearly drived her crazy! [3]She had always did well in high school. [4]But at college, everything feeled so new and strange. [5]She worried that she had taked on too big a job.

1. became
2. drove
3. done
4. felt
5. taken

Check Your Understanding

Underline the **five** mistakes in irregular verbs. Then write the correct form of the verbs in the spaces provided.

[1]Zamil knowed she needed to do something. [2]She decided to talk to her instructors. [3]She telled them where she was having problems, and they gived her advice. [4]She worked hard and growed more confident. [5]By the end of her freshman year, she felt she had beginned to win at the college game.

1. ______
2. ______
3. ______
4. ______
5. ______

A Note on Three Problem Verbs

Three common irregular verbs that confuse many writers are *be*, *do*, and *have*. Here are the correct present tense and past tense forms of these three verbs.

	Present Tense		Past Tense	
Be	I am	we are	I was	we were
	you are	you are	you were	you were
	he, she, it is	they are	he, she, it was	they were
Do	I do	we do	I did	we did
	you do	you do	you did	you did
	he, she, it does	they do	he, she, it did	they did
Have	I have	we have	I had	we had
	you have	you have	you had	you had
	he, she, it has	they have	he, she, it had	they had

Irregular Verbs: PRACTICE 1

Underline the mistakes in irregular verbs. Then write the correct form of the verbs in the spaces provided.

[1]Zamil taked an art class that she liked very much. [2]While she was taking the class, she spended hours in the library, looking through art books. [3]Here she has choosed a book about African art.

1. ________________

2. ________________

3. ________________

[1]When you can find the book you want in the library, it's great. [2]But sometimes that doesn't happen. [3]Sometimes the last person who borrowed it never bringed it back. [4]Maybe he or she just forgotted to return it. [5]Maybe the person moved away and keeped it. [6]In any case, books sometimes do disappear from the library forever.

4. ______________________________

5. ______________________________

6. ______________________________

[1]Zamil doesn't always eat in the cafeteria. [2]Today she eated there because there were grilled cheese sandwiches. [3]She likes them so much that she taked two. [4]When her friends seen her sit down, they comed over to join her for lunch.

7. ______________________________

8. ______________________________

9. ______________________________

10. ______________________________

Irregular Verbs: PRACTICE 2

For each sentence below, fill in the correct form of the verb in the space provided.

eaten, ate **1.** The alligators were very hungry. They ________________ everything the keeper gave them within two minutes.

done, did **2.** Sue was told she must not leave the house until she had ____________ all of her chores.

spended, spent **3.** Jose ________________ all his money on fast food and apps for his smart phone.

went, gone **4.** My boss was very unhappy when I suddenly quit my job because he had ________________ to a lot of trouble to train me.

drove, drived **5.** I ________________ over three hundred miles through Arizona before I reached Flagstaff.

catched, caught **6.** The left fielder ________________ the fly ball that resulted in his team winning the World Series.

bringed, brought **7.** They ________________ their daughter to see Santa Claus on the first day he was at the mall.

broke, broken **8.** Much to my embarrassment, my son ________________ the hand off the most expensive doll in the shop.

wrote, writed **9.** He ________________ an angry e-mail to his ex-girlfriend and regretted it as soon as he hit the send button.

chose, choosed **10.** The overweight man ________________ to walk to work, rather than drive, to get an hour's exercise done.

Irregular Verbs: PRACTICE 3

The following passage contains **ten** errors in irregular verbs. Cross out each error. Then, in the space provided, write the correct form of each verb.

[1]Zamil readed and writed a lot in high school. [2]Once she becomed a student at Haverford College, she finded that reading and writing were even more important in college. [3]She also learned that reading in her dorm room could be difficult. [4]Friends often camed by to visit her when she needed to be working. [5]At other times, she growed tired working in her room. [6]She even catched herself falling asleep. [7]She knowed that she needed to find other places to do her school work. [8]She taked her books to the library and tried studying there. [9]The library quickly became one of her favorite places. [10]It was beautiful and quiet. [11]She getted her work done more easily there. [12]Now, you can often find Zamil hard at work in the library.

1. ______________________________
2. ______________________________
3. ______________________________
4. ______________________________
5. ______________________________
6. ______________________________
7. ______________________________
8. ______________________________
9. ______________________________
10. ______________________________

Name ______________________________ Section ____________ Date ____________

Score: (Number right) ______ x 10 = ________ %

Irregular Verbs: TEST 1

Each of the items below contains **two** errors in irregular verbs. Find the errors and cross them out. Then, in the spaces provided, write the correct forms of the verbs.

NOTE To help you master irregular verbs, explanations are given for five of the sentences.

1. Once I seen a hawk dive from the top of a tall tree to capture a field mouse. The bird catched the tiny creature in its claws and flew back to its perch.

a. ______________

b. ______________

Use the past tense of the irregular verb *see* for the first correction needed.

2. I always have gave my little children household chores. This month, my son sets the table, and my daughter does some dusting. Last month, they both done some weeding in the backyard.

a. ______________

b. ______________

Use the past participle of the irregular verb *give* for the first correction needed.

3. My aunt be a big fan of Elvis Presley. Every time she hears "Love Me Tender," she becomes misty-eyed. Last year, she and my uncle gone on a trip to Graceland, Elvis's home. While there, she bought "Elvis Lives" bumper stickers for herself and all her friends.

a. ______________

b. ______________

Use the past tense of the irregular verb *go* for the second correction needed.

4. It is dangerous to shake a baby. Many babies who have been shook have suffered brain injuries. The adults who done this seldom meant to cause such harm.

a. ______________

b. ______________

Use the past tense of the irregular verb *do* for the second correction needed.

5. I was determined not to forget anything I needed at the store. I sat down and writed a long shopping list. Feeling proud of myself, I went to the store. Then I realized I had forgotted the list.

a. ______________

b. ______________

Use the past participle of the irregular verb *forget* for the second correction needed.

Name ______________________________ Section ______________ Date ______________

Score: (Number right) ______ x 10 = ____________ %

Irregular Verbs: TEST 2

Each of the items below contains **two** errors in irregular verbs. Find the errors and cross them out. Then, in the spaces provided, write the correct forms of the verbs.

1. "Whatever becomed of the boy I sat next to in high school history class?" I asked my best friend. She told me that he had growed a beard and joined a cult.

a. ______________

b. ______________

2. My uncle was a generous man. He gived me an iPad for my eighteenth birthday. I felt ashamed because I had not even gave him a card for his birthday.

a. ______________

b. ______________

3. Every one of my friends had saw the musical *A Lion King,* but no one be sure who played each part because of the stage makeup and costumes.

a. ______________

b. ______________

4. The man told his doctor that he only drinks fruit juice now. However, he admitted that he drinked a lot of wine over the previous twenty years. When all the wine in the house was drank, he would sometimes switch to whisky.

a. ______________

b. ______________

5. It taked a long time for me to finish my degree. However, I always knowed that I would finish eventually.

a. ______________

b. ______________

Name ______________________________ Section ______________ Date ______________

Score: (Number right) ________ x 10 = ____________ %

Irregular Verbs: TEST 3

Each of the following passages contains **five** errors in irregular verbs. Cross out each error. Then, in the space provided, write the correct form of each verb.

[1]Think of a time when you beginned something new in your life. [2]Maybe it was a new school, a new job, or even a new personal relationship. [3]Try to remember how you feeled at first. [4]Were you nervous? [5]Or were you confident you knowed what you were doing? [6]Zamil had did very well in high school. [7]But she finded out that college was very different. [8]Fortunately, Zamil was willing to do the hard work of "learning the ropes" at college. [9]Now she feels much more at home.

1. ______________________________

2. ______________________________

3. ______________________________

4. ______________________________

5. ______________________________

[1]"Who taked my food?" [2]The students living on the second floor of Smith Hall getted used to hearing that. [3]There was just one refrigerator on the floor, and many of them keeped snacks in it. [4]But lately, some of that food had been disappearing. [5]Nobody ever seed who took it. [6]Some students lefted notes for the thief, asking her to stop. [7]But nothing helped. [8]Finally some students placed dead mice in brown paper bags and put them in the refrigerator. [9]Two were stolen that night. [10]After that, the thief never struck again.

6. ______________________________

7. ______________________________

8. ______________________________

9. ______________________________

10. ______________________________

Name ______________________ Section ____________ Date ____________

Score: (Number right) ______ x 10 = ________ %

Irregular Verbs: TEST 4

Read each sentence below. Then choose the correct verb, fill in the blank, and write the letter of your choice in the space provided in the margin.

_____ 1. The boss ___________ his daughter to the office on Bring Your Child to Work Day.
a. bring c. brought
b. brang d. bringed

_____ 2. Loretta ___________ the flu from the kindergartners she taught who were all sick that week.
a. catched c. caught
b. catch d. caughted

_____ 3. We ___________ the employees they would all be laid off, but none of them believed us.
a. tell c. told
b. telled d. tolded

_____ 4. Mikhael has ___________ on vacation to Baja every summer for the last twenty years.
a. went c. go
b. wented d. gone

_____ 5. The newlyweds loved being with each other so much that they even ___________ to work together.
a. drived c. driven
b. drove d. droved

_____ 6. Just before arriving at the airport, Kendra exclaimed, "I can't go to London;

I ___________ my passport!"
a. forget c. forgotted
b. forgotten d. forgot

Name ______________________ Section ____________ Date ____________

Score: (Number right) ______ x 10 = ________ %

_____ **7.** The seventy-five-year-old actress has just ____________ her memoirs.

a. writed **c.** written

b. wrote **d.** write

_____ **8.** She was so absent minded that she ____________ the book from the library without checking it out.

a. take **c.** taked

b. took **d.** tooked

_____ **9.** I wish we had ____________ my aunt last Christmas because she died soon after New Year's.

a. seen **c.** seed

b. saw **d.** sawed

_____ **10.** If I had ____________ you were in town last week, you could have stayed with us.

a. knew **c.** knowed

b. known **d.** knewed

Name ______________________ Section __________ Date __________

Score: (Number right) ______ x 10 = ________ %

Irregular Verbs: TEST 5

Read each sentence below. Then choose the correct verb, fill in the blank, and write the letter of your choice in the space provided in the margin.

_____ **1.** Last July, Atinuke __________ an American citizen.
a. become **c.** became
b. becomed **d.** becamed

_____ **2.** The tiny, cute puppy has __________ into a ninety-pound monster.
a. grow **c.** growed
b. grew **d.** grown

_____ **3.** Last night, Natalie __________ nearly four hours on homework.
a. spent **c.** spended
b. spends **d.** spend

_____ **4.** Most people who traveled to Alaska during the Gold Rush never __________ anything.
a. finded **c.** find
b. founded **d.** found

_____ **5.** My father has __________ everything he can to keep our car in good shape.
a. did **c.** do
b. done **d.** doned

_____ **6.** I had __________ to do the assignment.
a. forget **c.** forgot
b. forgotten **d.** forgetted

_____ **7.** My family had __________ the whole pie before I got home.
a. eat **c.** eaten
b. ate **d.** eated

_____ **8.** The technology billionaire __________ all his money to charity.
a. left **c.** lefted
b. leave **d.** leaved

_____ **9.** Juanita has __________ the color gray for her bridesmaids' dresses.
a. chose **c.** choose
b. choosed **d.** chosen

_____ **10.** The story was about a man who foolishly __________ some money in an old trash barrel.
a. hide **c.** hided
b. hid **d.** hides

4 Subject-Verb Agreement

Basics about Subject-Verb Agreement

In a correctly written sentence, the subject and verb agree (match) in number. Singular subjects have singular verbs, and plural subjects have plural verbs.

In simple sentences of few words, it's not difficult to make the subject and verb agree:

- Our *baby* **sleeps** more than ten hours a day. Some *babies* **sleep** even longer.

However, not all sentences are as straightforward as the above examples. Here are two situations that can cause problems with subject-verb agreement.

WORDS BETWEEN THE SUBJECT AND VERB

A verb often comes right after its subject, as in this example:

- The sealed *boxes* **belong** to my brother.

Note Here and in the rest of the chapter, the *subject* is shown in *italic type*, and the **verb** is shown in **boldface type.**

However, at times the subject and verb are separated by a **prepositional phrase**. A prepositional phrase is a group of words that begins with a preposition and ends with a noun or pronoun. *By*, *for*, *from*, *in*, *of*, *on*, and *to* are common prepositions. (A longer list of prepositions is on page 246.) Look at the following sentences:

- A small *bag* of potato chips **contains** 440 calories.

  In this sentence, the subject and verb are separated by the prepositional phrase *of potato chips*. The verb must agree with the singular subject *bag*—not with a word in the prepositional phrase.

- The *tomatoes* in this salad **are** brown and mushy.

  Because the subject, *tomatoes*, is plural, the verb must also be plural. The prepositional phrase *in this salad* has no effect on subject and verb agreement.

- *Books* about baseball **fill** my son's room.

  The plural subject *books* takes the plural verb *fill*. *About baseball* is a prepositional phrase.

COMPOUND SUBJECTS

A **compound subject** is made up of two nouns connected by a joining word. Subjects joined by *and* generally take a plural verb.

- *Running* and *lifting* weights **are** good ways to keep in shape.
- *Fear* and *ignorance* **have** a lot to do with hatred.

Understanding Subject-Verb Agreement

The following passage contains **five** mistakes in subject-verb agreement. See if you can underline them. Then check your answers below.

[1]This is Teron Ivery, a teacher at a school in Philadelphia. [2]It's early in the day, and Teron has just gotten to work. [3]The children in his class hasn't arrived yet.

[4]This is Teron's first year as a teacher. [5]Some parts of his job still surprises him. [6]For example, preparation and paperwork takes up more time than he expected. [7]Those papers in Teron's hand contains his lesson plans for the day. [8]Every day, Teron learns more about what it means to be a good teacher. [9]One thing he knows is that a sense of humor and patience is qualities no teacher should be without.

1. The children in his class haven't arrived yet.
2. Some parts of his job still surprise him.
3. preparation and paperwork take up
4. Those papers in Teron's hand contain
5. a sense of humor and patience are

Check Your Understanding

The following passage has **five** errors in subject-verb agreement. Underline the errors. Then write the correct subject and verb in the space provided.

[1]The students in Teron's class is very young. [2]These boys and girls attends the school's pre-kindergarten class. [3]Most of them can't read yet. [4]But Teron and their other teachers reads to them every day. [5]Being read to is one way children learn to read themselves. [6]The boy on Teron's right love to read about insects. [7]Beetles and mosquitoes doesn't bother him! [8]He thinks that someday he might like to be a scientist who studies bugs.

1. ______________________________
2. ______________________________

3. ______________________________

4. ______________________________

5. ______________________________

Subject-Verb Agreement: PRACTICE 1

Each of the short passages below contains errors in subject-verb agreement. Underline the errors. Then correct them in the spaces provided.

[1]Recess time! [2]Reading and writing is important parts of the school day. [3]But games on the playground is, too. [4]The little kids in Teron's class loves racing around on these scooter-boards. [5]The exercise and fresh air benefits their bodies and minds.

1. ______________________________

2. ______________________________

3. ______________________________

4. ______________________________

[1]It's time to head back into class. [2]The smiles on the kids' faces makes Teron feel good. [3]They remind him of why he is a teacher. [4]Teron grew up in a poor neighborhood without his father around. [5]Drugs and crime was everywhere he looked. [6]The teachers in his own life was very important to him. [7]They let him know they believed he could succeed in life. [8]Adult support and encouragement makes a big difference in the life of a child. [9]Teron wants to provide that kind of support to the children he teaches.

5. ______________________________

6. ______________________________

7. ______________________________

8. ______________________________

[1]Boys and girls learns how to be adults from observing the grownups around them. [2]Teron saw lots of negative role models, such as drug dealers, as he was growing up. [3]But he focused on the positive people in his life. [4]He hopes the kids in his class does the same thing.

9. ______________________________

10. ______________________________

Subject-Verb Agreement: PRACTICE 2

For each sentence below, choose the correct form of the verb from the words in the margin, and write it in the space provided.

sleep, sleeps **1.** Susie and Maddie __________ in twin beds with identical sheets and bedspreads.

revolve, revolves **2.** The Earth and the other planets in our solar system __________ around the Sun.

is, are **3.** Those bags of trash __________ not for the charity shop; they are for the dump.

work, works **4.** Roses and tulips __________ well together in a floral arrangement.

has, have **5.** My mother and father __________ argued throughout my childhood, but they still are best friends.

run, runs **6.** John and his dogs __________ through the park every single day.

worry, worries **7.** The friends of the couple __________ about their deteriorating health.

is, are **8.** The potholes in the road __________ creating a driving hazard.

think, thinks **9.** Some citizens of this country __________ they do not have a duty to vote.

cry, cries **10.** Renaldo and Louise both __________ at very sad movies.

Subject-Verb Agreement: PRACTICE 3

Each of the short passages below contains **five** errors in subject-verb agreement. Underline the errors. Then correct them in the spaces provided.

[1]Parents and educators sometimes talks about "teachable moments." [2]A teachable moment can occur whenever an adult and a child is together. [3]Here, Teron and a little girl shares such a moment. [4]Teron is asking her about what she has written on the sidewalk. [5]The number of letters in her name become a little math lesson. [6]The color of the chalk marks are another mini-lesson. [7]The little girl doesn't know she's having a "teachable moment." [8]She just knows she's having fun.

1. ______________________________
2. ______________________________
3. ______________________________
4. ______________________________
5. ______________________________

[1]The students in Teron's class has gone home, and now he can, too. [2]Even though the seats on the bus is hard, he might fall asleep. [3]A long day of little kids wear him out! [4]But even when he is tired, the rewards of being a teacher satisfies him. [5]He thinks teaching small children are the best career in the world.

6. ______________________________
7. ______________________________
8. ______________________________
9. ______________________________
10. ______________________________

Name ______________________ Section __________ Date __________

Score: (Number right) _______ x 10 = __________ %

Subject-Verb Agreement: TEST 1

For each sentence, fill in the correct form of the missing verb.

NOTE To help you review subject-verb agreement, explanations are given for the first two sentences.

is, are **1.** Tall fences and locked gates ____________ essential safeguards for home swimming pools, whether or not there are small children in the family.

Fences and *gates* is a compound subject requiring a plural verb.

peep, peeps **2.** The harsh rays of the sun ____________ through my window curtains.

Rays, the subject, is a plural noun and so needs a plural verb. *Of the sun* is a prepositional phrase. The subject is never in—or affected by—a prepositional phrase.

look, looks **3.** A startled group of travelers ____________ to the sky when a sudden downpour occurs.

race, races **4.** Antoine and his cousin ____________ cars at the track almost every weekend.

is, are **5.** Ice skating and hockey ____________ the best sports to watch on television.

roll, rolls **6.** Pigs at the farm ____________ in the mud to protect their skin from sunburn.

crush, crushes **7.** The foot-stomping of the village women ____________ the red grapes into liquid for wine.

signal, signals **8.** The tolling of the bells ____________ the beginning of church.

squawk, squawks **9.** The chickens roosting in the hen house ____________ loudly each morning and each evening.

fly, flies **10.** The bee near the flowers ____________ around leisurely, looking for one to pollinate.

Name ______________________________ Section ______________ Date ______________

Score: (Number right) ______ x 10 = ____________ %

Subject-Verb Agreement: TEST 2

For each sentence, fill in the correct form of the missing verb.

have, has **1.** The ice cubes in the punchbowl ____________ melted.

is, are **2.** The old rotary telephones in my grandparents' home ____________ still in working order.

appear, appears **3.** Garlic and onions ____________ in almost everything my grandmother cooks.

wail, wails **4.** The tired, cranky baby ____________ while his mother tries to comfort him.

belong, belongs **5.** The leather cap and jacket on the desk ____________ to our teacher.

forget, forgets **6.** Members of the audience sometimes ____________ to turn off their cell phones during a performance.

is, are **7.** Goat and rabbit ____________ two of the more unusual items on the restaurant's menu.

greet, greets **8.** Moans and groans ____________ the teacher whenever she announces a pop quiz.

show, shows **9.** Dirt and grease ____________ clearly on the windows when the sun shines through them.

do, does **10.** Contrary to public opinion, cats and dogs ____________ not really hate each other.

Name ______________________________ Section ______________ Date ______________

Score: (Number right) ______ x 10 = ____________ %

Subject-Verb Agreement: TEST 3

The following passage contains **twelve** errors in subject-verb agreement. Cross out each wrong verb, and write the correction above the error. The first correction has been added for you as an example.

[1]More and more people ~~is~~ are considering a career in nursing. [2]In fact, in the current economic climate, nursing are considered to be the fastest-growing occupation. [3]The nursing profession have a large range of opportunities, geographic mobility, and job security. [4]Nursing is one profession that will not goes out of business. [5]Long thought to be a woman's career, nursing are becoming more and more popular among men. [6]Study after study demonstrates that men comes to the nursing profession for the same reasons women do. [7]They wants to care for sick and injured people, and they want reasonable job security with good wages. [8]Men reports also enjoying the competitive and challenging nature of this career. [9]As many Western nations faces a shortage of nurses, many governments and nursing schools are actively recruiting more men as nurses. [10]But there is still stereotypes and prejudice, and for some men it has not been easy to excel in the field of nursing. [11]Society are slowly becoming more comfortable with men as nurses, however. [12]Although people may feels a little uncomfortable at the first sight of a male nurse, they usually come to trust and respect him for his professionalism.

Name ______________________ Section ____________ Date ____________

Score: (Number right) ______ x 10 = ________ %

Subject-Verb Agreement: TEST 4

Read each sentence below. Then choose the correct verb, fill in the blank, and write the letter of your choice in the space provided in the margin.

_____ **1.** Our friends in the country ___________ rid of the insects in their yard without using poisonous sprays—they keep chickens.
a. get **b.** gets

_____ **2.** The chickens ___________ most of the insects. In addition, our friends get to enjoy fresh eggs.
a. eat **b.** eats

_____ **3.** The children and their mother ___________ disappointed in the frozen dinners. The peas look wrinkled and dry.
a. is **b.** are

_____ **4.** Also, mounds of soggy stuffing in the frozen dinners ___________ a small piece of meat.
a. cover **b.** covers

_____ **5.** Our kitchen is anything but quiet. The microwave and the dishwasher ___________ all kinds of noise.
a. produce **b.** produces

_____ **6.** Furthermore, the refrigerator in the kitchen hums, and the clock hanging over the cabinets ___________ every hour.
a. chime **b.** chimes

_____ **7.** The coins in the jar on my dresser ___________ almost three pounds. I wonder how much money is actually there.
a. weigh **b.** weighs

_____ **8.** Unfortunately, pennies and nickels ___________ up most of the total in the jar.
a. make **b.** makes

_____ **9.** The Bradleys have made their property much more attractive. Flowers and an evergreen bush now ___________ the sidewalk.
a. line **b.** lines

_____ **10.** Also, a birdbath near the front steps ___________ robins, blue jays, and other colorful birds.
a. attract **b.** attracts

Name ______________________ Section ____________ Date ____________

Score: (Number right) ______ x 10 = __________ %

Subject-Verb Agreement: TEST 5

Read each sentence below. Then choose the correct verb, fill in the blank, and write the letter of your choice in the space provided in the margin.

prefer, prefers **1.** Many cats ___________ places to people. This is in spite of the fact that they may be fond of their owners.

return, returns **2.** But cats after a move often ___________ to their previous home. Their sense of territory is stronger than their affection for people.

scare, scares **3.** The airbags in your car ___________ me. I know they might save your life, but they are pretty intense when deployed.

is, are **4.** Small women are considered the same as children. A person who weighs less than one hundred pounds ___________ liable to be injured by the airbag itself in a crash.

seem, seems **5.** Amelia is a great beauty. At least ten people in this restaurant ___________ to be staring at her.

is, are **6.** She does not seem to notice. She and the other servers ___________ more concerned with just doing their jobs.

swim, swims **7.** The ducks in the pond ___________ effortlessly. They are oblivious to the extremely cold weather.

marvel, marvels **8.** People shivering in heavy jackets ___________ at the ducks' fortitude.

study, studies **9.** My classmates and I ___________ very hard for each English exam.

grade, grades **10.** But some teachers at our university ___________ very strictly. Unfortunately, our English teacher is one of them!

5 Sentence Types

Basics about Sentence Types

There are three basic kinds of sentences in English:

SIMPLE SENTENCES

A **simple sentence** has only one subject-verb combination and expresses one complete thought.

- Our daughter cooked dinner tonight.
  Daughter is the subject, and *cooked* is the verb.

A simple sentence may have more than one subject or more than one verb:

- Shorts and T-shirts sway on the clothesline.
  Shorts and *T-shirts* are the two subjects; *sway* is the verb.
- The children splashed and squealed in the swimming pool.
  Children is the subject; *splashed* and *squealed* are the two verbs.

COMPOUND SENTENCES

A **compound sentence** is made up of two or more complete thoughts. Following are two complete thoughts, joined to form a compound sentence:

- Rose wants chili for dinner, but she forgot to buy beans.

By using a comma and a joining word such as *but*, we can combine what would otherwise be two simple sentences (*Rose wants chili for dinner* and *She forgot to buy beans*) into one compound sentence. In addition to *but*, the words *and* and *so* are the joining words most often used to connect two complete thoughts. Here are examples of *and* and *so* as joining words:

- The driver failed to signal, and he went through a stop sign.
- The meal was not hot, so we sent it back to the kitchen.

COMPLEX SENTENCES

A **complex sentence** is made up of one complete thought and a thought that begins with a dependent word like *after, although, as, because, before, if, since, unless, until, when, where,* and *while.*

Note A comma is placed after a dependent statement when it starts a sentence.

- Although I had a free ticket to the game, I was too tired to go.
- I set my alarm for 5 a.m. because I wanted to finish a paper.
- After the test was over, we got something to eat.

When you write, try to make your sentences varied and interesting. Using all three kinds of sentences will both help you express more complex thoughts and give your writing a lively style.

Understanding Sentence Types

Notice the different sentence types used in this passage about Vimul Ros, a Cambodian-American high-school student. Vimul's friends call him "V."

[1]Although Vimul Ros is only seventeen, he has traveled more than most people in their entire lives. [2]V's parents grew up in Cambodia. [3]They loved their country, but they had to leave upon the outset of war. [4]They fled to neighboring Thailand, where V was born. [5]After time in New York, Singapore, and Philadelphia, V is now a junior at Philadelphia's Charter School for Architecture and Design (CHAD). [6]He is at home in America, but he never wants to forget his Cambodian heritage.

Sentence 2 is a simple sentence. Sentences 3 and 6 are compound sentences. Sentences 1, 4, and 5 are complex sentences.

Check Your Understanding

Combine each group of simple sentences below into a compound or a complex sentence. Write your answers in the spaces provided. Use each of the following words in this order: **and**, **before**, **but**, **because**, and **so**.

1. V is excited about going to college. He is thinking carefully about where to apply.

____

____

____

2. He enrolled at CHAD. V attended another high school.

____

____

____

3. He did not work hard. He still made all A's.

____

4. He felt bored and unhappy. His adviser encouraged him to find another school.

____

____

5. V is interested in graphic design. CHAD is a good school for him.

____

Sentence Types: PRACTICE 1

Combine each group of simple sentences below into a compound or a complex sentence. Write your sentences in the spaces provided. Use each of the following words in this order: **because**, **and**, **so**, **but**, and **if**.

1. V has never seen Cambodia. He relies on his parents to tell him about it.
2. V's mother shares memories with her children. She also shows them sites such as the Cambodian temple in the picture.
3. "My parents want me to understand my background. They try all kinds of stuff."
4. "They put me in a group to learn Cambodian folk dance. I was really bad at that."
5. V has children of his own some day. He will want them to learn about the Cambodian culture.

1. ____

____

2. ____

____

3. ____

____

4. ____

____

5. ____

____

Combine each group of simple sentences below into a compound or a complex sentence. Write your sentences in the spaces provided. Use each of the following words in this order: **when, because, and, after**, and **so**.

6. V's father returned to Cambodia. V enrolled in elementary school.

7. Cambodia is a poor and troubled country. It needs educated people like Mr. Ros.

8. Mr. Ros sees his family only about once a year. They miss him very much.

9. His father left the United States. V lost interest in school for a while.

10. V realized he was endangering his own future. He made himself start working again.

Sentence Types: PRACTICE 2

A. Use a comma and a logical joining word to combine the following pairs of simple sentences into compound sentences. Choose from **and**, **but**, or **so**. Place a comma before the joining word.

> **HINT** Be sure to choose the logical joining word in each case. Keep in mind that
> **and** means *in addition*
> **but** means *however*
> **so** means *as a result*

1. My car broke down. I had to call a taxi to get to school on time.

2. I love anything to do with food. I especially enjoy cooking.

3. In the dark, I lost my keys in the bushes. I can't get into my house now.

4. The cat spends a lot of time cleaning herself. She cannot reach the back of her neck.

5. Harold cleans his house thoroughly every Saturday. On Sunday, he cleans his car.

B. Use a suitable dependent word to combine the following pairs of simple sentences into complex sentences. Choose from **although**, **because**, **since**, and **when**. Place a comma after a dependent statement when it starts a sentence.

6. Fran never talks about her family. She does have five brothers and sisters.

7. I decided to drop my math class. I failed four out of five exams.

8. My boyfriend has been ignoring my phone calls. His ex-girlfriend has been in town.

9. Peter has been sick with the flu for a week. He is returning to class tomorrow.

10. I have not mowed the yard in three weeks. The lawn mower is broken.

Sentence Types: PRACTICE 3

Combine each group of simple sentences below into a compound or a complex sentence. Use each of the following words in this order: **but**, **when**, **although**, **and**.

1. V's father cannot be with his family. They are proud of him.

2. He was living in the United States. He wrote two books for children, including *Brother Rabbit.*

3. Brother Rabbit is just a little bunny. He outwits a dangerous crocodile.

4. In a second book, *The Two Brothers*, one brother becomes rich. The other becomes king of Cambodia.

1. They proud of him, but V's father cannot be with his family.
2. When he was living in the United States, he wrote two books for children, including Brother Rabbit.
3. Although Brother Rabbit is just a little bunny, he
4. outwits a dangerous crocodile.

Combine each group of simple sentences below into a compound or a complex sentence. Use each of the following words in this order: **because, although, but, and, if, since.**

5. V was born into one culture but raised in another.
He has a foot in two worlds.
6. He lives surrounded by souvenirs of Cambodia. He wears a sweatshirt from a college in New Hampshire.
7. He is involved in Cambodian youth organizations.
He is friends with "all kinds of people."
8. He doesn't pay attention to people's color. His Asian, black, white, and Hispanic friends are proof of this.
9. V gets a chance to travel to Cambodia some day.
He would like to be of help there.
10. He was a little boy. V has seen himself as a citizen of the world.

5. Because V was born into one culture but raised in another, he
6. He wears a sweatshirt from college of New Hampshire although he lives surrounded by souvenirs of Cambodia.
7. He is involved in Cambodian youth organizations, but he is
8. And he doesn't pay attention to people's color, his Asian, black, white, and Hispanic friends are proof of this.
9. If V gets a chance to travel to Cambodia some day, he would
10. Since he was a little boy, V has seen himself as a

Name ______________________ Section ____________ Date ____________

Score: (Number right) ________ x 10 = ____________ %

Sentence Types: TEST 1

A. Use a comma and a suitable joining word to combine the following pairs of simple sentences into compound sentences. Choose from **and** (which means *in addition*), **but** (which means *however*), or **so** (which means *as a result*).

NOTE To help you master sentence combining, hints are given for the first two sentences.

1. The coffee is cold. It is also too strong.
   The coffee is cold; *in addition*, it is also too strong.
   ____

2. Our car runs well. Its body is dented and rusty.
   Our car runs well; however, its body is dented and rusty.
   ____

3. The book was very expensive. I didn't buy it.
   ____

4. Gene laughed throughout the movie. His date didn't laugh once.
   ____

5. The electricity was out. We had no flashlights or candles.
   ____

B. Use a suitable dependent word to combine the following pairs of simple sentences into complex sentences. Choose from **although**, **because**, **since**, and **when**. Place a comma after a dependent statement when it starts a sentence.

6. The ball game was postponed. It began to rain heavily.
   ____

7. Olivia practices her trumpet. The dog howls.
   ____

8. The house looks beautiful. It seems cold and unfriendly to me.
   ____

9. She doesn't drive. Mia must walk or take the bus to work.
   ____

10. The beautiful fireworks exploded. The audience gasped and applauded.
    ____

Name ______________________ Section ____________ Date ____________

Score: (Number right) ______ x 10 = ________ %

Sentence Types: TEST 2

A. Use a comma and a suitable joining word to combine the following pairs of simple sentences into compound sentences. Choose from **and**, **but**, or **so**.

1. Eddie was tired of his appearance. He shaved all the hair off his head.

2. Eddie bought new clothing in bright colors. He added an earring as well.

3. Twenty students were enrolled in the class. Only eight were present that stormy day.

4. Thirty percent of M&M's are brown. Twenty percent of them are red.

5. The stain did not wash out of my white pants. I dyed the pants tan.

B. Use a suitable dependent word to combine the following pairs of simple sentences into complex sentences. Choose from **although**, **because**, **since**, and **when**. Place a comma after a dependent statement when it starts a sentence.

6. I need to improve my grades. I will start taking more notes in class.

7. There used to be many small stores downtown. They are gone now.

8. The bus came into sight. Connie shouted "Goodbye!" and rushed out the door.

9. Mental illness is so little understood. It has always frightened people.

10. I'm allergic to most animals. Siamese cats don't bother me.

Name ______________________________ Section ______________ Date ______________

Score: (Number right) ________ x 10 = ____________ %

Sentence Types: TEST 3

Combine each group of simple sentences into compound or complex sentences. Combine the first two sentences into one sentence, and combine the last two sentences into another sentence. Use any of the following joining words and dependent words.

Joining words	**and**	**but**	**so**	
Dependent words	**after**	**although**	**because**	**when**

Two comma hints

1 Use a comma between two complete thoughts joined by **and**, **but**, or **so**.
2 Place a comma after a dependent statement when it starts a sentence.

1. It had rained for three days. The sun finally came out.
We wanted to have a picnic. The ground was too wet.

____

____

2. Roy saw a bright rainbow. He ran to get his camera.
He rushed back to take a picture. The rainbow had gone.

____

____

3. A long-winded neighbor was at my door. I pretended not to be home.
She rang the bell several times. She knocked on the door repeatedly.

____

____

4. Nadine hates her job. She won't leave it.
She likes the pension plan. She will stay until retirement.

____

____

5. I had to meet my girlfriend's mother. I was very nervous.
I was afraid of her opinion of me. She was very warm and friendly.

____

____

Name ______________________ Section ____________ Date ____________

Score: (Number right) ______ x 10 = ________ %

Sentence Types: TEST 4

In the space provided, write the letter of the combined sentence that reads most smoothly, clearly, and logically.

_____ **1.** **a.** Because my parents are both quite short, we kids are all on the tall side.
b. My parents are both quite short, so we kids are all on the tall side.
c. Although my parents are both quite short, we kids are all on the tall side.

_____ **2.** **a.** My cousin was falling behind in algebra class, but he decided to work with a tutor.
b. My cousin was falling behind in algebra class because he decided to work with a tutor.
c. Because my cousin was falling behind in algebra class, he decided to work with a tutor.

_____ **3.** **a.** The thunderstorm rattled the windows, but the dog hid in the closet.
b. Although the thunderstorm rattled the windows, the dog hid in the closet.
c. While the thunderstorm rattled the windows, the dog hid in the closet.

_____ **4.** **a.** The movie turned out to be too scary, so I took the children home.
b. The movie turned out to be too scary, but I took the children home.
c. Although the movie turned out to be too scary, I took the children home.

_____ **5.** **a.** Although the baby goat was cute and fluffy, it had a vicious temper.
b. The baby goat was cute and fluffy, and it had a vicious temper.
c. Because the baby goat was cute and fluffy, it had a vicious temper.

_____ **6.** **a.** Nobody was very hungry Thanksgiving night, but we ate cereal for dinner.
b. Nobody was very hungry Thanksgiving night, so we ate cereal for dinner.
c. Nobody was very hungry Thanksgiving night because we ate cereal for dinner.

_____ **7.** **a.** The mechanic called about our car, so he didn't have good news.
b. When the mechanic called about our car, he didn't have good news.
c. Before the mechanic called about our car, he didn't have good news.

_____ **8.** **a.** Alan is limping badly because he twisted his ankle playing basketball.
b. Because Alan is limping badly, he twisted his ankle playing basketball.
c. Alan is limping badly, and he twisted his ankle playing basketball.

_____ **9.** **a.** Before I met my new neighbor, I had never been friends with a blind person.
b. I met my new neighbor, but I had never been friends with a blind person.
c. I met my new neighbor, so I had never been friends with a blind person.

_____ **10.** **a.** You put masking tape around the windows and doors, but I'll get the paint and brushes.
b. Although you put masking tape around the windows and doors, I'll get the paint and brushes.
c. While you put masking tape around the windows and doors, I'll get the paint and brushes.

Name ______________________________ Section ____________ Date ____________

Score: (Number right) ______ x 10 = ________ %

Sentence Types: TEST 5

In the space provided, write the letter of the combined sentence that reads most smoothly, clearly, and logically.

_____ **1.** **a.** After I have an exam in the morning, I'd better get to bed early.
b. Although I have an exam in the morning, I'd better get to bed early.
c. I have an exam in the morning, so I'd better get to bed early.

_____ **2.** **a.** Because these shoes are comfortable, their price is reasonable.
b. These shoes are comfortable, but their price is reasonable.
c. These shoes are comfortable, and their price is reasonable.

_____ **3.** **a.** Although the clothes were being washed, we sat in the Laundromat reading magazines.
b. While the clothes were being washed, we sat in the Laundromat reading magazines.
c. The clothes were being washed, but we sat in the Laundromat reading magazines.

_____ **4.** **a.** I am afraid of heights, and flying in an airplane doesn't bother me.
b. Although I am afraid of heights, flying in an airplane doesn't bother me.
c. Because I am afraid of heights, flying in an airplane doesn't bother me.

_____ **5.** **a.** After rain began falling heavily, the umpires canceled the game.
b. Although rain began falling heavily, the umpires canceled the game.
c. Rain began falling heavily while the umpires canceled the game.

_____ **6.** **a.** When I always hang up on telemarketers, they keep calling.
b. Because I always hang up on telemarketers, they keep calling.
c. Although I always hang up on telemarketers, they keep calling.

_____ **7.** **a.** When my mother was a young girl, she quit school to help support her family.
b. Because my mother was a young girl, she quit school to help support her family.
c. My mother was a young girl, so she quit school to help support her family.

_____ **8.** **a.** The towels look soft and fluffy, so they feel scratchy.
b. When the towels look soft and fluffy, they feel scratchy.
c. Although the towels look soft and fluffy, they feel scratchy.

_____ **9.** **a.** We went to a movie last night until we stopped for ice cream.
b. After we went to a movie last night, we stopped for ice cream.
c. We went to a movie last night, but we stopped for ice cream.

_____ **10.** **a.** The newlyweds are trying to save money, so they clip coupons and buy items on sale.
b. Although the newlyweds are trying to save money, they clip coupons and buy items on sale.
c. The newlyweds are trying to save money, but they clip coupons and buy items on sale.

6 Fragments I

Basics about Fragments

To be a complete sentence, a group of words must contain a subject and a verb. It must also express a complete thought. If it lacks a subject, verb, or a complete thought, it is a **fragment**.

The most common kind of fragment is the **dependent-word fragment**, which has a subject and verb but does not express a complete thought. Here is an example:

- Because Laura was tired.

Although this word group contains a subject (*Laura*) and a verb (*was*), it is an incomplete thought. The reader wants to know **what happened** because Laura was tired. A word group that begins with *because* or another dependent word cannot stand alone; another idea is needed to complete the thought. For example, we could correct the above fragment like this:

- Because Laura was tired, **she took a nap.**

  The words *she took a nap* complete the thought.

Here are two more dependent-word fragments.

- When Joseph asked me on a date.
- After I turned off the television set.

Each of these word groups begins with a dependent word (*when, after*) and expresses an incomplete idea. See if you can add words to each fragment that would complete the thought.

- When Joseph asked me on a date, ______________________________.
- ______________________________ after I turned off the television set.

Here are some ways to complete the above fragments:

- When Joseph asked me on a date, **I said yes.**
- **I picked up a book** after I turned off the television set.

Punctuation note When a dependent-word group starts a sentence, follow it with a comma.

When you use a dependent word, take care that you complete the thought in the same sentence. Otherwise, a fragment may result. Here is a list of common dependent words:

after	even though	unless	wherever
although	even when	until	whether
as	if	what	which
because	since	when	while
before	that	whenever	who
even if	though	where	

Note that very often the way to correct a dependent-word fragment will be to connect it to the sentence that comes before or after it.

Understanding Fragments

The following passage about Donna Atkinson, a wife, mother, college student, and jobholder, contains **five** dependent-word fragments. See if you can underline the five fragments. Then look at how they are corrected.

[1]Although Donna is a wife and mother. [2]She is also a college student. [3]She wants to be an elementary teacher. [4]When she has earned her degree. [5]Since she is very busy with her son, her husband, her job, and her other duties. [6]She has decided to take college courses online, using her computer. [7]She is happy with her decision. [8]Because she does not have to travel to campus. [9]In order to take her classes, she reads assignments from her textbooks and then reads lectures online. [10]She has the option of taking tests online. [11]She is even able to ask her instructor questions. [12]Which she can do using e-mail.

1. Although Donna is a wife and mother, she is also a college student.
2. She wants to be an elementary teacher when she has earned her degree.
3. Since she is very busy with her son, her husband, her job, and her other duties, she has decided to take college courses online, using her computer.
4. She is happy with her decision because she does not have to travel to campus.
5. She is even able to ask her instructor questions, which she can do using e-mail.

Check Your Understanding

Underline the **five** dependent-word fragments. Then correct them in the spaces provided.

[1]Before she goes to bed at night, Donna gets ready for the next day. [2]Which will begin very early. [3]She will get up before sunrise. [4]Even if she stays up late studying. [5]She wakes up so early because she has her own office-cleaning business. [6]She does the cleaning jobs early in the morning. [7]Before the employees arrive at the office. [8]In the evening, she makes sure she has all her supplies together. [9]Because she doesn't want to forget anything. [10]Donna can't do everything she needs to do. [11]Unless she is well organized.

1. Before she goes to bed at night, Donna gets ready for the next day, which will begin very early.
2. She will get up before sunrise, even if she stays up late
3. She does the cleaning jobs early in the morning, before the employees
4. In the evening, she makes sure she has all her supplies together because she doesn't want to forget anything.
5. Donna can't do everything she needs to do, unless she is well organized

Fragments I: PRACTICE 1

Each of the short passages below contains dependent-word fragments. Underline each fragment. Then correct it on or above the line, crossing out unneeded periods, replacing unneeded capital letters with lowercase letters, and so on.

[1]When Sue and Fred both expressed an interest in learning to cook. [2]They enrolled in a Mexican cooking class. [3]The class was offered through an adult education program at the local junior college. [4]Which was located close to where they lived. [5]After paying a small fee of 20 dollars. [6]They were ready to begin the class. [7]Their teacher was a small, intense woman named Senora Gomez. [8]She assigned Sue and Fred to the same kitchen area. [9]Because she knew they wanted to learn together.

[1]Even though Sue and Fred loved to eat Mexican food. [2]They knew nothing about how to prepare it. [3]They did not know *masa* from *albondigas*! [4]Before they joined the class. [5]Senora Gomez assured them they would learn names of ingredients, cooking terms, and methods. [6]Before this class was over.

[1]Although the twelve weeks of class passed quickly. [2]Sue and Fred soon felt confident about their newfound knowledge of Mexican cooking. [3]The culmination of the class came with a visit to an authentic Mexican market, *El Mercado,* in Los Angeles. [4]Since shopping for quality ingredients was key to successful Mexican cooking. [5]When certificates of excellence were presented to the students at a grand banquet prepared by the class. [6]Everyone present, including family and friends, enjoyed the authentic meal very much.

Fragments I: PRACTICE 2

Underline the dependent-word fragment in each of the following items. Then correct it in the space provided. Add a comma after a dependent-word group that begins a sentence.

1. Because the movie was so violent. Some people left the theater.

   ____

2. Everything was peaceful. Before Martha stormed into the room.

   ____

3. Unless the refrigerator is fixed soon. All the food will spoil.

   ____

4. The batter argued with the umpire. While the crowd booed.

   ____

5. When two guests began to argue. The hostess moved the party outside.

   ____

6. After he bought some donuts. Virgil hurried to school.

   ____

7. We jumped up from the sofa. When we heard the crash in the kitchen.

   ____

8. Although the car was totaled. The passengers were unharmed.

   ____

9. Classes ended early today. Because of a leak in the water main.

   ____

10. Our neighbor is a quiet man. Who works as a nurse on a night shift.

    ____

Fragments I: PRACTICE 3

Each passage below contains **five** dependent-word fragments. Underline each fragment. Then correct it on or above the line, crossing out unneeded periods, replacing unneeded capital letters with lowercase letters, and so on.

[1]Meditation is becoming more and more popular among all age groups. [2]When we look at our increasingly stressful and busy lives. [3]It makes sense that people would seek something that can help them feel calmer. [4]Although there are many different types of meditation and different ways of meditating. [5]All meditation practices have something in common. [6]They all function to focus or train the mind and quiet busy thinking. [7]Meditation has been practiced since antiquity. [8]As a component of numerous religious traditions. [9]Since the 1960s, meditation has been the focus of scientific research. [10]And has been linked to changes in metabolism, blood pressure, brain activation, and other bodily processes. [11]It has been shown to dramatically reduce stress and pain and create a calm, peaceful state in the meditator. [12]Because of these positive results. [13]Meditation is often prescribed by doctors and other health care practitioners as a healing method.

[1]Regardless of your religious or scientific beliefs. [2]Meditation is worth a try. [3]If you are experiencing stress in your life. [4]Find a few moments in your busy day to sit with your eyes closed. [5]In a place where you won't be disturbed. [6]Morning is a good time to meditate as it sets the tone for the day. [7]First pay attention to sounds around you and notice the physical sensations in your body. [8]Next notice your breathing. [9]Watching the rise and fall of your chest and abdomen. [10]You may notice other things, like your thoughts or the sounds around you, but as soon as you notice your mind has wandered off, bring it back. [11]To noticing your breathing. [12]Do this for five minutes to start your day off right. [13]Over time you may notice that you feel better, less stressed, and more at ease.

Name ______________________________ Section ______________ Date ______________

Score: (Number right) ______ x 10 = ____________ %

Fragments I: TEST 1

Underline the dependent-word fragment in each of the following items. Then correct it in the space provided. Add a comma after a dependent-word group that begins a sentence.

NOTE To help you correct fragments, directions are given for the first two sentences.

1. Before I began violin lessons. I knew nothing about music.

The first word group begins with the dependent word *before.* Correct the fragment by adding it to the second word group.

____

2. I was worried about my daughter's cough. Until the doctor's diagnosis of bronchitis.

The second word group begins with the dependent word *until.* Correct the fragment by adding it to the first word group.

____

3. While we were driving down a dark, narrow street. We almost hit a man walking in the road.

____

____

4. If you see a penny lying on the sidewalk. Do you pick it up or leave it there?

____

5. I have never really idolized famous people. Who are only famous for acting or singing.

____

6. I saw a mother duck and her ducklings crossing the busy street. As if they had all the time in the world.

____

____

7. Whenever I think about my mother's cooking. I remember my favorite meal of pot roast, mashed potatoes, and biscuits.

____

____

8. Lucy is very upset at her husband. Because he forgot their tenth wedding anniversary.

____

9. Whether the boss is on time or two hours late to work. His employees still have to punch the time clock at exactly 9:00 in the morning.

____

____

10. We should arrive in Tulsa by 10:00 tonight. Unless the plane is very late.

____

Name ______________________ Section ____________ Date ____________

Score: (Number right) ______ x 10 = ________ %

Fragments I: TEST 2

Underline the dependent-word fragment in each of the following items. Then correct it in the space provided. Add a comma after a dependent-word group that begins a sentence.

1. Before the dog escaped from the fenced yard. He had tried to run away three other times.

2. We will never finish this project. Because we started on it so late.

3. I am really afraid to see the dentist. Even if I have a very painful toothache.

4. Although Susie had seen that man several times before. She could not remember his name.

5. Since the elm trees are all suffering from a fatal disease. They will all have to be cut down.

6. The new cheerleaders felt guilty celebrating their having been chosen. While some of their friends were left off the squad.

7. Sam and Maria asked to take part of their meals home. When the portions at this popular restaurant were huge.

8. Because John had more listings than anyone else in his office. He won salesman of the month.

9. Everyone at the party had a very good time. Although the host and hostess ran out of food early in the evening.

10. When the alarm clock awakened John. He turned it off because he forgot it was Monday.

Name ______________________________ Section ______________ Date ______________

Score: (Number right) ______ x 10 = ____________ %

Fragments I: TEST 3

Each passage below contains **five** dependent-word fragments. Underline each fragment. Then correct it on or above the line, crossing out unneeded periods, replacing unneeded capital letters with lowercase letters, and so on.

[1]Although most college students are in their teens or twenties. [2]Many are a good deal older. [3]Such people are often called "nontraditional students." [4]When they were younger. [5]They may have been too busy raising children to attend college. [6]Or maybe they have decided that going to college would be good for their careers. [7]Going to school as a "nontraditional" student has its own difficulties. [8]Which often include a job and family duties. [9]But older adults generally do very well in school. [10]Because they have strong goals. [11]Even if it means making personal sacrifices. [12]They are willing to do whatever it takes to get an education.

[1]Since the Internet was invented. [2]A real social revolution has taken place. [3]That revolution has affected many of our lives. [4]Going shopping in stores is a thing of the past for some people. [5]Who now order clothing, books, and supplies online. [6]Because e-mail is so fast and easy. [7]Some people don't use the telephone anymore. [8]Through Facebook, Twitter, and texting on smart phones, people form close relationships with each other. [9]Even though they've never met. [10]Before the "Internet revolution" took place. [11]None of these things would have been possible.

Name ______________________ Section __________ Date __________

Score: (Number right) ______ x 20 = ________ %

Fragments I: TEST 4

Read each group below. Then write the letter of the item that contains a fragment.

_____ **1.** **a.** Leon was very nervous. He had not studied for the exam. A failing grade could result in his failing the course.
b. Leon was very nervous because he had not studied for the exam. A failing grade could result in his failing the course.
c. Because Leon had not studied for the exam. He was very nervous. A failing grade could result in his failing the course.

_____ **2.** **a.** In 2005, the Oscar for Best Actor went to Morgan Freeman. Who had been nominated for four other Oscars.
b. In 2005, the Oscar for Best Actor went to Morgan Freeman. He had been nominated for four other Oscars.
c. In 2005, the Oscar for Best Actor went to Morgan Freeman, who had been nominated for four other Oscars.

_____ **3.** **a.** Before Tracy went to the party, she tried on six different outfits. She finally chose the one she'd tried on first.
b. Before Tracy went to the party. She tried on six different outfits. She finally chose the one she'd tried on first.
c. Tracy tried on six different outfits before she went to the party. She finally chose the one she'd tried on first.

_____ **4.** **a.** On our drive into the city, we came across an accident. Which had closed three of the four lanes of traffic. It added an extra hour to our trip.
b. On our drive into the city, we came across an accident, which had closed three of the four lanes of traffic. It added an extra hour to our trip.
c. On our drive into the city, we came across an accident. It had closed three of the four lanes of traffic, and it added an extra hour to our trip.

_____ **5.** **a.** Unless you are ready to work hard. Don't even think of enrolling in Dr. Reynold's class. She is a very demanding teacher.
b. Don't even think of enrolling in Dr. Reynold's class unless you are ready to work hard. She is a very demanding teacher.
c. Unless you are ready to work hard, don't even think of enrolling in Dr. Reynold's class. She is a very demanding teacher.

Name ______________________ Section ____________ Date ____________

Score: (Number right) ______ x 20 = ________ %

Fragments I: TEST 5

Read each group below. Then write the letter of the item that contains a fragment.

_____ **1.** **a.** Suzanne speaks several languages. She speaks English, German, French, and Greek, although her Greek is a little rusty.
b. Suzanne speaks several languages. She speaks English, German, French, and Greek. Although her Greek is a little rusty.
c. Suzanne speaks several languages. Although her Greek is a little rusty, she speaks English, German, French, and Greek.

_____ **2.** **a.** Until I speak to my mother, I will not know if my dad was all right after surgery. Then I will be able to rest easy.
b. I will not know if my dad was all right after surgery until I speak to my mother. Then I will be able to rest easy.
c. I will not know if my dad was all right after surgery. Until I speak to my mother. Then I will be able to rest easy.

_____ **3.** **a.** I love to attend the opera. Wherever one is playing. Even if I have to travel a long way, I do not mind.
b. Wherever one is playing, I love to attend the opera. Even if I have to travel a long way, I do not mind.
c. I love to attend the opera wherever one is playing. Even if I have to travel a long way, I do not mind.

_____ **4.** **a.** When my grandmother visits. I know she will bring a bag full of presents. I believe she loves to see us open the gifts, even more than we enjoy receiving them.
b. When my grandmother visits, I know she will bring a bag full of presents. I believe she loves to see us open the gifts, even more than we enjoy receiving them.
c. I know my grandmother will bring a bag full of gifts when she visits. I believe she loves to see us open the gifts, even more than we enjoy receiving them.

_____ **5.** **a.** Louise loved salsa dancing before she got married and had children. She wants to train as a salsa dancer as soon as the children are older.
b. Before she got married and had children, Louise loved salsa dancing. She wants to train as a salsa dancer as soon as the children are older.
c. Louise loved salsa dancing. Before she got married and had children. She wants to train as a salsa dancer as soon as the children are older.

7 Fragments II

More about Fragments

In addition to dependent-word fragments, there are three other common types of fragments:

FRAGMENTS WITHOUT A SUBJECT

Some fragments do have a verb, but they lack a subject.

Fragment Joe Davis lowered himself from the van into his wheelchair. And then rolled up the sidewalk ramp.
The second word group lacks a subject, so it is a fragment.

You can often fix such a fragment by adding it to the sentence that comes before it.

Sentence Joe Davis lowered himself from the van into his **wheelchair and** then rolled up the sidewalk ramp.

–ING AND *TO* FRAGMENTS

When *-ing* appears at or near the beginning of a word group, a fragment may result.

Fragment Hoping to furnish their new home cheaply. The newlyweds go to garage sales.
The first word group lacks both a subject and a verb, so it is a fragment.

A fragment may also result when a word group begins with *to* followed by a verb:

Fragment Leo jogged through the park. To clear his mind before the midterm.
The second word group is a fragment that lacks both a subject and a complete verb. (A word that follows *to* cannot be the verb of a sentence.)

You can often fix such fragments by attaching them to the sentence that comes before or after.

Sentence Hoping to furnish their new home **cheaply, the** newlyweds go to garage sales.

Sentence Leo jogged through the **park to** clear his mind before the midterm.

Punctuation note When an *-ing* or *to* word group starts a sentence, follow it with a comma.

EXAMPLE FRAGMENTS

Word groups that begin with words like *including, such as, especially,* and *for example* are sometimes fragments.

Fragment For class, we had to read several books. Including *The Diary of Anne Frank.*

Fragment My grandfather has many interests. For example, playing poker and watching old cowboy movies.

You can often fix such fragments by attaching them to the sentence that comes before, or by adding a subject and a verb.

Sentence For class, we had to read several **books, including** *The Diary of Anne Frank.*

Sentence My grandfather has many interests. For example, **he plays** poker and **watches** old cowboy movies.

Understanding Fragments

The following passage about Charlene Clarke, a single parent and student living in rural Virginia, contains five fragments. See if you can find and underline the five fragments. Then look at how they are corrected.

[1]This is Charlene Clarke. [2]Taking a moment to relax with her Boston terrier, Diamond. [3]Charlene doesn't have a lot of time to do things she enjoys. [4]Such as playing with her dog. [5]Working on her degree at the local business college. [6]She has a great deal of reading and studying to do. [7]In addition, she has other responsibilities. [8]Especially as the mother of four active young children. [9]There are plenty of days that Charlene feels overwhelmed. [10]But knows she must keep on going.

1. This is Charlene Clarke, taking a moment to relax with her Boston terrier, Diamond.
2. Charlene doesn't have a lot of time to do things she enjoys, such as playing with her dog.
3. Working on her degree at the local business college, she has a great deal of reading and studying to do.
4. In addition, she has other responsibilities, especially as the mother of four active young children.
5. There are plenty of days that Charlene feels overwhelmed but knows she must keep on going.

Check Your Understanding

Underline the **five** fragments in the following passage. Then correct them in the spaces provided.

[1]Charlene is studying to become a pharmacy technician. [2]She has to learn some very challenging material. [3]Such as the names of dozens of drugs and medical disorders. [4]Sometimes Charlene is amazed to find herself in school at all. [5]Considering how much she disliked school as a child. [6]She had trouble reading and spelling. [7]And was in special ed until seventh grade. [8]She has never forgotten how cruel other students could be. [9]Calling her names and making fun of her. [10]But she worked hard on her reading skills. [11]And was able to get back into regular classes. [12]Now she is earning A's and B's in school. [13]She even works part-time in the school library.

1. ______________________________

____

2. ______________________________

____

3. ______________________________

4. ______________________________

____

5. ______________________________

Fragments II: PRACTICE 1

Each of the short passages below contains fragments. Underline the fragments and then correct each in the space provided.

[1]Charlene has a number of reasons for enrolling in her job-training program. [2]Especially her four children, Kimmie, Nicole, Josh, and Sarah. [3]In the past, Charlene worked as an aide in a nursing home. [4]Handing out medications and feeding and helping residents. [5]She and her husband, Woodie, shared the job of raising the children. [6]But driving to work one morning. [7]Woodie was in a terrible automobile accident. [8]Charlene lost her husband, and the children lost their father. [9]Having to be a single parent. [10]Charlene has more responsibilities than ever. [11]She realized she needed a better job. [12]To provide for her children.

1. ______________________________

____

2. ______________________________

____

3. ______________________________

4. ______________________________

5. ______________________________

[1]The children are all in school now. [2]Remembering her own hard time in school. [3]Charlene is determined that her children will have a better experience. [4]She stays in touch with their teachers. [5]To learn about little problems before they become big ones. [6]She knows that teachers have their hands full with many students. [7]And wants to make sure her kids get the attention they need.

6. ____

____

7. ____

____

8. ____

____

[1]But being a parent isn't all about stress. [2]There are lots of fun times, too. [3]Such as reading about dinosaurs with Josh. [4]Charlene likes to see her children spend time with books. [5]Learning to enjoy reading for its own sake.

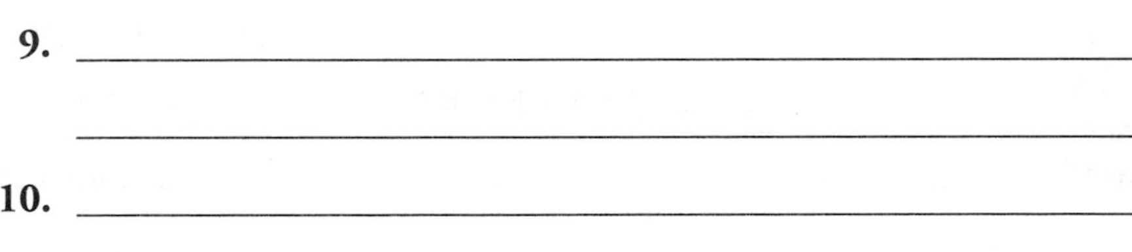

9. ____

____

10. ____

____

Fragments II: PRACTICE 2

Underline the fragment in each item that follows. Then rewrite and correct the fragment in the space provided.

1. Jan is talking out loud in her bedroom. Practicing a speech for her English class.

____

2. Puffing on a bad-smelling cigar. Mr. Bloom said, "You ought to take better care of your health."

____

____

3. I hung a sweater in the bathroom as the shower ran. To steam out the wrinkles.

____

4. Ticking loudly. The clock reminded me how little time I had to get ready.

____

5. We get forty-two channels on our TV. But don't have anything we want to watch.

____

6. Hank runs four miles every day after school. To get ready for track season.

____

7. Staring at me with an icy look on her face. The clerk refused to answer my question.

____

8. I eat only healthy snacks. Such as ice cream made with natural ingredients.

____

9. Crowds of fans hung around the theater all day. Hoping to see the famous actor.

____

10. Some nursery rhymes have unpleasant stories. One example, "Three Blind Mice."

____

Fragments II: PRACTICE 3

Each of the short passages below contains **five** fragments. Underline the fragments, and then correct each fragment in the space provided.

[1]A single mom in school has a lot of challenges. [2]Especially finding time for studying. [3]After school, the kids all want her attention. [4]To fix them a snack or listen to their stories. [5]Charlene then helps them with their homework and prepares dinner. [6]Then there are other chores to do. [7]Such as giving the younger children their baths. [8]Once the children are settled for the night, it's time for Charlene to sit down. [9]To do her own schoolwork. [10]Charlene admits that life is often difficult. [11]However, she knows that by going to school and working hard, she sets a good example for her kids. [12]And that Woodie would be proud of her.

1. ______________________________

2. ______________________________

3. ______________________________

4. ______________________________

____

5. ______________________________

____

[1]Pet nicknames are often used for Charlene's children. [2]Including Nicole and Sarah. [3]The family calls them "Noodie" and "Baby Sarah." [4]The two girls are six and five years old. [5]And are both in kindergarten. [6]They like to play with all kinds of toys. [7]Such as the sticker books they are holding. [8]When they see Charlene studying, they sometimes get out their books as well. [9]Wanting to imitate their mom. [10]It's a big responsibility for parents. [11]To realize how much influence they have over their children.

6. ______________________________

7. ______________________________

8. ______________________________

9. ______________________________

10. ______________________________

____

Name ______________________ Section ____________ Date ____________

Score: (Number right) ______ x 10 = ________ %

Fragments II: TEST 1

Underline the fragment in each item that follows. Then correct the fragment in the space provided.

NOTE To help you correct fragments, directions are given for the first three sentences.

1. Glancing at his watch frequently. The man seemed anxious to leave.
   The first word group lacks a subject and verb. Connect it to the complete statement that follows it.
   ____
2. There are many healthful desserts. Including sherbet and fruit salad.
   The second word group lacks a subject and verb. Connect it to the complete statement that comes before it.
   ____
3. Our instructor sometimes loses her temper. However, always apologizes afterward.
   Add a subject to the second word group to make it a complete thought.
   ____
4. To keep his bike from being stolen. Gilbert bought a padlock.
   ____
5. The small town is a beautiful place to visit. Especially in the spring.
   ____
6. Thomas lost the key to the front door. As a result, had to call a locksmith.
   ____
7. Certain dogs are well suited to be guide dogs. Including German shepherds and golden retrievers.
   ____
   ____
8. To get to school on time. I keep the clock in my room set ten minutes ahead.
   ____
9. Relaxing on the beach. Anna said, "I want to be a lifeguard."
   ____
10. Many towns in the United States have amusing names. Such as Boring, Oregon; Peculiar, Missouri; and Okay, Oklahoma.
    ____
    ____

Name ______________________ Section ____________ Date ____________

Score: (Number right) ______ x 10 = ________ %

Fragments II: TEST 2

Underline the fragment in each item that follows. Then correct the fragment in the space provided.

1. Melana refused the second helping of spaghetti. But ate three huge desserts.

   ____

2. I hate violent movies. Especially ones with lots of blood.

   ____

3. My cell phone rang at least ten times this morning. Then was silent the rest of the day.

   ____

4. We want to travel around the world before we settle down. For example, visit Mexico, Europe, and China.

   ____

5. To work off the calories from a huge meal. Greg likes to speed-walk for an hour around the neighborhood track.

   ____

   ____

6. Brainstorming ideas for a student essay is a good idea. Especially when you do it as soon as you receive an assignment.

   ____

   ____

7. Leroy was fed up and bored with school. Thinking seriously of dropping out.

   ____

8. Crying after being refused ice cream. The toddler screamed and stamped his feet.

   ____

9. My parents had many ideas for a name for my soon-to-be-born sister. Including Trisha, Louise, Sonja, and Deborah.

   ____

   ____

10. My uncle tried to signal to the car ahead of him that its lights were not on. Hoping to prevent an accident.

    ____

    ____

Name ________________________ Section ____________ Date ____________

Score: (Number right) ________ x 20 = ____________ %

Fragments II: TEST 3

The passage that follows contains **five** fragments. Underline the fragments and then correct them in the spaces provided.

[1]Throughout our lives, we humans have a deep need for affectionate touching. [2]That need begins as soon as we are born. [3]Infants can survive near-starvation, but they can actually die from lack of affection. [4]When they are regularly held and cuddled, they grow and thrive. [5]Sensing that they are loved.

[6]Children also need lots of loving touch from their parents, although they may seem to withdraw from it around age eight. [7]For instance, saying that hugs and kisses are "icky." [8]Parents must be sensitive to a child's growing need for independence. [9]But ready to give physical affection as needed.

[10]Teenagers often feel confused about touching. [11]Feeling a need for affection, but being embarrassed by it as well. [12]Some teens even turn to drugs or alcohol. [13]To fill that need. [14]Parents can help a self-conscious teen by providing as much friendly, casual touching as the teen can accept.

[15]The need for human touch never ends. [16]Surveys of successful marriages show that touching and hugging are key factors in a happy relationship.

1. ____________________

2. ____________________

3. ____________________

4. ____________________

5. ____________________

Name ______________________ Section ____________ Date ____________

Score: (Number right) ______ x 20 = __________ %

Fragments II: TEST 4

Read each group below. Then write the letter of the item in each group that contains a fragment.

_____ **1.** **a.** Lupe's heart skipped a beat. When she heard footsteps on the stairs outside her bedroom door. She was relieved when she realized the footsteps actually were coming from next door.

b. When she heard footsteps on the stairs outside her bedroom door, Lupe's heart skipped a beat. She was relieved when she realized the footsteps actually were coming from next door.

c. Lupe's heart skipped a beat when she heard footsteps on the stairs outside her bedroom door. She was relieved when she realized the footsteps actually were coming from next door.

_____ **2.** **a.** To get some ice cream, two-year-old Susie scooted a chair next to the freezer. Her mother heard her anguished cries as the little girl smacked her head on the freezer door.

b. Two-year-old Susie scooted a chair next to the freezer to get some ice cream. Her mother heard her anguished cries as the little girl smacked her head on the freezer door.

c. To get some ice cream. Two-year-old Susie scooted a chair next to the freezer. Her mother heard her anguished cries as the little girl smacked her head on the freezer door.

_____ **3.** **a.** Shouting and clawing her way to the surface. Lydia tried not to panic under the crushing snow of an avalanche. Luckily, her husband was nearby and was able to dig her out.

b. Shouting and clawing her way to the surface, Lydia tried not to panic under the crushing snow of an avalanche. Luckily, her husband was nearby and was able to dig her out.

c. Lydia tried not to panic under the crushing snow of an avalanche while shouting and clawing her way to the surface. Luckily, her husband was nearby and was able to dig her out.

_____ **4.** **a.** I have had many dogs over the years, including dachshunds, collies, and boxers. Although I loved my dogs, now I would like to try a cat.

b. I have had many dogs over the years. Including dachshunds, collies, and boxers. Although I loved my dogs, now I would like to try a cat.

c. I have had many dogs over the years. Those included dachshunds, collies, and boxers. Although I loved my dogs, now I would like to try a cat.

_____ **5.** **a.** Mary felt her entire body go limp while relaxing in a hot bath. This was the perfect remedy for a very stressful day.

b. While relaxing in a hot bath. Mary felt her entire body go limp. This was the perfect remedy for a very stressful day.

c. While relaxing in a hot bath, Mary felt her entire body go limp. This was the perfect remedy for a very stressful day.

Name ______________________ Section ____________ Date ____________

Score: (Number right) ______ x 20 = ________ %

Fragments II: TEST 5

Read each group below. Then write the letter of the item in each group that contains a fragment.

_____ **1.** **a.** Staring at the people standing outside, the tiger paced from one end of its cage to the other. It looked hungry.

b. The tiger paced from one end of its cage to the other. Staring at the people standing outside. It looked hungry.

c. The tiger paced from one end of its cage to the other, staring at the people standing outside. It looked hungry.

_____ **2.** **a.** Calling every half-hour, the man seemed extremely anxious to reach my father. "I have to talk to him," he kept saying.

b. The man who called every half-hour seemed extremely anxious to reach my father. "I have to talk to him," he kept saying.

c. Calling every half-hour. The man seemed extremely anxious to reach my father. "I have to talk to him," he kept saying.

_____ **3.** **a.** Robbie ran at full speed down the street. To try to get the letter in the mail before 5 p.m. He reached the post office at 5:02.

b. Robbie ran at full speed down the street to try to get the letter in the mail before 5 p.m. He reached the post office at 5:02.

c. Trying to get the letter in the mail before 5 p.m., Robbie ran at full speed down the street. He reached the post office at 5:02.

_____ **4.** **a.** There's an item on the dessert menu that contains most of my favorite ingredients. Such as chocolate, caramel, coconut, and nuts. I wonder if it's low in calories.

b. There's an item on the dessert menu that contains most of my favorite ingredients, such as chocolate, caramel, coconut, and nuts. I wonder if it's low in calories.

c. There's an item on the dessert menu that contains chocolate, caramel, coconut, and nuts, which are my favorite ingredients. I wonder if it's low in calories.

_____ **5.** **a.** People who can't read well run into constant problems. For example, they may have problems filling out a job application. They are often too embarrassed to admit they can't read it.

b. People who can't read well run into constant problems. For example, filling out a job application. They are often too embarrassed to admit they can't read it.

c. People who can't read well run into constant problems. Filling out a job application, for example, they are often too embarrassed to admit they can't read it.

8 Run-Ons and Comma Splices I

Basics about Run-Ons and Comma Splices

A **run-on** is made up of two complete thoughts that are incorrectly run together without a connection between them. Here is an example of a run-on:

- Dolphins have killed sharks they never attack humans.
  The complete thoughts are *dolphins have killed sharks* and *they never attack humans.*

A **comma splice** is made up of two complete thoughts that are incorrectly joined (or spliced) together with only a comma. A comma alone is not enough to connect two complete thoughts. Here's an example of a comma splice:

- Dolphins have killed sharks, they never attack humans.

How to Correct Run-Ons and Comma Splices

There are two common ways to correct run-ons and comma splices.

- **METHOD 1 Use a Period and a Capital Letter**

  Put each complete thought into its own sentence.

  Run-on The computer hummed loudly the sound was annoying.
  Comma splice The computer hummed loudly, the sound was annoying.
  Correct version The computer hummed **loudly. The** sound was annoying.

- **METHOD 2 Use a Comma and a Joining Word**

  Connect two complete thoughts into one sentence with a comma and a joining word. Perhaps the most common joining words are *and*, *but*, and *so*.

  Run-on Dolphins have killed sharks they never attack humans.
  Comma splice Dolphins have killed sharks, they never attack humans.
  Correct version Dolphins have killed **sharks, but they** never attack humans.

  Run-on The garden is overgrown the fence is falling down.
  Comma splice The garden is overgrown, the fence is falling down.
  Correct version The garden is **overgrown, and the** fence is falling down.

  Run-on The little boy appeared to be lost several women stopped to help him.
  Comma splice The little boy appeared to be lost, several women stopped to help him.
  Correct version The little boy appeared to be **lost, so** several women stopped to help him.

Understanding Run-Ons and Comma Splices

See if you can find and put a line (|) between the two complete thoughts in each run-on or comma splice.

[1]It's Monday morning at the Cardenas home. [2]Everyone is rushing to get out of the house early it's a busy time of day. [3]Alphonso, an air-conditioning installer, can give Korak a ride to high school, Jasmine will have to take the school bus to her middle school. [4]Maria wishes the family could have a quiet breakfast together their busy schedules don't allow time for that.

- "Everyone is rushing to get out of the house early" and "it's a busy time of day" are both complete thoughts. To connect them, use a comma plus the logical joining word *so,* which means "as a result."

  Correct Everyone is rushing to get out of the house **early, so** it's a busy time of day.

- "Alphonso, an air-conditioning installer, can give Korak a ride to high school" and "Jasmine will have to take the school bus to her middle school" are both complete thoughts. To connect them, use the logical joining word *but,* which means "however."

  Correct Alphonso, an air-conditioning installer, can give Korak a ride to high **school, but** Jasmine will have to take the school bus to her middle school.

- "Maria wishes the family could have a quiet breakfast together" and "their busy schedules don't allow time for that" are both complete thoughts. To correct the run-on, put each complete thought into its own sentence.

  Correct Maria wishes the family could have a quiet breakfast **together. Their** busy schedules don't allow time for that.

Check Your Understanding

Put a line (|) between the two complete thoughts in each run-on or comma splice in the following passage. Then correct the errors in the spaces provided.

[1]The family tries to rush out the door, the photographer begs them to wait. [2]They won't be together again until late tonight, he wants to get a family photo. [3]"Give your brother a hug!" he teases Jasmine, she throws her arms around Korak. [4]How does Korak feel about this?

1. ______________________________

2. ______________________________

3. ______________________________

Run-Ons and Comma Splices I: PRACTICE 1

Draw a line (|) between the two complete thoughts in each of the run-ons and comma splices that follow. Then rewrite each sentence. Correct it in one of two ways:

1 Use a period and a capital letter to create two sentences.

2 Use a comma and a logical joining word to connect the two complete thoughts. Choose from the following joining words:

and (which means *in addition*) **but** (which means *however*) **so** (which means *as a result*)

Do not use the same correction technique for all the sentences.

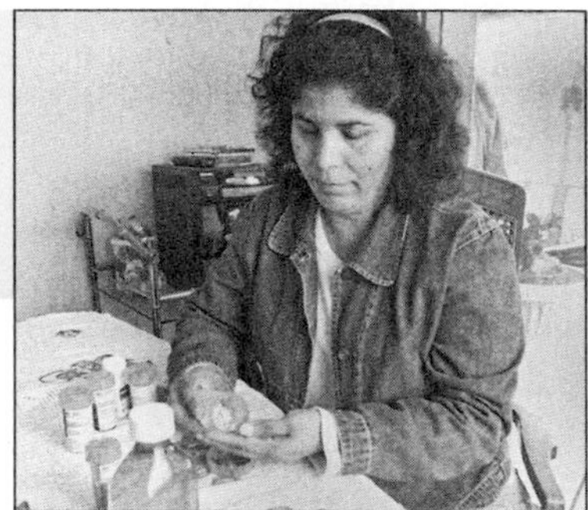

[1]The family is a happy one, they have a big problem. [2]Maria has a serious liver disease she has to take a lot of medicine. [3]Her liver cannot heal itself, she needs a liver transplant.

1. ______________________________

2. ______________________________

3. ______________________________

[1]Thousands of people are waiting for organ transplants Maria is just one of them. [2]Some of them need livers some of them need hearts or lungs. [3]Many healthy people have signed up to be organ donors when they die, many more are needed. [4]It's simple to become an organ donor, you just fill out a form on your driver's license.

4. ______________________________

5. ______________________________

6. ______________________________

____

7. ______________________________

[1]Antonietta could not be in the family picture she wasn't awake yet. [2]She worked late last night, she will leave for school in a few minutes. [3]She needs to give her parrot some attention first, he gets angry if she ignores him.

8. ______________________________

9. ______________________________

10. ______________________________

Run-Ons and Comma Splices I: PRACTICE 2

Draw a line (|) between the two complete thoughts in each of the run-ons and comma splices that follow. Then rewrite each sentence. Correct it in one of two ways:

1 Use a period and a capital letter to create two sentences.

2 Use a comma and a logical joining word to connect the two complete thoughts. Choose from the following joining words:

and (which means *in addition*) **but** (which means *however*) **so** (which means *as a result*)

Do not use the same correction technique for all the sentences.

1. Lawrence is going to the movies, he really wants to see an action film.

____

2. The entire team was very upset when they lost the championship game, they decided to forgo the after-game party.

____

____

3. My cousin is only four years old, he can already read on a fourth-grade level.

____

4. The hem of her skirt ripped in two pieces, Isabelle created a new look by tying the torn ends together.

____

____

5. I cannot find my car keys anywhere, I am going to be late for work—again!

____

6. The yellow house on the corner has a for-sale sign in its window I wish I could buy that house because I love it.

____

____

7. Whoever is knocking on the door is going to have to wait I am in the bathtub.

____

8. The heavy rain was interrupted by thunder the vibration shook the windows in my upstairs bedroom.

____

____

9. The party was gong to be full of loud, noisy strangers I decided to stay at home with a good book.

____

____

10. Aunt Gertrude loves knitting and crocheting she also enjoys many other crafts.

____

Run-Ons and Comma Splices I: PRACTICE 3

The following passage contains **ten** run-ons or comma splices. Correct each error in the space provided by using either **(1)** a period and capital letter, or **(2)** a comma and the joining word *and, so,* or *but.* Be sure to use both methods.

[1]When Maria was a little girl, she was a migrant worker her family traveled all the time. [2]She was never in the same school for very long sometimes she didn't go to school at all. [3]In classes she didn't understand what was going on she was too shy to ask for help. [4]Maria fell far behind in her studies, she had to work hard as an adult to catch up. [5]Now Maria is a wife and a mother she is also a college student. [6]She wants to be an elementary teacher, she will be able to help migrant children learn. [7]Here she is with one of her professors the professor's name is Dr. Olliff. [8]Dr. Olliff teaches a special kind of class, she shows students how to teach children to read. [9]She and Maria are looking at a very large book books like these are used in elementary classrooms. [10]This class will help prepare Maria for teaching she is looking forward to her first classroom of students.

1. ____
2. ____
3. ____
4. ____
5. ____
6. ____
7. ____
8. ____
9. ____

   ____

10. ____

    ____

Name ______________________ Section ____________ Date ____________

Score: (Number right) ________ x 10 = ____________ %

Run-Ons and Comma Splices I: TEST 1

Put a line (|) between the two complete thoughts in each of the following run-ons or comma splices. Then rewrite the sentences, using either **(1)** a period and a capital letter or **(2)** a comma and a joining word (*and, but,* or *so*).

NOTE To help you correct run-ons, directions are given for the first two sentences.

1. The sun was going down the air was growing chilly.
Use a logical joining word (*and, but,* or *so*) to connect the two complete thoughts.

____

2. Rick is not a good babysitter he treats his little brother like an insect.
Put each complete thought into its own sentence.

____

3. My throat is very sore a gallon of ice cream will relieve it.

____

4. The plumber repaired the water heater, the family can shower again.

____

5. Saturday is the worst day of the week to shop, people fill up many of the stores.

____

6. The phone rang someone knocked on the door at the same time.

____

7. The movie was boring at first it suddenly became interesting.

____

8. A burglar alarm went off three men raced away from the store.

____

9. The bear looked at me hungrily, I decided not to photograph him.

____

10. We decided to leave the restaurant, we were tired of waiting in line.

____

Name ______________________________ Section ______________ Date ______________

Score: (Number right) ________ x 10 = ______________ %

Run-Ons and Comma Splices I: TEST 2

Put a line (|) between the two complete thoughts in each of the following run-ons or comma splices. Then rewrite the sentences, using either **(1)** a period and a capital letter or **(2)** a comma and a joining word (*and, but,* or *so*).

1. Luis was very rude to the substitute teacher he did quiet down when she gave him a stern warning.

____

____

2. The dirty dishes in the sink had been there for several days Renee finally volunteered to wash them.

____

____

3. The toddler was crying so much she began to hiccup she really missed her mommy.

____

4. The policeman pulled me over for speeding on the freeway the ticket did not affect my car insurance premiums because this was my first citation.

____

____

5. My best friend moved far away I had a good cry and then felt better.

____

6. All the dogs at the shelter started to howl at the same time they could be heard two blocks away.

____

____

7. On Friday, I invited Raul over for dinner he had to work that night.

____

8. Sam flunked all of his classes last semester he was put on academic probation.

____

9. I gave Ron a cookbook when he moved out of his parents' house I also gave him a fire extinguisher just in case a recipe went wrong.

____

____

10. There was a giant sale on at Macy's the line of customers went around the block.

____

Name ______________________ Section ____________ Date ____________

Score: (Number right) ______ x 10 = ________ %

Run-Ons and Comma Splices I: TEST 3

Each of the short passages below contains **five** run-ons and comma splices. In the space between the lines, correct each error by using **(1)** a period and capital letter, or **(2)** a comma and the joining word *and, so,* or *but.* Be sure to use both methods. The first one is done for you as an example.

A. [1]There are many migrant workers in the United States, their children face special problems. [2]Many of them speak Spanish at home, they struggle with English at school. [3]They change schools often they get behind in their classes. [4]Some communities are trying to do a better job of helping migrant children get a good education. [5]They try this in a variety of ways, one of them is by hiring Spanish-speaking counselors to work with the families. [6]Another way is to help families get more involved in school activities, this can be done by offering child care and transportation. [7]A third is to develop classes that students can easily "drop in" and "drop out" of as they move. [8]It is good for everyone if migrant children can become well-educated citizens.

B. [1]Do you speak Spanish? [2]Maybe you say you don't you might know more Spanish than you think. [3]The English language has borrowed many words from Spanish, you probably use some of them every day. [4]Many food words were originally Spanish they include words such as *taco, burrito,* and *tortilla.* [5]Old-time Mexican and American cowboys often worked together, from them we borrowed Spanish words, including *lasso, rodeo,* and *ranch.* [6]We use many other words that have the same meaning in Spanish and English, a few of them are *tornado, mosquito, tobacco, vanilla,* and *patio.*

Name _______________ Section _______ Date _______

Score: (Number right) _______ x 10 = _______ %

Run-Ons and Comma Splices I: TEST 4

In each group below, **one** sentence is punctuated correctly. Write the letter of that sentence in the space provided.

_____ **1.** **a.** I really love dark chocolate I eat it only once a week so I won't gain weight.
b. I really love dark chocolate, I eat it only once a week so I won't gain weight.
c. I really love dark chocolate, but I eat it only once a week so I won't gain weight.

_____ **2.** **a.** I couldn't stand Phil at first then I grew to love him.
b. I couldn't stand Phil at first. Then I grew to love him.
c. I couldn't stand Phil at first, then I grew to love him.

_____ **3.** **a.** Wrestling is not a sport I enjoy watching my brother is addicted to the wrestling channel on cable television.
b. Wrestling is not a sport I enjoy watching, my brother is addicted to the wrestling channel on cable television.
c. Wrestling is not a sport I enjoy watching, but my brother is addicted to the wrestling channel on cable television.

_____ **4.** **a.** I refused to get out of bed when the phone rang it finally stopped after twenty rings.
b. I refused to get out of bed when the phone rang, so it finally stopped after twenty rings.
c. I refused to get out of bed when the phone rang, it finally stopped after twenty rings.

_____ **5.** **a.** The man camping on the church steps was homeless. He thanked me when I gave him five dollars.
b. The man camping on the church steps was homeless he thanked me when I gave him five dollars.
c. The man camping on the church steps was homeless, he thanked me when I gave him five dollars.

_____ **6.** **a.** I sanded the furniture for several hours my sister painted and moved them to the back of the house.
b. I sanded the furniture for several hours, and my sister painted and moved them to the back of the house.
c. I sanded the furniture for several hours, my sister painted and moved them to the back of the house.

_____ **7.** **a.** Tom did not have enough credits for a January graduation, so he applied to graduate in May.
b. Tom did not have enough credits for a January graduation he applied to graduate in May.
c. Tom did not have enough credits for a January graduation, he applied to graduate in May.

_____ **8.** **a.** Mr. Dobbs is friendly with his customers, he is rude to his workers.
b. Mr. Dobbs is friendly with his customers, but he is rude to his workers.
c. Mr. Dobbs is friendly with his customers he is rude to his workers.

_____ **9.** **a.** My back itched in a hard-to-reach place I scratched it on the doorpost.
b. My back itched in a hard-to-reach place, so I scratched it on the doorpost.
c. My back itched in a hard-to-reach place, I scratched it on the doorpost.

_____ **10.** **a.** June is a month of nice weather it is also the most popular month for weddings.
b. June is a month of nice weather, it is also the most popular month for weddings.
c. June is a month of nice weather. It is also the most popular month for weddings.

Name ______________________ Section ____________ Date ____________

Score: (Number right) ______ x 10 = ________ %

Run-Ons and Comma Splices I: TEST 5

In each group below, **one** sentence is punctuated correctly. Write the letter of that sentence in the space provided.

_____ **1. a.** Raoul is colorblind, so his wife lays out his clothes every morning.
b. Raoul is colorblind his wife lays out his clothes every morning.
c. Raoul is colorblind, his wife lays out his clothes every morning.

_____ **2. a.** The weatherman predicted a sunny day, it is cold and cloudy.
b. The weatherman predicted a sunny day it is cold and cloudy.
c. The weatherman predicted a sunny day, but it is cold and cloudy.

_____ **3. a.** The hammer and saw began to rust they had been left out in the rain.
b. The hammer and saw began to rust. They had been left out in the rain.
c. The hammer and saw began to rust, they had been left out in the rain.

_____ **4. a.** My final exams are next week, I am very worried about passing.
b. My final exams are next week, and I am very worried about passing.
c. My final exams are next week I am very worried about passing.

_____ **5. a.** I was sick a lot at the start of the semester, I was not able to keep up with the work.
b. I was sick a lot at the start of the semester I was not able to keep up with the work.
c. I was sick a lot at the start of the semester, so I was not able to keep up with the work.

_____ **6. a.** I do not enjoy feeling stress I never intend to get so far behind in class again.
b. I do not enjoy feeling stress, I never intend to get so far behind in class again.
c. I do not enjoy feeling stress. I never intend to get so far behind in class again.

_____ **7. a.** The children have been eating chocolate. It is smeared all over their faces.
b. The children have been eating chocolate it is smeared all over their faces.
c. The children have been eating chocolate, it is smeared all over their faces.

_____ **8. a.** The air is very stale in the library, and the lighting is poor.
b. The air is very stale in the library the lighting is poor.
c. The air is very stale in the library, the lighting is poor.

_____ **9. a.** My ancestors came from Greece, they arrived in this country in 1912.
b. My ancestors came from Greece they arrived in this country in 1912.
c. My ancestors came from Greece. They arrived in this country in 1912.

_____ **10. a.** The magician locked his assistant in a box then he cut her in half with a chainsaw.
b. The magician locked his assistant in a box, then he cut her in half with a chainsaw.
c. The magician locked his assistant in a box. Then he cut her in half with a chainsaw.

9 Run-Ons and Comma Splices II

Another Way to Correct Run-Ons and Comma Splices

The previous chapter described two ways to correct run-ons and comma splices:

- Use a period and a capital letter, dividing the thoughts into two sentences.
- Use a joining word (*and, but,* or *so*) to logically connect the two complete thoughts.

A third way is to add a **dependent word** to one of the complete thoughts. The sentence will then include one thought that depends upon the remaining complete thought for its full meaning. Here are some common dependent words:

after	because	since	when
although	before	unless	where
as	if, even if	until	while

For example, look at a run-on and comma splice considered in the previous chapter.

Run-on Dolphins have killed sharks they never attack humans.
Comma splice Dolphins have killed sharks, they never attack humans.

Using the dependent word *although,* the sentence can be corrected as follows:

Although dolphins have killed sharks, they never attack humans.

Below are other run-ons or comma splices that have been corrected by adding dependent words. In each case, a dependent word that logically connects the two thoughts has been chosen.

Punctuation note When a dependent thought begins a sentence, it is followed by a comma.

Run-on The roads are covered with ice school has been canceled.
Corrected **Because** the roads are covered with ice**,** school has been canceled.

Comma splice The water began to boil, I added ears of corn.
Corrected **After** the water began to boil, I added ears of corn.

Run-on The fish was served with its head on Carlo quickly lost his appetite.
Corrected **When** the fish was served with its head on**,** Carlo quickly lost his appetite.

Comma splice You'd better not store cereal in the basement, there are mice there.
Corrected You'd better not store cereal in the basement **since** there are mice there.

Understanding Run-Ons and Comma Splices II

See if you can find and put a line (|) between the two complete thoughts in each run-on or comma splice in the following passage.

[1]This is Fern Bertram, an 87-year-old woman with two sons and many grandchildren and great-grandchildren. [2]She stays in touch with everyone, her relatives call Fern "the glue that holds the family together."

[3]Her sons were born, Fern made a career as a homemaker. [4]She likes to say that she's "just an ordinary person." [5]"There were three of us girls," she says. [6]"One was an excellent nurse; the other could do anything with her hands. [7]Me, I'm just ordinary." [8]But other people say that Fern is an extraordinary person. [9]She maintains a cheerful attitude, her life has not been easy. [10]Her husband died when he was only 52, and she has dealt with serious illness. [11]Yet she insists, "I've had a good life. [12]We face struggles, but there are so many good things in the world." [13]The people who know Fern are inspired by her strength and optimism. [14]One nephew likes to say that Fern is made of "sunshine and steel."

1. The first run-on is in sentence 2. You can correct it by adding the dependent word *because:* **Because** she stays in touch with everyone, her relatives call Fern "the glue that holds the family together."
2. The second run-on is in sentence 3. You can correct it by adding the dependent word *after:* **After** her sons were born, Fern made a career as a homemaker.
3. The third run-on is in sentence 9. You can correct it by adding the dependent word *although:* She maintains a cheerful attitude **although** her life has not been easy.

Check Your Understanding

Draw a line (|) between the two complete thoughts in each of the **three** run-ons or comma splices that follow. Then correct the errors by adding a dependent word to one of the complete thoughts. Choose from these words: **when, after, although.**

[1]Fern has always loved to read, she doesn't choose books that are "heavy" or "educational." [2]She says, "At my age, I just read for entertainment." [3]Her favorite authors include Danielle Steele and Nora Roberts.

[4]Fern was about ten, she read a book that influenced her outlook on life. [5]The book, called *Pollyanna,* is about a girl who always manages to be happy. [6]At one point in the book, Pollyanna explains what she calls "the glad game." [7]Her family received a barrel of hand-me-downs from a missionary-aid society. [8]Pollyanna hoped there would be a doll in the barrel but found only a pair of child's crutches. [9]At first Pollyanna was disappointed. [10]She then decided to be happy because she was healthy and didn't need the crutches.

[11]Fern finished the book she decided to try to be like Pollyanna. [12]"She found something to be happy about, and I figured I could do the same. [13]I've tried to look at life that same way."

1. ______________________________

____

2. ______________________________

3. ______________________________

Run-Ons and Comma Splices II: PRACTICE 1

Draw a line (|) between the two complete thoughts in each of the **five** run-ons or comma splices that follow. Then correct each sentence by adding a dependent word to one of the complete thoughts. Choose from these words: **and, but, because, before, when, since, if.**

[1]Mardelle Pohlman exercises five days per week, even though she is ninety-one years old. [2]She has attended classes at the YMCA for over thirty years. [3]She started classes shortly after she retired she thought exercising might be fun. [4]At first, she only went to the Y three days a week, but found herself bored at home on her "days off." [5]In addition, she persuaded her husband Phil to join her. [6]Phil was reluctant at first he had only recently lost his eyesight from a rare medical condition. [7]Starting slowly, Phil soon found as much enjoyment in exercising as Mardelle did. [8]Phil told all of his friends, "My confidence is slowly returning because of my new-found fitness."

1. ______________________________

2. ______________________________

____

[1]Mardelle's first exercise class was an aqua-aerobics class, which met on Mondays, Wednesdays, and Fridays. [2]Because she had never been a swimmer, she had to buy a couple of suits for the class. [3]She went to the mall, she had no idea even what size suit she wore. [4]Not having worn a swimsuit for many years, the suits she tried on seemed skimpy and revealing. [5]A kindly saleswoman found several attractive, yet modest, suits for Mardelle to try on, they fit her slim figure very well. [6]The saleslady said to Mardelle, "If you do not feel comfortable wearing these suits, you may bring them back." [7]To get used to wearing the suits, she tried them on several times at home. [8]Then, Mardelle was ready to join the aqua-aerobics class.

3. ______________________________

4. ______________________________

____

[1]After one year of attending classes together, Mardelle had to leave Phil alone when she went out of town. [2]Phil was confident around the house and did everything for himself in spite of his sightlessness. [3]Phil practiced for a week walking to the Y on his own with only his cane to assist him Mardelle left. [4]Mardelle was nervous about leaving Phil on his own, but she knew he would be fine. [5]The day after she left, Phil made his way to the Y, which was five blocks from his house. [6]Before Mardelle returned, Phil went to his class on his own three more times, and he knew if he could do this, he could do just about anything, blind or not.

5. ______________________________

____

Run-Ons and Comma Splices II: PRACTICE 2

Correct each run-on or comma splice by adding the dependent word shown to one of the complete thoughts. Include a comma if the dependent word starts the sentence.

1. ***(although)*** These boots are supposed to be waterproof my feet are soaked.

   ____

2. ***(when)*** The driver jumped out quickly the car burst into flames.

   ____

3. ***(when)*** We waded into the lake tadpoles swirled around our ankles.

   ____

4. ***(if)*** You need to make a call you can borrow my cell phone.

   ____

5. ***(since)*** Ricardo was late to school, he had briefly lost his contact lens.

   ____

6. ***(while)*** It was still raining, a beautiful rainbow appeared in the west.

   ____

7. ***(until)*** The wet paint on the woodwork dries, you should not touch it.

   ____

8. ***(after)*** The players looked depressed the team lost the game.

   ____

9. ***(as)*** The sky darkened bats began to appear in the air.

____

10. ***(because)*** That pain killer has serious side effects you should take it only when needed.

____

Run-Ons and Comma Splices II: PRACTICE 3

Draw a line (|) between the two complete thoughts in each of the **five** run-ons or comma splices that follow. Then correct each sentence by adding a dependent word to one of the complete thoughts. Choose from these words: **when, although, if, after, because.**

[1]A good friend of mine has a doctorate and works as a linguist and as a teacher. [2]She is generally a responsible person, she is also chronically late. [3]She volunteers to pick me up for a work function, I start to feel anxious. [4]I always drive my own car it is important for me to be there on time. [5]She is a good person, but this is a major fault of hers. [6]She and I arrive at a function one or two hours late, then she wants to leave soon after our arrival. [7]I do not want to lose her friendship, usually I just get ready on time, and, if she is too late, I leave her a note saying I will see her there. [8]This compromise saves our friendship and keeps me from being late.

1. ____

____

2. ____

____

3. ____

____

4. ____

____

5. ____

____

Name ______________________ Section ____________ Date ____________

Score: (Number right) ________ x 10 = ____________ %

Run-Ons and Comma Splices II: TEST 1

Put a line (|) between the two complete thoughts in each of the following run-ons or comma splices. Then rewrite the sentences, correcting each one by adding a logical dependent word to one of the thoughts. Include a comma if the dependent word starts the sentence. Choose from these words: **because, after, although, if, when.**

NOTE To help you correct run-ons, directions are given for the first three sentences.

1. Nuts are high in protein they are a healthier snack than chips.

   ____

   Use *because* to begin the first complete thought.

2. Many people are afraid of spiders, most spiders are quite harmless.

   ____

   Use *although* to begin the second complete thought.

3. It starts to rain, bring in the clothes hanging on the line.

   ____

   Use *if* to begin the first complete thought.

4. The dishes were done we relaxed by watching some TV.

   ____

5. Elaine laid down the sleeping baby, she tiptoed out of the room.

   ____

6. You will be late to the party, let the host know ahead of time.

   ____

7. I haven't spent much time outdoors, it has been very cold.

   ____

8. Geneva apologized for yelling at Evan, she felt better.

   ____

9. You win the contest, what will you do with the prize money?

   ____

10. I could not open the childproof bottle, I was following the directions carefully.

    ____

    ____

Name ______________________ Section ____________ Date ____________

Score: (Number right) ________ x 10 = ____________ %

Run-Ons and Comma Splices II: TEST 2

Correct each run-on or comma splice by adding the dependent word shown to one of the complete thoughts. Include a comma if the dependent word starts the sentence.

1. ***(because)*** Nobody answered the phone the whole family had gone to bed early.

   ____

2. ***(after)*** Debbi took a self-defense course, she felt stronger and more confident.

   ____

3. ***(before)*** You start answering a multiple-choice question, read every one of the possible answers.

   ____

   ____

4. ***(because)*** My brother was tired of worrying how his hair looked, he shaved his head.

   ____

5. ***(although)*** Garlic may smell bad it tastes delicious.

   ____

6. ***(after)*** I finished watching the sad movie my eyes were red for hours.

   ____

7. ***(although)*** Mrs. Hunter is not an easy teacher her students love her.

   ____

8. ***(because)*** I am more alert in the morning, early classes are better for me.

   ____

9. ***(after)*** We had three hours of cleaning up to do, the party ended at 1 a.m.

   ____

10. ***(if)*** You want to be a rock star, you'd better have a second career plan just in case.

    ____

Name ______________________________ Section ______________ Date ______________

Score: (Number right) ________ x 20 = ____________ %

Run-Ons and Comma Splices II: TEST 3

Draw a line (|) between the two complete thoughts in each of the **five** run-ons or comma splices in the following paragraph. Then correct each sentence by adding a dependent word to one of the complete thoughts. Use each of the following dependent words once: **after, although, because, if, when.**

[1]How much do you know about your own family history? [2]Gathering family stories, photos, and keepsakes can be a fascinating hobby, and it can bring your whole family closer together. [3]Young people may not be interested in such things, they may regret their lack of knowledge later. [4]People reach middle age, they often begin to wish they knew more about their family history. [5]That's why it is a great idea to get an early start on your own family's stories. [6]Probably the best way to begin is to interview older relatives, they're such good sources of information. [7]Chances are you'll have a good time doing it. [8]You're concerned about bothering people, you probably shouldn't worry. [9]Elderly family members are usually pleased and surprised when younger relatives ask questions about the past. [10]The questions don't have to be complicated ones. [11]You might start by asking things like, "Where were you born? [12]Where did your parents come from? [13]What kind of work did they do? [14]What kind of school did you go to?" [15]You do a few such interviews, you'll be on your way to becoming the family historian.

1. ____

____

2. ____

____

3. ____

____

4. ____

____

5. ____

____

Name ______________________ Section ____________ Date ____________

Score: (Number right) ______ x 10 = ________ %

Run-Ons and Comma Splices II: TEST 4

In each group below, **one** sentence is punctuated correctly. Write the letter of that sentence in the space provided.

_____ **1.** **a.** Because I was in a hurry. I locked my keys in the car.
b. Because I was in a hurry, I locked my keys in the car.
c. I was in a hurry I locked my keys in the car.

_____ **2.** **a.** Try to remember everything then you will not have to come back.
b. If you try to remember everything. Then you will not have to come back.
c. If you try to remember everything, then you will not have to come back.

_____ **3.** **a.** I really want a cigarette, I am trying very hard to quit.
b. Although I really want a cigarette, I am trying very hard to quit.
c. Although I really want a cigarette. I am trying very hard to quit.

_____ **4.** **a.** The doctor will be here in a minute. After he completes his rounds at the hospital.
b. The doctor will be here in a minute, after he completes his rounds at the hospital.
c. The doctor will be here in a minute he completes his rounds at the hospital.

_____ **5.** **a.** My sister is suffering from a broken heart because the man she loved left her.
b. Because the man she loved left her. My sister is suffering from a broken heart.
c. My sister is suffering from a broken heart the man she loved left her.

_____ **6.** **a.** Rochelle was a brilliant student. Before she suddenly dropped out of school.
b. Rochelle was a brilliant student she suddenly dropped out of school.
c. Rochelle was a brilliant student before she suddenly dropped out of school.

_____ **7.** **a.** The recipe is a very simple one, even a beginner can make it.
b. When the recipe is a very simple one. Even a beginner can make it.
c. When the recipe is a very simple one, even a beginner can make it.

_____ **8.** **a.** Before I can return the library books, I will have to find them in my very messy dorm room.
b. Before I can return the library books. I will have to find them in my very messy dorm room.
c. I must return the library books I will have to find them in my very messy dorm room.

_____ **9.** **a.** Because he ate so much for lunch, even the thought of dinner made him feel ill.
b. Because he ate so much for lunch. Even the thought of dinner made him feel ill.
c. He ate so much for lunch even the thought of dinner made him feel ill.

_____ **10.** **a.** John is determined to attend college. Although no one in his family had previously done so.
b. John is determined to attend college, although no one in his family had previously done so.
c. John is determined to attend college no one in his family had previously done so.

Name ______________________________ Section ____________ Date ____________

Score: (Number right) ______ x 10 = ____________ %

Run-Ons and Comma Splices II: TEST 5

In each group below, **one** sentence is punctuated correctly. Write the letter of that sentence in the space provided.

_____ **1.** **a.** Although friends had told us the restaurant was very good, we had a dreadful meal.
b. Friends had told us the restaurant was very good, we had a dreadful meal.
c. Although friends had told us the restaurant was very good. We had a dreadful meal.

_____ **2.** **a.** You don't enjoy the party, we can leave early.
b. If you don't enjoy the party, we can leave early.
c. If you don't enjoy the party. We can leave early.

_____ **3.** **a.** I nearly had a heart attack. When the smoke alarm started shrieking at 2 a.m.
b. I nearly had a heart attack, the smoke alarm started shrieking at 2 a.m.
c. I nearly had a heart attack when the smoke alarm started shrieking at 2 a.m.

_____ **4.** **a.** I let myself eat that chocolate cake, I will finish my homework.
b. Before I let myself eat that chocolate cake. I will finish my homework.
c. Before I let myself eat that chocolate cake, I will finish my homework.

_____ **5.** **a.** Kristen came back from her blind date, she said, "Never, ever, ever again."
b. After Kristen came back from her blind date, she said, "Never, ever, ever again."
c. After Kristen came back from her blind date. She said, "Never, ever, ever again."

_____ **6.** **a.** Although I love spicy Mexican food. I do not love the heartburn it gives me.
b. Although I love spicy Mexican food, I do not love the heartburn it gives me.
c. I love spicy Mexican food, I do not love the heartburn it gives me.

_____ **7.** **a.** The two brothers seldom speak because they had an argument ten years ago.
b. The two brothers seldom speak. Because they had an argument ten years ago.
c. Because they had an argument ten years ago. The two brothers seldom speak.

_____ **8.** **a.** You are afraid of snakes, you might not want to go on the hike with us.
b. You might not want to go on the hike with us. If you are afraid of snakes.
c. If you are afraid of snakes, you might not want to go on the hike with us.

_____ **9.** **a.** The soup was too hot to eat, I dropped in two ice cubes to cool it off.
b. Because the soup was too hot to eat. I dropped in two ice cubes to cool it off.
c. Because the soup was too hot to eat, I dropped in two ice cubes to cool it off.

_____ **10.** **a.** The neighbors saw a police car pull up outside. They turned off their lights and watched through the window.
b. When the neighbors saw a police car pull up outside, they turned off their lights and watched through the window.
c. When the neighbors saw a police car pull up outside. They turned off their lights and watched through the window.

10 The Comma

Basics about the Comma

Here are three main uses of the comma:

1 The comma is used to separate three or more items in a series.

- The school cafeteria has learned not to serve broccoli, spinach, or Brussels sprouts.
- The letters *k*, *j*, *x*, *z*, and *q* are the least frequently used letters of the alphabet.
- Our tasks for the party are blowing up balloons, setting the table, and planning the music.

2 The comma is used to separate introductory material from the rest of the sentence.

- After taking a hot shower, Vince fell asleep on the sofa.
- When covered with chocolate syrup, frozen yogurt is not a diet food.
- As the movie credits rolled, we stretched and headed toward the exits.

3 The comma is used between two complete thoughts connected by *and*, *but*, or *so*.

- Lee broke her leg in the accident, and her car was badly damaged.
- The forecast called for rain, but it's a beautiful sunny day.
- My glasses broke, so I mended them with duct tape.

NOTES

- A comma often marks a slight pause, or break, in a sentence. When you read a sentence aloud, you can often hear the points where slight pauses occur.
- In general, use a comma only when a comma rule applies or when a comma is otherwise needed to help a sentence read clearly.
- Regarding Rule 3 above, do not use a comma just because a sentence contains *and*, *but*, or *so*. Use a comma only when the *and*, *but*, or *so* comes between two complete thoughts. Each of the two thoughts must have its own subject and verb.
  - ***Comma*** Lee broke her leg in the accident, and her car was badly damaged.
    Each complete thought has a subject and a verb: *Lee broke* and *car was damaged.*
  - ***No comma*** Lee broke her leg in the accident and badly damaged her car.
    This sentence expresses only one complete thought. The subject *Lee* has two verbs: *broke* and *damaged.*

Understanding the Comma

See if you can find the **three** sentences where commas are needed in the following passage about Julia Burney, a retired police officer and community leader in Racine, Wisconsin. Then look below to see the corrections.

[1]Julia Burney's family was very poor when she was a little girl. [2]This photograph shows Julia her mother her father and her baby sister. [3]If you look closely you can see the hem is hanging out of four-year-old Julia's dress. [4]Her little coat is missing most of its buttons. [5]Her parents had to work hard for a living and there wasn't extra money for books. [6]That was the worst thing of all about being poor for a book-lover like Julia.

1. This photograph shows Julia**,** her mother**,** her father**,** and her baby sister.
   Commas are needed to separate items in a series.
2. If you look closely**,** you can see the hem is hanging out of four-year-old Julia's dress.
   A comma is needed after introductory words.
3. Her parents had to work hard for a living**,** and there wasn't extra money for books.
   A comma is needed between complete thoughts joined by *and*, *but*, or *so*.

Check Your Understanding

Insert commas where needed in the following passage. **Five** commas are missing.

[1]When she grew up Julia became a police officer. [2]She would often meet children without books in their homes so she decided to ask people in the community to donate children's books. [3]She began handing the books out to kids in their homes in the parks at the police station and anywhere else she met them. [4]Other police officers were inspired by what Julia was doing and joined her in the effort to get books into the hands of kids.

The Comma: PRACTICE 1

Insert commas where needed in each of the short passages below. **Ten** commas are needed.

[1]The idea for thc "Cops 'n Kids Reading Program" began to take off. [2]After a business owner heard about the program, he donated an old building. [3]The building needed a good deal of work so many volunteers pitched in to help clean and repair it. [4]They wanted to help Julia turn it into a reading center where kids could come in to read relax and learn.

[1]As the work got under way the producers of the Oprah Winfrey program heard about the project. [2]Oprah invited Julia to appear on her TV show. [3]While Julia was in Chicago the Oprah people sprang into action. [4]They installed beautiful carpets, furniture, a crafts center, a computer lab, and a piano. [5]Artists even painted a giant mural on the wall. [6]Julia then appeared on the show and Oprah surprised her with pictures of what they had done. [7]Julia was so happy that she cried.

[1]Julia's idea is not just a dream anymore. [2]In the city of Racine today the Cops 'n Kids Reading Center is a wonderful reality. [3]It provides an after-school program a summer program and lots of special events for the local children. [4]The kids can borrow from a library of more than 5,000 books. [5]If the books are late or lost there are no overdue fines or fees. [6]Julia has retired from the police force to become the Center's full-time director. [7]The picture shows Julia and a staff member sorting through some of the newest books people have donated.

The Comma: PRACTICE 2

On the lines provided, write the word or words in each sentence that need to be followed by a comma. Include each missing comma as well.

1. Before I die, I want to learn to ski to swim to play basketball and to play cricket.

 ____

2. In the middle of the night John fell out of his bed and broke his arm.

 ____

3. Holding on to the safety bar for dear life I really enjoyed my first rollercoaster ride.

 ____

4. After a very filling meal Mr. Edwards fell fast asleep on the couch.

 ____

5. Albert screamed, "I need help" but no one heard him.

 ____

6. My eighty-six-year-old aunt still rode horses hunted deer and kept a vegetable garden.

 ____

7. I work full time as an administrative assistant and I attend college full time.

 ____

8. I applied to college too late for the fall semester so I will try again in the spring.

 ____

9. The overnight freeze produced slick ice on the sidewalks strange frozen spider webs on the plants and one-inch ice on the pond.

 ____

10. The kindergartners' drawings were of older siblings cartoon characters and best friends.

 ____

The Comma: PRACTICE 3

Passage A Insert commas where needed in the following passage. **Fifteen** commas are missing.

[1]As Julia thinks about her childhood she remembers that no one ever read stories to her. [2]She is now in her 50s but that memory still hurts. [3]She is making sure the kids at the Reading Center have better memories. [4]Every day those children sit down get comfortable and enjoy a story. [5]Julia often sits down and listens too.

[6]Although a staff member reads the story today that is not often the case. [7]Much of the time volunteers from the community come in to read. [8]"Guest readers" have included local teachers school principals police officers news photographers and others.

[9]This group of children is of kindergarten age. [10]This picture was taken close to Mother's Day so some of the children were making cards for their moms. [11]Others were painting pictures or practicing uppercase and lowercase letters. [12]Older children who attend the Center might read newspapers talk about current events or take part in a book club.

Passage B Insert commas where needed in the following passage. **Seven** commas are missing.

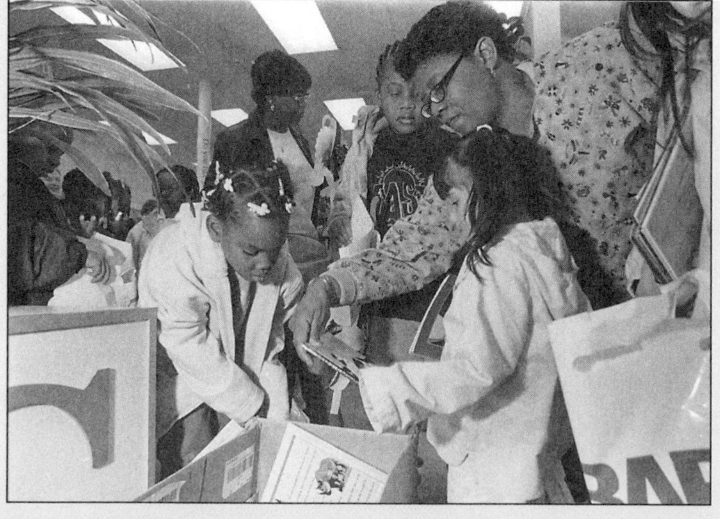

[1]The day's program is over and it's time to go home. [2]The children always borrow books to take home read and return. [3]But on days when the Center has plenty of extra books children are invited to select books to keep. [4]Today is one of those days. [5]As you can see in this photo the children are enjoying picking out books of their own. [6]When Julia Burney sees scenes like this she almost cries with joy. [7]She grew up in a home without books but she has brought books into the homes of the children in her community.

Name ______________________ Section ____________ Date ____________

Score: (Number right) ______ x 10 = ________ %

The Comma: TEST 1

Add commas where needed in each sentence. Then refer to the box below and, in the space provided, write the letter of the comma rule that applies.

a	**Between items in a series**
b	**After introductory material**
c	**Between complete thoughts**

NOTE To help you master the comma, explanations are given for the first three sentences.

__b__ **1.** If my cat kills one more bird I am going to confine her to the house.
Use a comma after introductory material.

__a__ **2.** My eighteen-year-old brother's dream was an apartment of his own a new car with racing stripes and a beautiful girlfriend with a good job.
A comma is needed after each item in a series.

__c__ **3.** The grocery store closed at nine so I had to look for bread at the minimart.
Use a comma between complete thoughts.

__a__ **4.** Benedict was afraid of flying swimming and driving.

__c__ **5.** I am going to go camping and I hope to do some fishing as well.

__b__ **6.** Wishing he was two inches taller the little boy failed the height test for the rollercoaster ride.

__c__ **7.** The rain was coming down in torrents so we decided to stay inside for the afternoon.

__b__ **8.** Before John asked Sheila to marry him he bought her a beautiful engagement ring.

__b__ **9.** Barbara believed that friends should be fiercely loyal good listeners and interesting conversationalists.

__b__ **10.** In spite of her age the elderly woman was a very fast runner.

Name ______________________ Section ____________ Date ____________

Score: (Number right) ______ x 10 = __________ %

The Comma: TEST 2

Add commas where needed in each sentence. Then refer to the box below and, in the space provided, write the letter of the comma rule that applies.

a	**Between items in a series**
b	**After introductory material**
c	**Between complete thoughts**

_____ **1.** These shoes are my usual size but they are still too small for me.

_____ **2.** If you ask me that milk has gone bad.

_____ **3.** The car is badly rusted and the rear window is cracked.

_____ **4.** Lainie's chills fever and headache warned her she was coming down with something.

_____ **5.** While I enjoy reading books I hate having to write a book report.

_____ **6.** The dog bared its teeth flattened its ears and snarled when it saw me.

_____ **7.** Unused to the silence of the forest the campers found it hard to sleep.

_____ **8.** Every day starts with bringing in the newspaper turning on a morning news show and feeding the cat.

_____ **9.** Because it increases unrest among inmates prison overcrowding is dangerous.

_____ **10.** I had forgotten my glasses so I could not read the fine print on the test.

Name ______________________________ Section ______________ Date ______________

Score: (Number right) ________ x 10 = ______________ %

The Comma: TEST 3

Add commas where needed in each sentence. Then refer to the box below and, in the space provided, write the letter of the comma rule that applies.

a	**Between items in a series**
b	**After introductory material**
c	**Between complete thoughts**

_____ **1.** When Thomas Edison was a little boy he suffered from scarlet fever.

_____ **2.** It was thought that an illness caused his injury but later he attributed it to an accident on a train.

_____ **3.** His teachers believed he was stupid so he left school after only three months.

_____ **4.** His mother home-schooled him he read a lot on his own and he had a very inquisitive mind.

_____ **5.** Having had many jobs from an early age he was always a hard worker.

_____ **6.** He was married two times and he had six children altogether.

_____ **7.** He was a very successful inventor who held 1,093 patents in the United States and others in Germany France and the United Kingdom.

_____ **8.** Some of his most famous inventions were the phonograph the light bulb and the microphone.

_____ **9.** Thomas Edison was a very prolific inventor and he was a very successful businessman as well.

_____ **10.** In a lasting tribute to him the United States Congress designated his February 11 birthdate as National Inventors' Day.

Name ______________________ Section ____________ Date ____________

Score: (Number right) ______ x 10 = ____________ %

The Comma: TEST 4

In each group below, **one** sentence uses the comma correctly. Write the letter of that sentence in the space provided.

_____ **1.** **a.** The smoke detector was buzzing and we, could smell something burning.
b. The smoke detector was buzzing, and we could smell something burning.
c. The smoke detector was, buzzing, and we could smell something burning.

_____ **2.** **a.** When my sister was little she thought lima beans, were stuffed with mashed potatoes.
b. When my sister was little she thought lima beans were stuffed, with mashed potatoes.
c. When my sister was little, she thought lima beans were stuffed with mashed potatoes.

_____ **3.** **a.** The driving instructor asked me to turn on my headlights, windshield wipers, and emergency flashers.
b. The driving instructor, asked me to turn on my headlights windshield wipers and emergency flashers.
c. The driving instructor asked, me to turn on my headlights windshield wipers, and emergency flashers.

_____ **4.** **a.** I woke up feeling cheerful, but my mood soon changed.
b. I woke up, feeling cheerful but my mood soon changed.
c. I woke up feeling cheerful but, my mood soon changed.

_____ **5.** **a.** Many people are afraid of spiders, and I can certainly understand why.
b. Many people are afraid of spiders and I, can certainly understand why.
c. Many people, are afraid of spiders and I can certainly understand why.

_____ **6.** **a.** Looking embarrassed the man asked, if he could borrow bus fare.
b. Looking embarrassed the man asked if he could, borrow bus fare.
c. Looking embarrassed, the man asked if he could borrow bus fare.

_____ **7.** **a.** You'll need to have some onions, garlic carrots tomatoes, and parsley.
b. You'll need to have some, onions garlic carrots tomatoes and parsley.
c. You'll need to have some onions, garlic, carrots, tomatoes, and parsley.

_____ **8.** **a.** If you are approached, by a vicious dog you should stand still.
b. If you are approached by a vicious dog, you should stand still.
c. If you are approached by a vicious dog you should, stand still.

_____ **9.** **a.** The little boy said that, his favorite subjects were lunch gym and recess.
b. The little boy said that his favorite subjects were lunch gym, and recess.
c. The little boy said that his favorite subjects were lunch, gym, and recess.

_____ **10.** **a.** Without a sound, the thief quickly emptied the cash register.
b. Without a sound the thief, quickly emptied the cash register.
c. Without a sound the thief quickly, emptied the cash register.

Name ______________________ Section ____________ Date ____________

Score: (Number right) ______ x 10 = ________ %

The Comma: TEST 5

In each group below, **one** sentence uses the comma correctly. Write the letter of that sentence in the space provided.

_____ **1.** **a.** Susan, Mary and Roberta were all supposed to have their babies on the same due date.
b. Susan Mary and Roberta, were all supposed to have their babies on the same due date.
c. Susan, Mary, and Roberta were all supposed to have their babies on the same due date.

_____ **2.** **a.** The list of super foods includes spinach, blueberries broccoli, and flaxseed.
b. The list of super foods includes, spinach blueberries, broccoli, and flaxseed.
c. The list of super foods includes spinach, blueberries, broccoli, and flaxseed.

_____ **3.** **a.** By the last week of the term, half of the advanced math class had dropped out.
b. By the last week of the term half of the advanced, math class had dropped out.
c. By the last week of the term half of the advanced math class, had dropped out.

_____ **4.** **a.** My cat was only eight months old when she gave birth to kittens, so we thought she might not be a good mother.
b. My cat, was only eight months old when she gave birth, to kittens so we thought she might not be a good mother.
c. My cat was only eight months old, when she gave birth to kittens so we thought she might not be a good mother.

_____ **5.** **a.** My little nephew wanted to be, a clown, a fireman, a farmer, or a policeman when he grew up.
b. My little nephew wanted to be a clown, a fireman, a farmer, or a policeman when he grew up.
c. My little nephew wanted to be a clown a fireman a farmer, or a policeman when he grew up.

_____ **6.** **a.** The speeding motorist could not control his car, so it careened off the highway into a ditch.
b. The speeding motorist could not control his car so it careened off the highway into a ditch.
c. The speeding motorist could not control his car so, it careened off the highway into a ditch.

_____ **7.** **a.** At the post office I had, to wait in line for over twenty minutes.
b. At the post office, I had to wait in line for over twenty minutes.
c. At the post office I had to wait in line for over twenty minutes.

_____ **8.** **a.** I need some new running shoes but, I do not have the money right now.
b. I need some new running shoes but I do not have the money, right now.
c. I need some new running shoes, but I do not have the money right now.

Name ______________________________ Section ______________ Date ______________

Score: (Number right) ________ x 10 = ____________ %

______ **9.** **a.** During the last election, the number of people who did not vote was 45 percent of the population.
b. During the last election the number, of people who did not vote was 45 percent of the population.
c. During the last election the number of people who did not vote, was 45 percent of the population.

______ **10.** **a.** The dog's sloppy grin wagging tail, and pleading eyes made me get up in the night to feed him.
b. The dog's sloppy grin wagging tail and pleading eyes, made me get up in the night to feed him.
c. The dog's sloppy grin, wagging tail, and pleading eyes made me get up in the night to feed him.

11 The Apostrophe

Basics about the Apostrophe

There are two main uses of the apostrophe:

1 The apostrophe takes the place of one or more missing letters in a contraction. (A **contraction** is a word formed by combining two or more words, leaving some of the letters out.)

- I am sleepy. —> **I'm** sleepy.
  The letter *a* in *am* has been left out.
- Hank did not know the answer. —> Hank **didn't** know the answer.
  The letter *o* in *not* has been left out.
- They would keep the secret. —> **They'd** keep the secret.
  The letters *woul* in *would* have been left out.

Here are a few more common contractions:

it + is = **it's** (the *i* in *is* has been left out)
does + not = **doesn't** (the *o* in *not* has been left out)
do + not = **don't** (the *o* in *not* has been left out)
she + will = **she'll** (the *wi* in *will* has been left out)
he + is = **he's** (the *i* in *is* has been left out)
we + have = **we've** (the *ha* in *have* has been left out)
could + not = **couldn't** (the *o* in *not* has been left out)
will + not = **won't** (the *o* replaces *ill*; the *o* in *not* has been left out)

2 The apostrophe shows that something belongs to someone or something. (This is called **possession.**)

- the fin of the shark —> the **shark's** fin
  The apostrophe goes after the last letter of the name of the owner, *shark*. The *'s* added to *shark* tells us that the fin belongs to the shark.
- the grades of Nina —> **Nina's** grades
  The apostrophe goes after the last letter of the name of the owner, *Nina*. The *'s* added to *Nina* tells us that the grades belong to Nina.

  Note No apostrophe is used with simple plurals such as *grades,* which simply means "more than one grade."

- the cheering of the crowd —> the **crowd's** cheering
  The apostrophe goes after the last letter of the name of the owner, *crowd*. The *'s* added to *crowd* tells us that the cheering belongs to the crowd.

For added information about the apostrophe, see page 291.

Understanding the Apostrophe

Notice how the apostrophe is used in the following passage about Beth Johnson's three children.

[1]The day's work for this suburban family begins over breakfast. [2]Isaac is finishing his Spanish homework. [3]Sam notices that the calculator's batteries are getting low. [4]Because Maddie's bus doesn't come until after the boys leave, she's still in her bathrobe.

1. **The day's work** means "the work of the day."
2. The second apostrophe, in **calculator's batteries**, means "the batteries belonging to the calculator."
3. The third apostrophe, in **Maddie's bus**, means "the bus for Maddie."
4. The fourth apostrophe, in **doesn't**, takes the place of the missing letter in *does not.*
5. The fifth apostrophe, in **she's**, takes the place of the missing letter in *she is.*

Check Your Understanding

Read the passage below. Then fill in the missing word or words in each sentence.

[1]After the boys have gone, Maddie plays school. [2]She pretends her dolls haven't learned to read, and she's teaching them by reading a book out loud. [3]At night, the little girl's bed is so covered with dolls that there's hardly room for her to sleep. [4]She never removes any dolls despite her mom's suggestion that she do so.

1. The apostrophe in **haven't** takes the place of the missing letter in thc word ____________.
2. The apostrophe in **she's** takes the place of the missing letter in the word ____________.
3. The apostrophe in **girl's bed** means *the bed belonging to the* ____________________.
4. The apostrophe in **there's** takes the place of the missing letter in the word ____________.
5. The apostrophe in **her mom's suggestion** means *the suggestion belonging to* ____________.

The Apostrophe: PRACTICE 1

Each of the short passages below contains words that need apostrophes. Underline the words that need apostrophes. Then write each word, with its apostrophe, in the space provided.

[1]Harrys friend, Sara, lives in the same apartment building. [2]On a beautiful Saturday afternoon he calls her to go on a picnic, but she isnt home. [3]Sara's sister, Olivia, says shell go instead.

1. ______________________
2. ______________________
3. ______________________

[4]Olivia asks Harry if her brothers friend, Jonah can join them. [5]"I didnt know Jonah was your brother's friend," Harry said. [6]"Youre welcome to invite him."

4. ______________________
5. ______________________
6. ______________________

[7]Harry, Olivia, and Jonah borrow their friends bicycles and head off to have a picnic. [8]Their local park is a great place to go and they dont need a permit. [9]As they approach the perfect spot, they see Saras bike leaning on a tree. [10]The four friends enjoy the day together and arent worried about the huge rain clouds in the distance.

7. ______________________
8. ______________________
9. ______________________
10. ______________________

The Apostrophe: PRACTICE 2

Each of the sentences below contains **one** word that needs an apostrophe. Write each word, with its apostrophe, in the space provided.

1. A lobsters claws are used to crush prey and then tear it apart.

 ____

2. We havent seen our waitress since she gave us menus twenty minutes ago.

 ____

3. My cousins know the stores owner, a man named Mr. Sherwin.

 ____

4. The mystery books final ten pages were missing.

 ____

5. School wont be opening until noon because of the power failure.

 ____

6. A dogs collar should not be too tight.

 ____

7. We watched a TV movie about an adult who couldnt read.

 ____

8. For Halloween, Barry dressed up in a cheerleaders outfit.

 ____

9. There was a rumor that some employees would be laid off, but it wasnt true.

 ____

10. The models teeth were so white that they did not look real.

 ____

The Apostrophe: PRACTICE 3

Each sentence in the following passage contains **one** word that requires an apostrophe. Underline the ten words. Then, on the lines following the passage, write the corrected form of each word.

Note To help you master the apostrophe, explanations are given for five of the sentences.

[1]Smart phones are a great invention, but what they shouldnt become is an addiction. [2]They can take over peoples lives, rather than make them easier. [3]With a smart phone, youre never alone. [4]You can now talk on the phone, send text messages, listen to music, surf the Web if you dont have a computer nearby, play games, and check your e-mail. [5]Many people enjoy checking their Facebook and Twitter accounts while crossing the street and often they arent aware of oncoming traffic. [6]Theyre completely focused on the screen of their smart phone. [7]The smart phones main attraction is its applications, or "apps." [8]Theres an application for games, horoscopes, pedometers, music software, and recording devices. [9]The fun and convenience of a smart phone can certainly make peoples lives easier. [10]It is important to remember, however, that smart phones cant take the place of face-to-face interaction.

1. ____________ The contraction of *should not* needs an apostrophe.
2. ____________
3. ____________ The contraction of *you are* needs an apostrophe.
4. ____________
5. ____________ The contraction of *are not* needs an apostrophe.
6. ____________
7. ____________ The writer means "the main attraction of the phone."
8. ____________
9. ____________ The writer means "the lives of people."
10. ____________

Name ______________________________ Section ____________ Date ____________

Score: (Number right) ________ x 10 = ____________ %

The Apostrophe: TEST 1

Each of the sentences below contains **one** word that needs an apostrophe. Underline the word. Then write the word, with its apostrophe, in the space provided.

NOTE To help you master the apostrophe, explanations are given for the first three sentences.

1. My fathers thunderous snores can be heard all over the house.
   The snores belong to the father. *Snores* is a simple plural; no apostrophe is used.

   ____

2. The movie star wore a hat and dark glasses, but she couldnt fool her waiting fans.
   An apostrophe should take the place of the missing *o* in the contraction.

   ____

3. The tigers pacing never stopped as it watched the crowd of zoo visitors.
   The pacing belongs to the tiger. *Visitors* is a simple plural; no apostrophe is used.

   ____

4. Some students are unhappy about the schools decision to remove soft-drink machines.

   ____

5. Even though they didnt finish elementary school, my grandparents want me to get a college degree.

   ____

6. The grasshoppers powerful hind legs allow the insect to jump many times its own height.

   ____

7. Sheer white curtains and fresh lilacs added to the rooms simple charm.

   ____

8. The hypnotists only tools are a soothing voice and a watch that ticks very loudly.

   ____

9. If you keep eating the cheese dip, there wont be enough to serve our guests.

   ____

10. Since lemons are so cheap right now, Im going to buy enough to make lemonade, lemon cake, and lemon chicken.

    ____

Name ______________________ Section ____________ Date ____________

Score: (Number right) ______ x 10 = ________ %

The Apostrophe: TEST 2

Each of the sentences below contains **one** word that needs an apostrophe. Underline the word. Then write the word, with its apostrophe, in the space provided.

1. Arvels route to work involves a bus, train, and subway.

____

2. My dads truck is perfect for moving furniture.

____

3. Isnt my dog Ziggy the best companion a person could ever have?

____

4. I couldnt get that scary movie last night out of my mind.

____

5. Rogers plaid cap became his signature as he always wore it to school.

____

6. The poor football players havent won a game since the season began.

____

7. Orlando unscrewed the bottles cap after thumping it repeatedly on the sidewalk.

____

8. They discovered that they werent ready to run a marathon after only one month of training.

____

9. The mans toupee fell off when he began to dance.

____

10. The smart phones apps are easy to download.

____

Name ______________________ Section ____________ Date ____________

Score: (Number right) ________ x 10 = ____________ %

The Apostrophe: TEST 3

Each sentence in the passages below contains a word that needs an apostrophe. Underline the **ten** words that need apostrophes. Then, on the lines following the passages, write the corrected form of each word.

A. [1]Some students are morning people, and some just arent. [2]The morning people are awake as soon as the suns rays hit the window, so they are ready to hop out of bed and get ready for school. [3]But given a choice, many people would prefer a beds warmth for a few more hours. [4]Their brains dont start functioning until about 10 a.m. [5]Couldnt there be one school for the morning people and another for the rest of us?

1. ____________________

2. ____________________

3. ____________________

4. ____________________

5. ____________________

B. [1]If you could choose, would you rather be your familys only child, or would you want to have siblings? [2]Sherry, an only child I once knew, never had to share her toys or her mothers attention. [3]When I first realized that, I wanted to put my brothers photograph on a "for sale" sign. [4]But later I decided I didnt really want to be an "only." [5]Without my brother, I wouldnt have had anybody to blame when I did something wrong!

6. ____________________

7. ____________________

8. ____________________

9. ____________________

10. ____________________

Name ______________________ Section ____________ Date ____________

Score: (Number right) ______ x 10 = ________ %

The Apostrophe: TEST 4

In each group below, **one** sentence uses apostrophes correctly. Write the letter of that sentence in the space provided.

_____ **1.** **a.** The mans beard and the woman's hair were both stark white.
b. The man's beard and the womans hair were both stark white.
c. The man's beard and the woman's hair were both stark white.

_____ **2.** **a.** I havent so much as smelled a cigarettes smoke in ten days.
b. I haven't so much as smelled a cigarette's smoke in ten days.
c. I haven't so much as smelled a cigarettes smoke in ten days.

_____ **3.** **a.** The boy's grades haven't been good since he left his old school.
b. The boys grades haven't been good since he left his old school.
c. The boy's grades havent been good since he left his old school.

_____ **4.** **a.** My nephew's house is up for sale, but he doesnt want to move until summer.
b. My nephew's house is up for sale, but he doesn't want to move until summer.
c. My nephews house is up for sale, but he doesn't want to move until summer.

_____ **5.** **a.** The classes books haven't arrived yet.
b. The classes books' haven't arrived yet.
c. The classes' books haven't arrived yet.

_____ **6.** **a.** We'll be surprised if the new tenants' lease allows them to have pets.
b. We'll be surprised if the new tenants lease allows them to have pets.
c. Well be surprised if the new tenants' lease allows them to have pets.

_____ **7.** **a.** My pet rats cage and my pet snakes aquarium are right next to each other.
b. My pet rat's cage and my pet snakes aquarium are right next to each other.
c. My pet rat's cage and my pet snake's aquarium are right next to each other.

_____ **8.** **a.** Hayley wont eat any vegetables grown in her mothers garden.
b. Hayley won't eat any vegetables grown in her mothers garden.
c. Hayley won't eat any vegetables grown in her mother's garden.

_____ **9.** **a.** My computer's hard drive has crashed, so I can't get any work done.
b. My computer's hard drive has crashed, so I cant get any work done.
c. My computers hard drive has crashed, so I can't get any work done.

_____ **10.** **a.** I didn't remember to change the cars oil.
b. I didnt remember to change the car's oil.
c. I didn't remember to change the car's oil.

Name ______________________________ Section ______________ Date ______________

Score: (Number right) ________ x 10 = ____________ %

The Apostrophe: TEST 5

In each group below, **one** sentence uses apostrophes correctly. Write the letter of that sentence in the space provided.

______ **1.** **a.** My aunts hairstyle hasnt changed in twenty years.
b. My aunt's hairstyle hasnt changed in twenty year's.
c. My aunt's hairstyle hasn't changed in twenty years.

______ **2.** **a.** The veterinarian's assistant quickly examined our puppy's hurt paws.
b. The veterinarian's assistant quickly examined our puppys hurt paw's.
c. The veterinarians assistant quickly examined our puppy's hurt paws.

______ **3.** **a.** The romance novel's cover showed a woman fainting in a man's arms.
b. The romance novel's cover showed a woman fainting in a man's arm's.
c. The romance novels cover showed a woman fainting in a man's arm's.

______ **4.** **a.** Sheila's boyfriend work's part-time in his fathers barbershop.
b. Sheilas boyfriend work's part-time in his father's barbershop.
c. Sheila's boyfriend works part-time in his father's barbershop.

______ **5.** **a.** The police didn't show up until four hour's after wed called them.
b. The police didn't show up until four hours after we'd called them.
c. The police didnt show up until four hour's after we'd called them.

______ **6.** **a.** I can't believe youve never eaten in a Chinese restaurant.
b. I can't believe you've never eaten in a Chinese restaurant.
c. I cant believe you've never eaten in a Chinese restaurant.

______ **7.** **a.** The witch's gingerbread house wasn't visible to grownups.
b. The witch's gingerbread house wasnt visible to grownups.
c. The witchs gingerbread house wasn't visible to grownup's.

______ **8.** **a.** The oceans floor isn't flat, but contains mountain's, plains, and ridges.
b. The ocean's floor isnt flat, but contains mountain's, plains, and ridges.
c. The ocean's floor isn't flat, but contains mountains, plains, and ridges.

______ **9.** **a.** An ostrich eggs shell is as thick as a nickel and can't be easily broken.
b. An ostrich egg's shell is as thick as a nickel and can't be easily broken.
c. An ostrich egg's shell is as thick as a nickel and cant be easily broken.

______ **10.** **a.** The homeless man's feet were wrapped in page's of yesterdays newspaper.
b. The homeless mans feet were wrapped in page's of yesterday's newspaper.
c. The homeless man's feet were wrapped in pages of yesterday's newspaper.

12 Quotation Marks

Basics about Quotation Marks

Use quotation marks to set off all exact words of a speaker or writer.

- The little girl's mother said, "It wasn't nice to fill up the sugar bowl with salt."
  The mother's exact words are enclosed within quotation marks.
- "I'm afraid," the mechanic muttered to Fred, "that your car is in big trouble."
  The mechanic's exact words are enclosed within quotation marks.
- "Our math teacher is unfair," complained Wanda. "He assigns two hours of homework for each class. Does he think we have nothing else to do?"
  Wanda's exact words are enclosed within quotation marks. Note that even though Wanda's second set of exact words is more than one sentence, only one pair of quotation marks is used. Do not use quotation marks for each new sentence as long as the quotation is not interrupted.
- "We cannot solve a problem by hoping that someone else will solve it for us," wrote psychiatrist M. Scott Peck.
  The exact words that Dr. Peck wrote are enclosed in quotation marks.

NOTES

- Quoted material is usually set off from the rest of the sentence by a comma. When the comma comes at the end of quoted material, it is included inside the quotation marks. The same is true for a period, exclamation point, or question mark that ends quoted material:

  Incorrect "Watching golf", complained Rosie, "is like watching grass grow".
  Correct "Watching golf," complained Rosie, "is like watching grass grow."

  Incorrect "Aren't you ready yet"? Dad yelled. "Hurry up, or we're leaving without you"!
  Correct "Aren't you ready yet?" Dad yelled. "Hurry up, or we're leaving without you!"

- Notice, too, that a quoted sentence begins with a capital letter, even when it is preceded by other words:

  Incorrect The diner asked suspiciously, "is this fish fresh?"
  Correct The diner asked suspiciously, "Is this fish fresh?"

Understanding Quotation Marks

Notice how quotation marks are used in the following interview with Dr. Richard Kratz, president of Reading Area Community College in Reading, Pennsylvania. All of the words Dr. Kratz actually spoke aloud are set off in quotation marks.

[1]If you had told Dr. Kratz when he was a teenager that he would someday be a college president, he would have laughed at you.

[2]"My family believed in education. [3]In fact, my father was superintendent of schools, and my mother was a teacher," Dr. Kratz says. [4]"But somehow, I didn't get on board at first."

[5]He was a poor student in high school.

[6]"I think I was fifth in my class," he says, "but I mean fifth from the bottom." [7]He didn't like to read, and he didn't write well. [8]But then in college, something happened to Dr. Kratz.

[9]"I took a course in which we read some amazing novels," he remembers. [10]"The ones I remember best are *Brave New World* and *1984.* [11]I discovered a passion for reading, and I've been a reader ever since."

[12]Dr. Kratz doesn't mean that he never had any more trouble in school. [13]"I had to take basic English in college," he says, "and I still don't write as well as I would like. [14]But I realized that writing was a skill I could acquire, if I worked at it."

Check Your Understanding

Use **five** sets of quotation marks (" ") to enclose the words that Dr. Kratz says out loud.

[1]Here is Dr. Kratz in the cafeteria with some students. [2]Dr. Kratz has a lot of respect for his students. [3]According to him, many of them are dealing with difficult obstacles.

[4] Many of our students are the first in their families to go to college, he says. [5] That can make it tough. [6]When I got back my first college English paper, it was so covered with red marks it looked like a Christmas tree. [7]My parents told me not to worry, that the same thing had happened to them. [8]If I hadn't had anybody at home to tell me that, I might have panicked and given up.

[9]Dr. Kratz also explains that community-college students face other challenges, too. [10]He says, The average age of our students is 28. [11]For many of them, school is about the fourth priority. [12]I hear them talking about job problems, transportation problems, and family problems.

[13]Dr. Kratz then continues, Women students have their own special issues. [14]Too often, there's no support at home. [15]If nobody is offering extra help with the kids or the housework, I can understand how they end up feeling they can't handle it all.

[16]Finally, Dr. Kratz cites the special problems of minority students: Some people criticize them for working hard in school. [17]They accuse them of thinking they're better than their friends.

[18]For all these reasons, Dr. Kratz is very proud of his students for being in college and doing their best there.

Quotation Marks: PRACTICE 1

Each of the short passages below contains words that need quotation marks. Add the **four** sets of missing quotation marks in the passage below.

[1]Dr. Kratz loves to tell success stories about his former and current students.

[2]One of his favorites is about the college's commencement speaker several years ago. [3]She had been a student at the college, and one day her biology instructor got into a conversation with her.

[4] What are you majoring in? he asked.

[5] I'm going to be a legal secretary, she answered. [6] I'm not really interested in it, but I'm a single mother on welfare, and I just need to get some job training quickly. [7]I'd really like to work in medical research, but someone like me can't do that.

[8]The biology instructor encouraged the woman not to settle for a career she wasn't excited about. [9]She decided to find a way to make her education a priority. [10]She graduated from community college, went on to earn a bachelor's degree, and is now finishing her doctorate at a major medical center. [11]When she spoke at the community college's commencement, she said, Don't accept the idea that you can't. [12]Find out what you *can* do, and do it.

Add the **five** sets of missing quotation marks.

[1]These students are looking forward to their own graduations. [2]Commencement at the college is always an exciting day.

[3] It's the greatest thing in the world, says Dr. Kratz. [4] Everybody is hooting and hollering for their friends and relatives.

[5]He says the enthusiasm is very contagious. [6]He then tells this story: A few years ago, the mayor of Philadelphia came to speak at commencement. [7]I expected he would just give his speech and leave early. [8]But the mayor got so caught up in the excitement that he ended up hanging around for the whole evening.

[9]Dr. Kratz gets caught up in the excitement, too. [10] I know many of these students have sacrificed in order to make it to this day, he says. [11] I'm as proud of them as if they were my own kids.

Add the **one** set of missing quotation marks.

[1]Here Dr. Kratz stands nearby as a library staff member helps a student do computer research. [2]He explains, Cooperation is at the heart of what community college is all about. [3]We will meet you wherever you are and help you become the best that you can be.

Quotation Marks: PRACTICE 2

Insert quotation marks where needed in the following sentences. Look at the example below.

Example The game announcer called out, "Looks like we have a winner!"

1. I won't take any more criticism, Kylie said to her boyfriend. Our relationship is over.

2. The 911 operator stated, Please stay calm. Help is on the way.

3. Let's all turn on our computers, the instructor said.

4. The label on the chlorine bleach says, Do not mix this product with other cleansers.

5. This is a movie that will scare everyone in the family, the reviewer said.

6. The boat captain said sternly, Please keep your arms and legs inside the boat. Failure to do so will make the alligators very happy.

7. In his book *Think Big*, Dr. Benjamin Carson writes, I had been in the fifth grade not even two weeks before everyone considered me the dumbest kid in the class and frequently made jokes about me.

8. Cut the onions into thin slices, the cooking instructor explained. Then place them in the hot skillet.

9. Could you turn the radio down just a little? the passenger shouted to the taxi driver.

10. Anne Frank wrote the following in her diary: It's a wonder I haven't abandoned all my ideals, which seem so absurd and impractical. Yet I cling to them because I still believe, in spite of everything, that people are truly good at heart.

Quotation Marks: PRACTICE 3

Five sets of quotation marks are missing from each of the following passages. Insert the quotation marks where needed.

Passage 1

[1]Dr. Richard Kratz knows that, of course, college isn't only about studying.

[2] Let's go see if anyone's in the student union, Dr. Kratz says.

[3]When he gets there, he finds a number of students watching TV, talking, and playing pool.

[4] Hey, how are you guys doing? Dr. Kratz says to the pool players. [5] Do you mind if we take some pictures here?

[6]The guys don't mind at all. [7] Put me in the picture! says one student.

[8]Another jokes, Why would you put him in when you can have my good-looking self in it?

[9]In the end, all the guys get in the picture.

Passage 2

[1]Community colleges have been part of America since 1901. [2]Today, the more than one thousand community colleges educate over half the undergraduate college students in the United States. [3]Community colleges are gaining in popularity for a number of reasons. [4]According to *U.S. News and World Report,* Some students have started off at two-year schools because they aren't ready, either academically or emotionally, for big universities.

[5]But the magazine goes on to say that many students who could go directly to a four-year college are choosing a community college instead. [6]Here's an excerpt from the magazine: Chantel Bain wanted a college with small classes, caring professors, and diverse course offerings. [7]She found her perfect match at Santa Barbara City College, a two-year college.

[8]One person posting on an online message board had this to say about the advantages of community colleges: My student loans are going to be only a quarter of what they would have been, thanks to my attending a community college rather than a four-year school. [9]She went on to praise the flexibility she found at her school: Community colleges attract students who have other full-time obligations, such as work or family. [10]Most instructors understand this and are willing to accommodate.

[11]In an interview, Dr. Richard Kratz notes, Community colleges are the only sector of American education that is truly American. [12]Everything else has been borrowed from British education.

[13]For all the above reasons, it is likely that community colleges will continue growing in importance in the American educational system.

Name ______________________________ Section ______________ Date ______________

Score: (Number right) _______ x 10 = ____________ %

Quotation Marks: TEST 1

On the lines provided, rewrite the following sentences, adding quotation marks as needed.

NOTE To help you master quotation marks, explanations are given for the first three sentences.

1. My mother said, Take some vitamin C for your cold.
   The mother's words and the period at the end of the sentence should be included within quotation marks.

   ____

2. Do not discuss the trial during your break, the judge reminded the jury.
   The judge's words and the comma at the end of his words should be enclosed within quotation marks.

   ____

3. That movie, my friend complained, is full of nonstop violence.
   Each of the two parts of the friend's words requires a set of quotation marks. The words *my friend complained* do not get quotation marks because he did not speak them aloud.

   ____

4. The children's voices sang, Row, row, row your boat, gently down the stream.

   ____

5. My computer screen is frozen, I said to the instructor.

   ____

6. Let's eat, Rochelle said, before we go to the movie.

   ____

7. A sign on my father's desk reads, In the rat race, only the rats win.

   ____

8. Who would like another slice of turkey? Mr. Brandon asked the dinner guests.

   ____

9. Keep your voice down! the little boy shouted loudly to the woman using a cell phone.

   ____

10. Take a lot of notes, my friend warned, if you want to do well on tests.

    ____

Name ______________________ Section ______________ Date ______________

Score: (Number right) ______ x 10 = ______ %

Quotation Marks: TEST 2

On the lines provided, rewrite the following sentences, adding quotation marks as needed.

1. I know you are sorry, the mother said, but you must apologize to your sister for yelling at her.

 ____

 ____

2. The kindergartners all wanted to be called upon, so they shouted to their teacher, Me! Me! Me! as they all raised their hands.

 ____

 ____

3. I am totally exhausted, the mother of six exclaimed.

 ____

4. Phillip's response to his jilted fiancée was, I'm just not ready to get married.

 ____

5. The little girl sighed, I wish I could have a brand-new baby brother!

 ____

6. Mark Twain quipped, Always do right. This will gratify some people and astonish the rest.

 ____

7. The warning sign stated, You will die if you touch these wires.

 ____

8. The headline of the local newspaper read, Serial Killer Strikes Again.

 ____

9. All women and children in the life boats! shouted the ship's captain.

 ____

10. How do you have such lovely skin? my friend Nereida asked.

 ____

Name ______________________ Section ____________ Date ____________

Score: (Number right) _______ x 10 = ____________ %

Quotation Marks: TEST 3

Place quotation marks where needed in the short passages that follow. Each passage needs **two** sets of quotation marks.

1. After serving the couple expensive lobster dinners, the waitress was upset to find that they had left her only fifty cents for a tip. Wait, mister, she called after the man. You can use this more than I can.

2. The interviewer poked her head out of the office door and called out, Please come in, Mr. Taylor. She asked him a few questions about his experience. Then she said, We've had twenty-five applicants for this position. Tell me why you deserve to be hired rather than any of those others.

3. Pointing to a headline in the tabloid newspaper at the supermarket counter, the boy said, It looks as if space aliens have landed in Minnesota.

   You'd have to be from outer space to believe those newspapers, stated his father.

4. My uncle and aunt have different ways of dealing with guests who stay too long. My aunt will hint politely, Well, it sure has been nice having you folks over. My uncle is much more direct. He says, Let's call it a night, Norma, and let these nice people go home.

5. The Hollywood tourist asked the handsome man in the coffee shop for his autograph. He graciously signed her menu. When she read the signature, she sputtered, James Dixon? You're nobody famous!

   The man shrugged. I didn't say I was. You're the one who asked for my autograph.

Name ______________________ Section ____________ Date ____________

Score: (Number right) ______ x 10 = ________ %

Quotation Marks: TEST 4

In each group below, **one** sentence uses quotation marks correctly. Write the letter of that sentence in the space provided.

_____ **1.** **a.** "My grades are going downhill, Laura whispered.
b. My grades are going downhill," Laura whispered.
c. "My grades are going downhill," Laura whispered.

_____ **2.** **a.** The movie star said, "I only ride in limousines.
b. "The movie star said, I only ride in limousines."
c. The movie star said, "I only ride in limousines."

_____ **3.** **a.** "Why are your eyes closed? the instructor asked Simon."
b. "Why are your eyes closed?" the instructor asked Simon.
c. "Why are your eyes closed? the instructor asked Simon.

_____ **4.** **a.** The instructions say, "Open the battery compartment. Insert 4 AA batteries."
b. The instructions say, "Open the battery compartment." Insert 4 AA batteries.
c. "The instructions say, Open the battery compartment. Insert 4 AA batteries."

_____ **5.** **a.** "It says right here in our lease," "The landlord is responsible for taking care of the yard."
b. "It says right here in our lease," The landlord is responsible for taking care of the yard.
c. It says right here in our lease, "The landlord is responsible for taking care of the yard."

_____ **6.** **a.** "I hate that music, said my brother, "and you know it.
b. "I hate that music," said my brother, "and you know it."
c. "I hate that music, said my brother, and you know it."

_____ **7.** **a.** The sign in the restaurant window reads, "Breakfast served anytime."
b. "The sign in the restaurant window reads, "Breakfast served anytime."
c. The sign in the restaurant window reads, "Breakfast served anytime.

_____ **8.** **a.** As I sat at the baseball game, I heard someone call, "Get your fresh hot peanuts."
b. As I sat at the baseball game, "I heard someone call, Get your fresh hot peanuts."
c. "As I sat at the baseball game, I heard someone call," Get your fresh hot peanuts.

_____ **9.** **a.** Dale said, "If that salesman were covered in gravy and dropped into a pit of lions, he could talk them into becoming vegetarians.
b. Dale said, "If that salesman were covered in gravy and dropped into a pit of lions, he could talk them into becoming vegetarians."
c. "Dale said, If that salesman were covered in gravy and dropped into a pit of lions, he could talk them into becoming vegetarians."

_____ **10.** **a.** "The first line in the novel *1984* reads," It was a bright cold day in April, and the clocks were striking thirteen.
b. The first line in the novel *1984* reads, "It was a bright cold day in April, and the clocks were striking thirteen."
c. "The first line in the novel *1984* reads," "It was a bright cold day in April, and the clocks were striking thirteen."

Name ______________________________ Section ______________ Date ______________

Score: (Number right) ______ x 10 = ______________ %

Quotation Marks: TEST 5

In each group below, **one** sentence uses quotation marks correctly. Write the letter of that sentence in the space provided.

_____ **1.** **a.** I don't like your lollipops, "the little girl said to the dentist."
b. "I don't like your lollipops," the little girl said to the dentist.
c. "I don't like your lollipops, the little girl said to the dentist."

_____ **2.** **a.** Rachel announced, "I can open the locked door with a bent coat hanger.
b. "Rachel announced, I can open the locked door with a bent coat hanger."
c. Rachel announced, "I can open the locked door with a bent coat hanger."

_____ **3.** **a.** The boss advised, "Don't be late again. If you are, I'll fire you."
b. The boss advised, Don't be late again. If you are, I'll fire you."
c. The boss advised, "Don't be late again. If you are, I'll fire you.

_____ **4.** **a.** "Albert Einstein wrote, Will it matter that I was?"
b. Albert Einstein wrote, "Will it matter that I was?"
c. Albert Einstein wrote, "Will it matter that I was?

_____ **5.** **a.** How do you like it? "Cindy asked, showing off her new purple fake-fur jacket."
b. "How do you like it?" Cindy asked, showing off her new purple fake-fur jacket.
c. "How do you like it? Cindy asked, showing off her new purple fake-fur jacket."

_____ **6.** **a.** Her mother paused and then said, "Well, it certainly is a cheerful color."
b. Her mother paused and then said, "Well, it certainly is a cheerful color.
c. Her mother paused and then said, Well, it certainly is a cheerful color."

_____ **7.** **a.** Her brother was less tactful. You look like a giant purple marshmallow, he said.
b. Her brother was less tactful. "You look like a giant purple marshmallow, he said."
c. Her brother was less tactful. "You look like a giant purple marshmallow," he said.

_____ **8.** **a.** Most people don't plan to fail, "the counselor said," but they fail to plan.
b. "Most people don't plan to fail," the counselor said, but they fail to plan.
c. "Most people don't plan to fail," the counselor said, "but they fail to plan."

_____ **9.** **a.** "Reading is to the mind what exercise is to the body," wrote Richard Steele.
b. "Reading is to the mind what exercise is to the body, wrote Richard Steele."
c. Reading is to the mind what exercise is to the body, "wrote Richard Steele."

_____ **10.** **a.** Mother Teresa said, "Kind words can be easy to speak, but their echoes are truly endless."
b. Mother Teresa said, "Kind words can be easy to speak, but their echoes are truly endless.
c. "Mother Teresa said, "Kind words can be easy to speak, but their echoes are truly endless."

13 Homonyms

Basics about Homonyms

Homonyms are two or more words that have the same sound but different spellings and meanings. The following four groups of homonyms cause writers the most trouble.

its belonging to it
it's contraction of *it is*

- **It's** a shame that the shiny car lost **its** muffler and now roars like an old truck.
  It is a shame that the shiny car lost *the muffler belonging to it* and now roars like an old truck.

  Spelling hint In *it's,* the apostrophe takes the place of the *i* in the word *is.*

their belonging to them
there (1) in or to that place; (2) used with *is, are, was, were,* and other forms of the verb *to be*
they're contraction of *they are*

- Our neighbors are health-food addicts. When we attend parties at **their** home, they serve pizza with broccoli florets on top. **They're** also fond of serving carrot juice. I hope they won't be offended if we don't go **there** very often.
  Our neighbors are health-food addicts. When we attend parties at the home *belonging to them,* they serve pizza with broccoli florets on top. *They are* also fond of serving carrot juice. I hope they won't be offended when we don't go *to that place* very often.

  Spelling hints *There, where,* and *here,* which all end in *-ere,* all refer to places.
  In *they're,* the apostrophe takes the place of the *a* in *are.*

to (1) used before a verb, as in "to serve"; (2) so as to reach
too (1) overly or extremely; (2) also
two the number 2

- I'll take these **two** letters **to** the post office for you, but you'll need **to** put more postage on one of them. It is **too** heavy for only one stamp.
  I'll take these *2* letters *so as to reach* the post office for you, but you'll need *to put* more postage on one of them. It is *overly* heavy for only one stamp.

  Spelling hint *Too* has one *o,* and it **also** has another one.

your belonging to you
you're contraction of *you are*

- **You're** going to need a first-aid kit and high boots for **your** camping trip.
  You are going to need a first-aid kit and high boots for the camping trip *belonging to you.*

  Spelling hint In *you're,* the apostrophe takes the place of the *a* in *are.*

Understanding Homonyms

In the following passage about a married couple, Joe and Terri Davis, **five** homonym mistakes are underlined. The correct spelling of each word is then shown in the spaces below.

[1]Joe and Terri live in Philadelphia. [2]The too of them have been married for thirteen years. [3]They met after Terri had an operation on her knee. [4]While she was recovering, she had too ride in a special bus for people with disabilities. [5]Because he has a spinal-cord injury, Joe used that bus two. [6]It was their on the bus that they began getting acquainted. [7]You never know where your going to meet someone special!

1. The meaning is "the number 2," which is spelled two.
2. The spelling before a verb (here, to ride) is always to.
3. The meaning is "also," which is spelled too.
4. The meaning is "at that place," which is spelled there.
5. The meaning is "you are," which is spelled you're. (The apostrophe takes the place of the missing a in you are.)

Check Your Understanding

Underline the **five** mistakes in homonyms. Then write the correct spellings of the words in the five spaces provided.

[1]Now Joe and Terri have a lift for Joe's wheelchair in there own van. [2]It's gas pedal and brake have been changed so that Joe can operate them by hand. [3]Joe and Terri both work downtown. [4]In this picture, their about to head on there way home. [5]Joe is using the lift to get into the van. [6]He'll then drive too a corner near Terri's office and pick her up.

1. ______________ 2. ______________

3. ______________ 4. ______________ 5. ______________

Other Common Homonyms

brake — slow or stop
break — to cause to come apart

hear — take in by ear
here — in this place

hole — an empty spot
whole — complete

know — to understand
no — the opposite of *yes*

right — correct
write — to form letters and words

whose — belonging to whom
who's — contraction of *who is* or *who has*

Homonyms: PRACTICE 1

In the passages below, underline the correct word in the **fifteen** sets of parentheses.

[1]We all like to save money if we have the chance. [2]Next time (your, you're) going grocery shopping, consider using coupons. [3]Once you (no, know) a few couponing tips, it's one of the easiest ways to spend less and save more. [4]First you'll need to get hold of some coupons. [5]The best places to look for coupons are in newspapers, magazines, on the products themselves, or on store shelves. [6]Don't forget to check (whether, weather) there's a coupon printed out with your sales receipt, (two, to, too)!

[1]On the Web you can find printable coupons, and often (your, you're) junk mail will contain coupons for local, neighborhood products and services and discounts for (knew, new) restaurants. [2]So don't forget to look (through, threw) your mail before you toss it!

[1](You're, your) probably wondering how to organize all your coupons. [2]The key to organizing these valuable bits of paper is to find the approach that works best for you. [3](Here, hear) are some clipping options to consider: clip all the coupons you find, clip just the coupons that you intend to use, or clip coupons on an "as-needed" basis. [4]Next you will need (to, too, two) develop a filing system and organize them (wear, where) you'll remember to use them—a storage container, a binder, or a pouch in (your, you're) bag. [5]Keep your coupons with you at all times as you never (know, no) when you'll be able to match up a coupon you have with the product you (knead, need). [6]Once you get the hang of it, couponing can be like a game to (see, sea) how much money you can save.

Homonyms: PRACTICE 2

For each sentence, underline the correct word in parentheses.

1. There is only one (write, right) answer to a math problem.
2. No child will be able to (break, brake) this toy.
3. We drove (through, threw) the entire state in only three hours.
4. Everyone wants (piece, peace) in the world.
5. I forgot (where, wear) I stored the Christmas presents.
6. Are you going to order a half or a (hole, whole) barbecued chicken?
7. The (weather, whether) in England is rainy much of the time.
8. Ray and Coral, who just got married, want all (new, knew) furniture in their house.
9. People who cannot (hear, here) often communicate by American Sign Language.
10. The sign in the bus said, "(There, They're, Their) is no excuse for domestic violence."

Homonyms: PRACTICE 3

In the passage below, underline the correct word in each set of parentheses. **Ten** corrections are needed.

[1]Working at home can be better than going to an office every day. [2]It can depend on (weather, whether) or not you are an organized person. [3]Each (piece, peace) of your personal life can intrude upon your working life if you are not careful. [4]If you need to (write, right) e-mails to someone (whose, who's) business you need to keep, then you cannot be distracted by a sink full of dirty dishes. [5]You can also be driven away from work tasks if you (here, hear) the doorbell ring and stop working (to, too, two) answer it. [6]One technique is to get (threw, through) as many household chores as you can before shutting yourself into your work office at a set, predetermined time every day. [7]Creating a designated workplace (wear, where) home life cannot intrude is helpful, (to, too, two). [8]Working effectively at home can be done with just (plain, plane) careful planning. [9]Between nine o'clock and five o'clock each day, you are at work, as if you actually got into your car and drove there. [10]One of the greatest things about working at home is once five o'clock hits, you are home—no gridlock for you!

Name ______________________ Section ____________ Date ____________

Score: (Number right) ______ x 10 = ________ %

Homonyms: TEST 1

Cross out the **two** homonym mistakes in each sentence. Then write the correct words in the spaces provided.

NOTE To help you review some of the homonyms in the chapter, definitions are given in four of the sentences.

________ **1.** Who's job is it too clean the erasers today?
________ *The job that belongs to* who *is "to clean," which is the infinitive of the verb.*

________ **2.** Your the write man for the job.
________ *You are the correct man for the job.*

________ **3.** The breaks on there car didn't work in time to prevent the collision.
________ *The part of the car that stops it belongs to them.*

________ **4.** I here the plain had to make a crash landing.
________ *I hear with my ears that the airplane had to make a crash landing.*

________ **5.** Whose in charge of the piece march this Saturday?
____

________ **6.** I have been commissioned to right the hole story of the courageous rescue.
____

________ **7.** Its a good idea to no how to drive a car with a manual transmission.
____

________ **8.** Please don't brake the knew dishes by washing them so carelessly.
____

________ **9.** I didn't no weather to go there when I heard it was snowing in the mountains.
____

________ **10.** He swore that he through the trash in the bin, but I know he left it they're.
____

Name ______________________________ Section ______________ Date ______________

Score: (Number right) ________ x 10 = ____________ %

Homonyms: TEST 2

Cross out the **two** homonym mistakes in each sentence. Then write the correct words in the spaces provided.

________ **1.** The words on the tombstone read, "I'd rather be wear your standing."

____

________ **2.** In the hole world, there are only a few hundred Siberian tigers. In fact, their almost extinct.

____

________ **3.** Their is a custom at a Jewish wedding for the groom to step on a glass and brake it.

____

________ **4.** In really cold whether, Jeremy always wears to pairs of socks.

____

________ **5.** The doctor says its going to take at least six weeks for Jenna's sprained foot too heal.

____

________ **6.** Please place each of these knew books in it's proper place on the shelves.

____

________ **7.** Many young people don't no where there ancestors came from.

____

________ **8.** The test was full of silly questions I didn't no how to answer, such as "Whose buried in Grant's Tomb?"

____

________ **9.** My wasteful sister through out a pepperoni pizza because she prefers plane pizza.

____

________ **10.** If fortunetellers really no the future, why aren't they all lottery winners? They should be able to choose the write numbers.

____

Name ______________________ Section ____________ Date ____________

Score: (Number right) ______ x 10 = __________ %

Homonyms: TEST 3

The passage below contains **ten** errors in homonyms. Find these errors and cross them out. Then write the correct words in the spaces provided.

[1]Amelia Earhart was famous during her lifetime for being a daring pilot. [2]After her death—or at least, after what was probably her death—she became even more famous, as the center of a mystery. [3]As a young woman, Earhart earned her pilot's license and became something of a wanderer. [4]When she flew across the Atlantic Ocean with too men in 1928, the unusual trip made headlines. [5]In 1937, Earhart began her boldest trip yet. [6]With a navigator named Fred Noonan to assist her, she set out to fly around the world. [7]Their plain took off from Miami, Florida, in June. [8]They flew to New Guinea, wear they stopped to rest and make repairs before taking off for an island in the Pacific on July 1. [9]But on that date, Earhart's radio messages stopped. [10]The aircraft and it's crew had disappeared.

[11]Earhart may have simply run out of fuel over the Pacific. [12]Or perhaps unexpected bad whether caused the airplane to brake up into pieces. [13]But another theory says that Earhart was murdered. [14]In 1937, Japan was building strong military defenses on some Pacific islands. [15]Some historians believe that Earhart was forced down by Japanese troops who were afraid that she had spotted there secret military buildup. [16]After all these years, no one knows who's theory is write. [17]Threw the years since, many have searched for the missing aircraft, but no sign of it has been found. [18]And Amelia Earhart remains one of the most famous pilots in the world.

1. ______________
2. ______________
3. ______________
4. ______________
5. ______________
6. ______________
7. ______________
8. ______________
9. ______________
10. ______________

Name ______________________ Section ____________ Date ____________

Score: (Number right) ________ x 10 = ________ %

Homonyms: TEST 4

In each group below, **one** sentence uses homonyms correctly. Write the letter of that sentence in the space provided.

_____ **1.** **a.** Its raining so hard that the hikers will get all of their gear completely soaked.
b. It's raining so hard that the hikers will get all of their gear completely soaked.
c. It's raining so hard that the hikers will get all of there gear completely soaked.

_____ **2.** **a.** Please leave those two figurines alone before you brake them.
b. Please leave those too figurines alone before you break them.
c. Please leave those two figurines alone before you break them.

_____ **3.** **a.** Your house is so beautiful that it's as if it's from a fairytale.
b. You're house is so beautiful that it's as if it's from a fairytale.
c. Your house is so beautiful that its as if it's from a fairytale.

_____ **4.** **a.** Your worried about the hole family coming to dinner, while I am worried they will never leave.
b. You're worried about the hole family coming to dinner, while I am worried they will never leave.
c. You're worried about the whole family coming to dinner, while I am worried they will never leave.

_____ **5.** **a.** There are so many ways a cat can lose it's nine lives.
b. Their are so many ways a cat can lose its nine lives.
c. There are so many ways a cat can lose its nine lives.

_____ **6.** **a.** Its going to be a miracle if your history test is postponed.
b. It's going to be a miracle if your history test is postponed.
c. It's going to be a miracle if you're history test is postponed.

_____ **7.** **a.** Your mother called me at Thanksgiving to remind me that it's my turn to cook Christmas dinner this year.
b. You're mother called me at Thanksgiving to remind me that its my turn to cook Christmas dinner this year.
c. Your mother called me at Thanksgiving to remind me that its my turn to cook Christmas dinner this year.

_____ **8.** **a.** The soldier on the write was afraid to brake ranks when he felt ill.
b. The soldier on the right was afraid to break ranks when he felt ill.
c. The soldier on the right was afraid to brake ranks when he felt ill.

_____ **9.** **a.** I believe they're in for a surprise if it is my opinion you're asking.
b. I believe their in for a surprise if it is my opinion you're asking.
c. I believe they're in for a surprise if it is my opinion your asking.

_____ **10.** **a.** I no you were here before because I saw you.
b. I know you were hear before because I saw you.
c. I know you were here before because I saw you.

Name ______________________ Section ____________ Date ____________

Score: (Number right) ______ x 10 = ________ %

Homonyms: TEST 5

In each group below, **one** sentence uses homonyms correctly. Write the letter of that sentence in the space provided.

_____ **1.** **a.** Now that Mrs. Ringwald is in the hospital, no one nos whose going to teach her class.
b. Now that Mrs. Ringwald is in the hospital, no one knows whose going to teach her class.
c. Now that Mrs. Ringwald is in the hospital, no one knows who's going to teach her class.

_____ **2.** **a.** Here in Detroit, many people earn their living in the automobile industry.
b. Hear in Detroit, many people earn their living in the automobile industry.
c. Hear in Detroit, many people earn they're living in the automobile industry.

_____ **3.** **a.** Excuse me, but you're radio is playing too loudly for the other passengers.
b. Excuse me, but your radio is playing to loudly for the other passengers.
c. Excuse me, but your radio is playing too loudly for the other passengers.

_____ **4.** **a.** Too many people write unsigned letters to the newspaper.
b. To many people right unsigned letters to the newspaper.
c. Two many people write unsigned letters to the newspaper.

_____ **5.** **a.** To brake the habit of smoking takes a whole lot of willpower.
b. To break the habit of smoking takes a hole lot of willpower.
c. To break the habit of smoking takes a whole lot of willpower.

_____ **6.** **a.** You're wasting to much time worrying about things you can't control.
b. Your wasting to much time worrying about things you can't control.
c. You're wasting too much time worrying about things you can't control.

_____ **7.** **a.** After two weeks, the lost cat returned, thin and dirty and without its collar.
b. After too weeks, the lost cat returned, thin and dirty and without it's collar.
c. After to weeks, the lost cat returned, thin and dirty and without its collar.

_____ **8.** **a.** Unfortunately, it's easy to take you're family and friends for granted.
b. Unfortunately, it's easy to take your family and friends for granted.
c. Unfortunately, its easy to take your family and friends for granted.

_____ **9.** **a.** Their are too many empty storefronts in the downtown area.
b. There are too many empty storefronts in the downtown area.
c. They're are two many empty storefronts in the downtown area.

_____ **10.** **a.** Where will the party be held if the weather turns bad?
b. Wear will the party be held if the whether turns bad?
c. Where will the party be held if the whether turns bad?

14 Capital Letters

Basics about Capital Letters

Here are six main uses of capital letters:

1 THE FIRST WORD IN A SENTENCE OR DIRECT QUOTATION

- The ice-cream man said, "Try one of the frozen banana bars."

2 THE WORD "I" AND PEOPLE'S NAMES

- Because I was the first caller in the radio contest, I won two backstage passes to the Lady Gaga concert. My friend Maria Santana went with me.

3 NAMES OF SPECIFIC PLACES, INSTITUTIONS, AND LANGUAGES

- Janice, who lives in Boston and works as a lab technician at Newton Hospital, grew up on a farm in Kokomo, Indiana.
- The signs in the airport terminal were written in Spanish, English, and Japanese.

4 PRODUCT NAMES

Capitalize the brand name of a product, but not the kind of product it is.

- Every morning Ben has Tropicana orange juice and Total cereal with milk.

5 CALENDAR ITEMS

Capitalize the names of days of the week, months, and holidays.

- At first, Thanksgiving was celebrated on the last Thursday in November, but it was changed to the fourth Thursday of the month.

6 TITLES

Capitalize the titles of books, TV or stage shows, songs, magazines, movies, articles, poems, stories, papers, and so on.

- Sitting in the waiting room, Dennis nervously paged through issues of *Newsweek* and *People* magazines.
- Gwen wrote a paper titled "Portrayal of Women in Rap Music Videos" that was based on videos shown on MTV.

NOTES

- The words *the*, *of*, *a*, *an*, *and*, and other little, unstressed words are not capitalized when they appear in the middle of a title. That is why *of* and *in* are not capitalized in "Portrayal of Women in Rap Music Videos."

Understanding Capital Letters

Notice how capital letters are used in the following passage about Mark Wilson, a Philadelphia high-school student.

[1]This is Mark Wilson. [2]Mark is a sophomore at Furness High School in Philadelphia. [3]Mark lives with his family on Algard Street on the other side of Philadelphia. [4]"To get to school," Mark says, "I take two buses and a train. [5]The trip lasts an hour and a half." [6]Today is a Sunday in March, so Mark gets to stay home and relax. [7]Mark travels so far to school because he is determined to be the best that he can be, no matter what the obstacles are.

In Sentence 1, capitals are used for the first word in the sentence (and the first words in all the sentences that follow) and for Mark Wilson's name.

In Sentences 2 and 3, capitals are used for specific institutions (Furness High School) and places (Algard Street, Philadelphia).

In Sentences 4 and 5, capitals are used for Mark's name and the word "I."

In Sentence 6, capitals are used for calendar items: a day of the week (Sunday) and a month (March).

Check Your Understanding

The following passage contains **five** errors in capitalization. Underline those words, and then write them, properly capitalized, in the spaces that follow.

[1]Mark decided to attend furness in order to enroll in the school's law enforcement program. [2]He is interested in a career in federal law enforcement. [3]because of that interest, Mark says, "I also took part in a summer 'boot camp' program held at a military base in willow Grove, Pennsylvania." [4]There, Mark learned about military life, military history, and military discipline. [5]He has taken part in other special programs, too. [6]For four days last february, he attended an academic enrichment program at dartmouth College in New Hampshire.

1. ______________________

2. ______________________

3. ______________________

4. ______________________

5. ______________________

Capital Letters: PRACTICE 1

Each of the short passages that follow contains **five** errors in capitalization. Underline the words that need capitalizing. Then write these words correctly in the spaces provided.

[1]Mark has always been a young man who thinks for himself. [2]peer pressure doesn't influence him. [3]He says, "most kids care too much about what other kids think. [4]You've got to be your own person." [5]His parents have encouraged him to aim high. [6]They want Mark and his younger brother kenny involved in school and extra-curricular activities. [7]"I didn't finish high school myself," says Mark's dad. [8]"Now i work in a furniture warehouse over in kensington. [9]I've taken Mark in to work so he can see what it's like to work your tail off in 100-degree heat. [10]He knows that doing well in school is the key to getting a job where he uses his head, not his back."

1. ______________________
2. ______________________
3. ______________________
4. ______________________
5. ______________________

[1]Although he works hard in school and out of it, Mark is in most ways a typical teenager. [2]on this sunday, when he was in the kitchen with his mom, the photographer told him to act natural. [3]In response, he put out his hand and asked, "can i have some money?" [4]Do you think he wants some new nike sneakers?

6. ______________________
7. ______________________
8. ______________________
9. ______________________
10. ______________________

Capital Letters: PRACTICE 2

Underline the **two** words that need capitalizing in each sentence. Then write these words correctly in the spaces provided.

1. I do love to eat candy bars late at night, especially snickers and mounds.

   ____________________ ____________________

2. I love chicago and plan to visit there in march.

   ____________________ ____________________

3. my friend is always asking me to visit and says, "come anytime!"

   ____________________ ____________________

4. I am glad that thanksgiving always falls on a thursday.

   ____________________ ____________________

5. Barack Obama was born in hawaii and lived in indonesia when he was a young boy.

   ____________________ ____________________

6. On easter, I love to eat campbell's tomato soup for breakfast.

   ____________________ ____________________

7. My computer is a macintosh, but my parents have a gateway.

   ____________________ ____________________

8. I hope to be home in california for my april birthday.

   ____________________ ____________________

9. I used to live on studebaker road before I moved.

   ____________________ ____________________

10. I cannot find my *oprah* magazine that had an ad for a television show on the discovery channel.

    ____________________ ____________________

Capital Letters: PRACTICE 3

Each of the short passages that follow contains **five** errors in capitalization. Underline the words that need capitalizing. Then write these words correctly in the spaces provided.

[1]It's rare to find Mark without a book. [2]He began reading a lot as a way to pass the time during his long trip to school. [3]The first books he remembers really liking were a series of novels by W. E. B. Griffin. [4]The novels, which take place within the philadelphia police department, include such titles as *men at war* and *Honor Bound.* [5]After Mark worked his way through that series, his english teacher recommended some historical fiction. [6]Mark also likes biographies, and he is pictured here reading a biography of John Wanamaker, the founder of a famous department store. [7]It's nice to spend a lazy sunday afternoon just lying on the couch with a good book.

1. ______________________
2. ______________________
3. ______________________
4. ______________________
5. ______________________

[1]One of the reasons Mark wants to do well in school is that he knows his younger brother Kenny is watching him. [2]Kenny notices Mark's efforts, and he tells a visitor, "don't be a fool. stay in school." [3]He adds, "Mark and I are alike in some ways. [4]We both play the trumpet." [5]He asks Mark, "Would you rather go to Dartmouth College or temple university here in Philadelphia?" [6]Kenny is only in fifth grade, but he's learned that people have to plan ahead to get the things that they want. [7]But on this beautiful march day, all he really wants is to go skating with his friends.

6. ______________________
7. ______________________
8. ______________________
9. ______________________
10. ______________________

Name ______________________ Section ____________ Date ____________

Score: (Number right) ______ x 10 = ________ %

Capital Letters: TEST 1

Underline the **two** words that need to be capitalized in each sentence. Then write the words correctly in the spaces provided.

NOTE To help you master capitalization, explanations are given for the first four sentences.

1. Last summer, my mother and i visited my aunt in New orleans.
   Capitalize the word *I* and the names of specific places.

   ______________ ______________

2. The car salesman said, "here's a used buick you folks might be interested in."
   Capitalize the first word of a direct quotation and the brand name of a car.

   ______________ ______________

3. Every wednesday after school, Cara goes to chinese-language school.
   Capitalize the days of the week and the names of foreign languages.

   ______________ ______________

4. The november issue of *time* magazine had an article you could use for your report.
   Capitalize the months of the year and the titles of magazines, but not the word *magazine.*

   ______________ ______________

5. My grandfather's real name is henrik, but when he left norway, he started calling himself Hank.

   ______________ ______________

6. When i was a little girl, I thought that cheerios grew on a cereal bush.

   ______________ ______________

7. Being located right on Lake michigan makes chicago a very windy city.

   ______________ ______________

8. Every other july, the members of the baker family get together for a big reunion.

   ______________ ______________

9. To celebrate my birthday next thursday, my family is taking me out to my favorite vietnamese restaurant.

   ______________ ______________

10. At least once a year, my cousin james and I make popcorn, sit down, and watch the movie *The Wizard of oz.*

    ______________ ______________

Name ______________________ Section ____________ Date ____________

Score: (Number right) ______ x 10 = ____________ %

Capital Letters: TEST 2

Underline the **two** words that need to be capitalized in each sentence. Then write the words correctly in the spaces provided.

1. Knott's Berry farm in Garden grove, California, is a really fun place to go.

   ____________________ ____________________

2. My friend likes mcDonald's hamburgers; I prefer Burger king's chicken.

   ____________________ ____________________

3. I am very health conscious, so the article "fit, not fat" caught my eye.

   ____________________ ____________________

4. My uncle went to crufts, a famous dog show in england.

   ____________________ ____________________

5. I used to buy running shoes on brond Street, but now I shop on Halax road.

   ____________________ ____________________

6. My favorite month is march because I always order girl scout cookies from my local troop.

   ____________________ ____________________

7. Once every four years, my friend marta has her birthday on february 29.

   ____________________ ____________________

8. In california, you can buy hadley's dates.

   ____________________ ____________________

9. do you know anyone who speaks estonian?

   ____________________ ____________________

10. In french class, we will read *The Little prince* in its original language.

    ____________________ ____________________

Name ____________________ Section ____________ Date ____________

Score: (Number right) ______ x 20 = ________ %

Capital Letters: TEST 3

Underline the **two** words that need to be capitalized in each sentence. Then write the words correctly in the spaces provided.

1. Last may, my grandmother visited colorado. She bought a beautiful shawl there and claims she has never been cold since.

   ____________________ ____________________

2. Because Randall has an evening class on thursdays, he often stays on campus for dinner. He usually carries some ritz peanut-butter crackers to eat before class.

   ____________________ ____________________

3. A sleek black sports car with tinted windows came to a sudden stop on spruce street. A woman and her large sheepdog then came out of a pet store and hopped into the back seat.

   ____________________ ____________________

4. The best christmas gift I ever got was a wii game set. The best part is my whole family can play it with me.

   ____________________ ____________________

5. During a break in our english class, I asked Reba why she was moving out of her apartment. She replied, "my neighbors in the apartment above me are as quiet as mice—mice in combat boots, that is."

   ____________________ ____________________

Name ______________________ Section ____________ Date ____________

Score: (Number right) ______ x 10 = ________ %

Capital Letters: TEST 4

In each group below, **one** sentence uses capital letters correctly. Write the letter of that sentence in the space provided.

_____ **1.** **a.** Before moving into the house, lynn scrubbed the floors with lysol.
b. Before moving into the house, Lynn scrubbed the floors with lysol.
c. Before moving into the house, Lynn scrubbed the floors with Lysol.

_____ **2.** **a.** Ellen's dinner was a Roast Beef Sandwich from Arby's and a Salad from Wendy's.
b. Ellen's dinner was a roast beef sandwich from Arby's and a salad from Wendy's.
c. Ellen's dinner was a roast beef Sandwich from Arby's and a Salad from Wendy's.

_____ **3.** **a.** Our hostess asked, "Have you ever visited Nashville before?"
b. Our hostess asked, "have you ever visited Nashville before?"
c. Our hostess asked, "have You ever visited Nashville before?"

_____ **4.** **a.** My little niece often watches her DVD of *Beauty and the beast.*
b. My little niece often watches her DVD of *Beauty and The Beast.*
c. My little niece often watches her DVD of *Beauty and the Beast.*

_____ **5.** **a.** Brian foolishly complained to the police officer, "But sir, i never stop at that Stop Sign."
b. Brian foolishly complained to the police officer, "But sir, I never stop at that stop sign."
c. Brian foolishly complained to the police officer, "but sir, I never stop at that stop sign."

_____ **6.** **a.** On the last Friday in May, Ross Hospital stopped admitting emergency patients.
b. On the last friday in may, Ross hospital stopped admitting emergency patients.
c. On the last Friday in May, ross hospital stopped admitting emergency patients.

_____ **7.** **a.** On Memorial day and the Fourth of july, our dog howls when she hears the fireworks.
b. On Memorial day and the fourth of July, our dog howls when she hears the fireworks.
c. On Memorial Day and the Fourth of July, our dog howls when she hears the fireworks.

_____ **8.** **a.** Grandpa heated up some Log Cabin syrup to pour over his Eggo waffles.
b. Grandpa heated up some Log Cabin Syrup to pour over his Eggo Waffles.
c. Grandpa heated up some Log cabin syrup to pour over his Eggo waffles.

_____ **9.** **a.** When I visited Mexico, I had a chance to practice my spanish.
b. When I visited Mexico, I had a chance to practice my Spanish.
c. When I visited mexico, I had a chance to practice my Spanish.

_____ **10.** **a.** On Monday, I must have a paper titled "Hate Crimes" ready for my english class.
b. On Monday, I must have a paper titled "Hate crimes" ready for my english class.
c. On Monday, I must have a paper titled "Hate Crimes" ready for my English class.

Name ______________________________ Section ______________ Date ______________

Score: (Number right) _______ x 10 = ____________ %

Capital Letters: TEST 5

In each group below, **one** sentence uses capital letters correctly. Write the letter of that sentence in the space provided.

_____ **1.** **a.** I am going to see a movie this Friday called *The King's Speech.*
b. I am going to see a movie this friday called *The King's Speech.*
c. I am going to see a movie this Friday called *The King's speech.*

_____ **2.** **a.** We ran to our visiting uncle and said, "did you bring us any presents From Borneo?"
b. We ran to our visiting uncle and said, "Did you bring us any presents from borneo?"
c. We ran to our visiting uncle and said, "Did you bring us any presents from Borneo?"

_____ **3.** **a.** The man was so perplexed, he forgot to ask, "does anyone have the key to the bathroom?"
b. The man was so perplexed, he forgot to ask, "Does anyone have the key to the bathroom?"
c. the man was so perplexed, he forgot to ask, "Does anyone have the key to the bathroom?"

_____ **4.** **a.** In october, I am going on a Caribbean vacation.
b. In October, I am going on a Caribbean vacation.
c. In October, I am going on a caribbean vacation.

_____ **5.** **a.** The article in the magazine was called "The Meaning of Life."
b. The Article in the magazine was called "The Meaning of Life."
c. The article in the magazine was called "The Meaning of life."

_____ **6.** **a.** I want to get my degree in german studies at Cornell.
b. I want to get my degree in German studies at cornell.
c. I want to get my degree in German studies at Cornell.

_____ **7.** **a.** An articulated truck crashed into a guard rail at Logan and Divine.
b. An Articulated truck crashed into a guard rail at Logan and Divine.
c. An articulated truck crashed into a guard rail at logan and divine.

_____ **8.** **a.** Before nike coined the phrase, "Just do it," my mom used to say that.
b. Before Nike coined the phrase, "just do it," my mom used to say that.
c. Before Nike coined the phrase, "Just do it," my mom used to say that.

_____ **9.** **a.** American express is a card I use every September when I throw myself a birthday party.
b. American Express is a card I use every september when I throw myself a birthday party.
c. American Express is a card I use every September when I throw myself a birthday party.

_____ **10.** **a.** Susan graduated with honors from Lincoln High School.
b. Susan graduated with honors from Lincoln high school.
c. Susan graduated with honors from lincoln High School.

15 Parallelism

Basics about Parallelism

Two or more equal ideas should be expressed in **parallel**, or matching, form. The absence of parallelism is jarring and awkward to read. Parallelism will help your words flow smoothly and clearly. Here's an example:

Not parallel The new restaurant has fresh food, reasonable prices, and service that is fast.

The first two features of the restaurant—*fresh food* and *reasonable prices*—are described in parallel form. In each case, we get a descriptive word followed by the word being described:

fresh food, reasonable prices

But with the last feature, we get the word being described first and then a descriptive word:

service that is fast

To achieve parallelism, the nonparallel item must have the same form as the first two:

Parallel The new restaurant has fresh food, reasonable prices, and **fast service.**

Here are some additional examples of problems with parallelism and explanations of how to correct them:

Not parallel The children were arguing in the lobby, talked during the movie, and complained on the ride home.

Talked and *complained* are similar in form. But *were arguing* is not. It must be changed so that it has the same form as the other two.

Parallel The children **argued** in the lobby, talked during the movie, and complained on the ride home.

Not parallel Our neighbors spend a lot of time shopping online, visiting friends, and they go to the movies.

The sentence lists a series of activities. *Shopping* and *visiting* both end in *-ing*. To be parallel, *they go to the movies* must be revised to include an *-ing* word.

Parallel Our neighbors spend a lot of time shopping online, visiting friends, and **going to the movies.**

Not parallel My aunt is selfish, impatient, and she is not a kind person.

To be parallel, *she is not a kind person* should have a form that matches *selfish* and *impatient.*

Parallel My aunt is selfish, impatient, and **unkind.**

Not parallel Every morning I have to feed the dog and bringing in the mail.

Feed the dog and *bringing in the mail* are not parallel. For parallelism, both must be in the same form.

Parallel Every morning I have to feed the dog and **bring in the mail.**

Understanding Parallelism

See if you can underline the **three** errors in parallelism in the following passage. Then look at the corrections below.

[1]This is Jasmin Santana. [2]In this picture, Jasmin is laughing, answering the telephone, and she works at the computer. [3]It is typical for Jasmin to be doing several things at once. [4]She is a full-time employee and a full-time student as well. [5]Jasmin has to be very organized, efficient, and with discipline to get everything done. [6]Sometimes she is discouraged by how busy she is. [7]But she knows she will feel pride, happiness, and relieved when she earns her college degree.

1. working at the computer.
2. disciplined
3. relief

Check Your Understanding

Underline the **three** mistakes in parallelism in the following passage. Then write the correct forms in the spaces provided.

[1]Jasmin works for an organization called Philadelphia Futures. [2]Philadelphia Futures helps motivated high-school students in many ways. [3]The organization matches them with mentors and teaches them good study skills. [4]Jasmin is the Philadelphia Futures receptionist. [5]She spends a lot of time answering the phone, the typing of letters, and greeting visitors. [6]But she also works directly with the students in the program. [7]She provides them with information, encouragement, and she is their friend. [8]In this picture, Jasmin is shown with Virgen on the left, Julio in the middle, and on the right is Kimberly.

1. ______________________
2. ______________________
3. ______________________

Parallelism: PRACTICE 1

Each of the short passages below contains errors in parallelism. Underline the errors. Then correct them in the spaces provided.

[1]When she lived at home, Jasmin loved her grandmother's cooking. [2]But now she lives on her own, and she doesn't have much time to prepare meals. [3]After work, she usually makes a sandwich, heats up some soup, or she might scramble some eggs. [4]Then she's off to campus, where she spends the evening listening to a lecture, she takes notes, and asking questions. [5]But sometimes she has to take a break. [6]"I call Grandma and say, 'I am so stressed out!'" Jasmin says. [7]"And she says, 'Come over, and I'll cook for you.' [8]I go over and she feeds me, babies me, and is talking Spanish to me. [9]That always makes me feel better."

1. ______________________________
2. ______________________________
3. ______________________________

[1]Jasmin moved into her own apartment when she was just 17. [2]She could have lived at home and saved money, time, and making a lot of effort. [3]But back in her neighborhood, she was too distracted by friends who didn't understand why college was so important to her. [4]They wanted her to hang out, party, and having fun. [5]Jasmin likes to have fun, too, but doing well in school is more important to her. [6]Sometimes living alone is boring, depressing, and it makes her feel lonely. [7]Other times she loves feeling independent, grown-up, and having a sense of responsibility. [8]Even when she feels lonely, she is sure her decision will pay off in the end.

4. ______________________________
5. ______________________________
6. ______________________________
7. ______________________________

[1]When she gets home after a long night of classes, Jasmin reviews her notes, reads her next day's assignments, and is studying for any upcoming tests. [2]She often falls asleep over her textbooks. [3]It's hard to find time to clean her apartment, shop for groceries, and the doing of laundry. [4]She sometimes envies other students who work only part time or don't have to work at all. [5]She sees them attending class during the day and go out with their friends when they want to. [6]"I'd like to have more time for a social life," she admits, "but that's not my top priority right now."

8. ______________________________

9. ______________________________

10. ______________________________

Parallelism: PRACTICE 2

The part of each sentence that needs revising is *italicized.* On the line, rewrite this part to make it match the other item(s) listed.

1. Simone thinks she will either go to the movies or *she is thinking about staying home.*

   ____

2. Chang bought a brown jacket, a red tie, and *a shirt that was white.*

   ____

3. Russell always wanted to visit a remote area with clean streams, *places for camping,* and wilderness areas.

   ____

4. The outdoor barbeque would have been perfect if it weren't for burned hamburgers and *guests who were drunk.*

   ____

5. In my dreams, I am often a beautiful, graceful ballerina; *a scientist who is brilliant and famous*; or a talented rock musician.

   ____

6. Jogging and *taking a walk* are both great for aerobic exercise.

   ____

7. The post office has a lot of trouble with inadequate postage, *stamps not sticking,* and oversized envelopes.

   ____

8. I not only have a runny nose but also *a throat that is sore.*

   ____

9. Greek fraternities, uninterested instructors, and *students that are rowdy* are the things I hate about university life.

   ____

10. I'd rather eat nails than *having to endure a root canal.*

    ____

Parallelism: PRACTICE 3

The passage below contains **five** errors in parallelism. Underline the errors. Then correct them in the spaces provided.

[1]In spite of her difficult schedule, Jasmin is smiling, focused, and she stays positive. [2]She keeps her goals in mind. [3]Those goals are to do well in college and getting admitted to law school. [4]She wants to earn her law degree, become a judge, and working to help the Latino community. [5]"I see so many people around me get in trouble, go to jail, and giving up on themselves," she says. [6]"As a judge, I'll be in a position to see that people get the help they need."

[7]Jasmin is grateful for the support of her family as she works to achieve her dreams. [8]"My mom and my aunts are my best friends. [9]And Grandma is terrific. [10]She'd like to see me settling down, get married, and having kids, but if going to school is what makes me happy, she respects that, too."

1. ______________________________
2. ______________________________
3. ______________________________
4. ______________________________
5. ______________________________

Name ______________________ Section __________ Date __________

Score: (Number right) ________ x 10 = ________ %

Parallelism: TEST 1

The part of each sentence that needs revising is *italicized.* On the line, rewrite this part to make it match the other item(s) listed.

NOTE To help you master parallelism, explanations are given for the first three sentences.

1. Laughing children, creaking swings, and *dogs that bark* are all part of going to the park.
   Dogs that bark must be changed to the same form as *laughing children.*

   ____

2. Lizette has an overdrawn checkbook and *a savings account that is low.*
   A savings account that is low must be changed to the same form as *overdrawn checkbook.*

   ____

3. When you're on vacation, shopping in local markets and *staying in hotels that are economical* can save you a lot of money.
   Staying in hotels that are economical must be changed to the same form as *shopping in local markets.*

   ____

4. Last night, I enjoyed a movie, *was making dinner,* and phoned my parents.

   ____

5. My landlord is upset by late rent and *checks that bounce.*

   ____

6. The U.S. army wants soldiers who will be patriotic, stay in shape, and *be willing to travel the world.*

   ____

7. In this ethical dilemma, I want to do the right thing, *staying out of jail,* and to keep my best friend.

   ____

8. The doctor diagnosed the patient with high blood pressure, collapsed lungs, and *a heartbeat that is rapid.*

   ____

9. If you want to establish a relationship, *learning about the other person* and to live happily ever after are the steps to pure bliss.

   ____

10. That movie was intense, *full of violence,* and funny.

    ____

Name ______________________ Section ____________ Date ____________

Score: (Number right) ______ x 10 = ________ %

Parallelism: TEST 2

The part of each sentence that needs revising is *italicized.* On the line, rewrite this part to make it match the other item(s) listed.

1. In emergencies, Charles feels either totally helpless or *as if he is in charge,* nothing in between.

   ____

2. Sadie is fond of rare steaks, *vegetables that are crisp,* and fattening desserts.

   ____

3. I know I can pass my exams by studying with my wife, reviewing with my tutor, and *with my entire being, praying.*

   ____

4. Some of my quirky relatives include an amateur opera singer, *an undertaker that is twenty years old,* and a used-boat salesman.

   ____

5. She begged us to book the camping trip or *the vacation should be canceled.*

   ____

6. Prior to departure, the airplane staff requested that we buckle our seat belts tightly, *that our seats be upright,* and store our baggage appropriately.

   ____

7. Broken promises, *lies that were hurtful,* and repeated infidelity all caused Louise heartbreak.

   ____

8. Unfortunately, my grandmother's wardrobe consisted of tight trousers, *blouses that were low cut,* and flashy jewelry.

   ____

9. The soccer forward passed the ball to the right, blocked another player beside him, and *was regaining the ball* in time to score.

   ____

10. The nurse wore baggy jeans, scuffed shoes, and *a shirt that was stained.*

    ____

Name ______________________ Section ______________ Date ______________

Score: (Number right) ________ x 10 = ______________ %

Parallelism: TEST 3

There are **ten** problems with parallelism in the following selection. Cross out each error in parallelism, and write the correction above the line.

[1]The novel *Les Miserables* was written in the 1800s by French author Victor Hugo. [2]It tells the story of Jean Valjean. [3]Poor and being full of hunger, Valjean stole a loaf of bread one day. [4]He was arrested and receiving a sentence of five years as a slave in a galley ship. [5]His attempts to escape added years to his sentence. [6]In the end, Valjean served nineteen years for stealing the bread. [7]He left prison bitter, vengeful, and full of anger. [8]But a surprising event changed Valjean's mind and was softening his heart.

[9]Valjean could find nothing to eat and no place for sleeping because everyone was afraid of him. [10]Finally, he stormed angrily into the house of a bishop. [11]He demanded a scrap of food and was asking for permission to sleep in the stable. [12]To Valjean's surprise, the bishop welcomed him kindly and in a warm fashion. [13]He ate dinner with Valjean and then led him to a comfortable bedroom.

[14]During the night, Valjean sneaked out of bed and was stealing the knives and forks from the dining room. [15]In the morning, soldiers brought him and the silverware to the bishop's door. [16]The bishop greeted him as a friend and was responding, "I am glad you took the silverware I gave you." [17]Convinced that Valjean was innocent, the soldiers went away. [18]Valjean spent the rest of his life helping people, sharing with them, and he showed them the kindness the bishop had shown him.

Name ______________________ Section ____________ Date ____________

Score: (Number right) ______ x 10 = ______ %

Parallelism: TEST 4

In each group below, **one** sentence uses parallelism correctly. Write the letter of that sentence in the space provided.

_____ **1.** **a.** Mowing the lawn and to weed the garden are two chores I must complete on Saturday.
b. To mow the lawn and weeding the garden are two chores I must complete on Saturday.
c. Mowing the lawn and weeding the garden are two chores I must complete on Saturday.

_____ **2.** **a.** The old dog and the young kitten were the best of friends.
b. The dog that was old and the young kitten were the best of friends.
c. The old dog and the kitten that was young were the best of friends.

_____ **3.** **a.** After my ten-mile hike in the desert, I was thirsty, hungry, and I was so tired.
b. After my ten-mile hike in the desert, I was thirsty, felt hungry, and was tired.
c. After my ten-mile hike in the desert, I was thirsty, hungry, and tired.

_____ **4.** **a.** I remember my dance instructor asking me to stand up straight, concentrate deeply, and to listen carefully.
b. I remember my dance instructor asking me to stand up straight, concentrate deeply, and listen carefully.
c. I remember my dance instructor asking me to stand up straight, make sure I concentrated deeply, and to listen carefully.

_____ **5.** **a.** All around us after the earthquake were fallen trees, overturned cars, and traffic lights that were broken.
b. All around us after the earthquake were trees that were fallen, cars that were overturned, and broken traffic lights.
c. All around us after the earthquake were fallen trees, overturned cars, and broken traffic lights.

_____ **6.** **a.** After a persistent phone solicitor calls, I mutter curse words, stamp my feet, and practice deep breathing.
b. After a persistent phone solicitor calls, I mutter curse words, stamping my feet occurs, and practice deep breathing.
c. After a persistent phone solicitor calls, I mutter curse words, stamp my feet, and deep breathing is practiced.

_____ **7.** **a.** Singing in the shower, laughing at my own jokes, and dancing to pop tunes are three activities done best alone.
b. Singing in the shower, to laugh at my own jokes, and dancing to pop tunes are three activities done best alone.
c. Singing in the shower, laughing at my own jokes, and to dance to pop tunes are three activities done best alone.

Name ______________________________ Section ______________ Date ______________

Score: (Number right) ________ x 10 = ______________ %

_____ **8.** **a.** Eyes like limpid pools and lips like ripe cherries are what make my girlfriend so exquisite.

b. Eyes that look like limpid pools and lips looking like ripe cherries are what make my girlfriend so exquisite.

c. Eyes that look like limpid pools and lips like ripe cherries are what make my girlfriend so exquisite.

_____ **9.** **a.** The route to your heart's desire is either to work fourteen hours per day or to look into your beloved's face.

b. The route to your heart's desire is either to work fourteen hours per day or looking into your beloved's face.

c. The route to your heart's desire is either working fourteen hours per day or to look into your beloved's face.

_____ **10.** **a.** Cats make wonderful pets because they are independent, dainty, and they clean themselves.

b. Cats make wonderful pets because they are independent, dainty, and clean.

c. Cats make wonderful pets because they are independent, usually very dainty, and clean.

Name ______________________ Section ____________ Date ____________

Score: (Number right) ______ x 10 = ________ %

Parallelism: TEST 5

In each group below, one sentence uses parallelism correctly. Write the letter of that sentence in the space provided.

_____ **1.** **a.** Peeling paint and windows that were broken made the old house look sad.
b. Peeling paint and the breaking of windows made the old house look sad.
c. Peeling paint and broken windows made the old house look sad.

_____ **2.** **a.** The loud voices, air that has smoke in it, and stale smells in the room all made me want to leave quickly.
b. The loud voices, smoky air, and stale smells in the room all made me want to leave quickly.
c. Voices that were loud, smoky air, and stale smells in the room all made me want to leave quickly.

_____ **3.** **a.** Joe sucked in his stomach, stopped breathing, and was trying to pull the zipper up.
b. Joe sucked in his stomach, was not breathing, and tried to pull the zipper up.
c. Joe sucked in his stomach, stopped breathing, and tried to pull the zipper up.

_____ **4.** **a.** The book, with its tattered pages and cover that was missing, had been read many times.
b. The book, with its tattered pages and that had a cover missing, had been read many times.
c. The book, with its tattered pages and missing cover, had been read many times.

_____ **5.** **a.** Students from lower-income families often have to hold jobs, go to school, and take care of children all at the same time.
b. Students from lower-income families often have to hold jobs, go to school, and caring for children all at the same time.
c. Students from lower-income families often have to hold jobs, going to school, and take care of children all at the same time.

_____ **6.** **a.** The movie featured terrible acting, excessive violence, and plot twists that were ridiculous.
b. The movie featured terrible acting, excessive violence, and ridiculous plot twists.
c. The movie featured terrible acting, violence to excess, and ridiculous plot twists.

_____ **7.** **a.** Attending class regularly and taking notes carefully are real keys to success in school.
b. Attending class regularly and to take notes carefully are real keys to success in school.
c. To attend class regularly and taking notes carefully are real keys to success in school.

Name ______________________ Section ____________ Date ____________

Score: (Number right) ______ x 10 = ________ %

_____ 8. a. The babysitter's nails, long and red, heavy eye makeup, and jangling jewelry all frightened the twins.
b. The babysitter's long red nails, heavy eye makeup, and jangling jewelry all frightened the twins.
c. The babysitter's long red nails, eye makeup that was heavy, and jangling jewelry all frightened the twins.

_____ 9. a. The driving rain turned the park into a swamp and the highway was a river.
b. The driving rain turned the park into a swamp and the highway into a river.
c. The driving rain turned the park into a swamp and made a river of the highway.

_____ 10. a. I know not how others may feel, but as for me, give me liberty or give me death.
b. I know not how others may feel, but as for me, give me liberty or else I would prefer to die.
c. I know not how others may feel, but as for me, liberty or give me death.

PART TWO Extending the Skills

PART TWO
Extending the Skills

PREVIEW

Part Two presents some topics not included in Part One:

It also includes additional information about many of the topics presented in Part One:

16 Preparing a Paper

Basics about Preparing a Paper

Here are important guidelines for preparing a paper.

THE TITLE

Most of your school papers will begin with a title. The title of a paper prepared on a computer should be about an inch and a half from the top of the page. The title of a handwritten paper should be on the top line of the first page. For example, here are the title and the opening part of a paper about the author's brother.

	A Shy Brother
	My older brother is the shyest person I know. Whenever there
	are more than two people in a group, he will stop talking. He has
	never raised his hand to answer a question in class...

Use the above correctly written example to identify each of the following statements as either true (**T**) or false (**F**).

_____ **1.** The title should be set off in quotation marks.

_____ **2.** The title should have a period after it.

_____ **3.** The title should be capitalized.

_____ **4.** The title should be centered on the page.

_____ **5.** A line should be skipped between the title and the first sentence.

You should have answered "False" for the first two items and "True" for the last three. Here is a checklist for how to handle a title:

- Type the title about an inch and a half below the top of the first page. For handwritten papers, put the title on the top line of the first page.
- Center the title.
- Do not use quotation marks around the title or put a period after the title.
- Capitalize each word in the title. (The only exceptions are small words such as *a, the, and, of, in,* and *for* in the middle of a title.)
- Skip a line between the title and the first sentence of the paper.

INDENTING THE FIRST LINE

The first line of a paragraph should be **indented**—that is, set in—about one-half inch from the left-hand margin. (Note the indentation of the first line of the paper about the shy brother.) Do not indent the other sentences in a paragraph.

MARGINS

Leave enough margin on all four sides of a paper to avoid a crowded look. The standard margins on a typed paper are about an inch and a half on the top and sides of the paper and an inch on the right and at the bottom.

OTHER GUIDELINES

1 Use full-sized paper ($8\frac{1}{2}$ by 11 inches).

2 Write or type on only one side of the paper.

3 Ideally, type your paper using double-spacing. If you are writing by hand, do the following:
   - Use blue or black ink—never pencil.
   - Use wide-lined paper, or write on every other line of narrow-lined paper.
   - Write letters and punctuation marks as clearly as you can, taking care to distinguish between small and capital letters.

4 If your teacher so requests, include a cover page on which you put your name, the date, the title, and the section number of your course.

Practice

What **five** corrections are needed in the student paper shown below? Explain the corrections needed in the five numbered spaces below.

	Family meetings
	My family has found various ways to get along well. One way is having
	family meetings. We meet twice a month to discuss and handle our
	problems before they get out of hand. This has saved the members of
	my family a great deal of aggravation. For instance, when my brother . . .

1. ______________________________

2. ______________________________

3. ______________________________

4. ______________________________

5. ______________________________

17 Punctuation Marks

Eight Types of Punctuation Marks

This chapter first describes three marks of punctuation that are used to end a sentence: the period (.), the question mark (?), and the exclamation point (!). The chapter then describes five additional marks of punctuation: the colon (:), semicolon (;), hyphen (-), dash (—), and parentheses ( ).

THE PERIOD (.)

Use a **period** at the end of a statement, a mild command, or an indirect question.

- The children jumped over all the rain puddles.
  (A statement)
- Hand me the red pen.
  (A mild command)
- I wonder if there will be a surprise quiz today.
  (An indirect question)

THE QUESTION MARK (?)

Use a **question mark** after a sentence that asks a question.

- Are you ready for the test?
- How did the car get scratched?
- "Can I have your phone number?" Susanne asked Phil.

Indirect questions tell the reader about questions, rather than asking them directly. They end with periods, not question marks.

- The teacher asked if we were ready for the test.
- I wonder how the car got scratched.
- Susanne asked Phil if she could have his phone number.

THE EXCLAMATION POINT (!)

Use an **exclamation point** after a word or statement that expresses extreme emotion or that gives a strong command.

- Help!
- Wow!
- I just got a huge raise!
- Cut that out!

Note Exclamation points lose their power if they are used too frequently. Use them only when you wish to emphasize strong emotion.

Practice 1

Place a period, question mark, or exclamation point at the end of each of the following sentences.

Example Will we see each other again?

1. Marisol and Andrea are the best of friends
2. Where in the world is my umbrella
3. Look out for that falling beam
4. I wish I could see my best friend, who lives five hundred miles away
5. Mr. Shaw is a very sneaky private detective my brother knows
6. Why did you park your car so close to mine
7. When will we ever see each other again
8. Stop that fighting, or I will call the police
9. I do not understand why there are so many hungry people in a world with so many natural resources
10. Will you come with me to the prom on May 14

THE COLON (:)

The **colon** directs attention to what follows. It has three main uses:

1 Use a colon to introduce a list.

- On her first day of vacation, Carrie did three things: she watched a funny movie, took a long nap, and ate at her favorite restaurant.

2 Use a colon to introduce a long or formal quotation.

- The autobiography of Arthur Ashe begins with the following biblical quotation: "Since we are surrounded by so great a cloud of witnesses, let us lay aside every weight, and the sin which so easily ensnares us, and let us run with endurance the race that is set before us."

3 Use a colon to introduce an explanation.

- Bert suddenly canceled his evening plans for a simple reason: his car was out of gas.

The use of a colon in the opening of a letter is explained on page 287.

Practice 2

Add **one** colon to each sentence.

1. I have only one reason to continue my marriage the children.
2. He went to the store for butter and came back with six other items bread, apples, toothpaste, gum, cigarettes, and soda.
3. Francine felt a rush of emotion when the door opened James was home from his trip.
4. The teacher's heavy bag contained only the essentials books, exams, and handouts.
5. St. Thomas Aquinas stated this "An unjust law is a human law that is not rooted in eternal law and natural law."

THE SEMICOLON (;)

A **semicolon** indicates that the reader should pause. It has three main uses:

1 Use a semicolon to join two complete thoughts that are closely related, but are not connected by a joining word (such as *and*, *but*, or *so*).

- Our cat knocked over a can of Coca-Cola**;** the soda foamed over the white carpet.

2 Use a semicolon to join two closely related complete thoughts with a transitional word or word group (such as *afterwards*, *however*, *instead*, *therefore*, and *on the other hand*). Follow the transitional word or word group with a comma.

- LeQuita began school without knowing any English**;** nevertheless, she will graduate at the top of her class.

The use of a semicolon to join two complete thoughts is explained in "More about Run-Ons and Comma Splices" on pages 281–284.

3 Use semicolons to separate items in a series when the items themselves contain commas.

- Driving down Sunset Strip, we passed La Boutique, which sells women's clothing**;** The Friendly Cafe, which serves twenty different kinds of coffee**;** and Pet Palace, which sells snakes, parrots, and spiders.

Practice 3

Add one or more semicolons to each sentence.

1. Some of the relatives who showed up for the family reunion were Aunt Julie, from Rhode Island Grandma Betty, from Arizona and Cousin Louis, from Alaska.
2. I love most domesticated animals however, I do not like snakes.
3. Disneyland was filled to capacity with happy guests for the first time, the park had to turn people away.
4. I ate far too much for Sunday dinner however, I did find room for pie.
5. The fly ball seemed to hover over the crowd one young fan finally caught it.

THE HYPHEN (-)

Hyphens are used within a word or between two words. Following are three main uses of hyphens:

1 Use a hyphen to divide a word at the end of a line of writing.

- The lawyer stood up, put on her jacket, shoved a bundle of papers into her brief-case, and hurried to court.

Note Here are rules for dividing a word at the end of a line:

a Never divide a word that has only one syllable.
b Divide words only between syllables.
c Never divide a word in a way that leaves only one or two letters alone on a line.
d When dividing a word that already contains a hyphen, divide where the hyphen is.

2 Use a hyphen to join two or more words that act together to describe a noun that follows them.

- The sports car swerved around the slow-moving truck.

3 Put a hyphen in any number from twenty-one to ninety-nine and in a fraction that is written out, such as one-fourth or two-thirds.

Note Words made up of two or more words are sometimes hyphenated (for example, *baby-sit* and *fine-tune*). There is no clear rule to cover such cases, so when you're unsure about whether or not to hyphenate such words, check your dictionary.

Practice 4

Add a hyphen to each sentence.

1. Polls show that two thirds of the voters would support higher taxes.
2. You've handed in a very well written story.
3. That angry looking boss actually has a sweet personality.
4. Although Trudy turned thirty last month, she tells everyone she's twenty eight.
5. José was telling me about a beautiful green eyed girl he saw on the subway.

THE DASH (—)

While the hyphen is used within or between individual words, the **dash** is used between parts of a sentence. Following are three common uses of the dash:

1 Dashes may be used to set off and emphasize interrupting material. Use them when you wish to give special attention to words that interrupt the flow of the sentence.

- Everyone in that family—including the teenagers—has a weight problem.

2 Use a dash to signal the end of a list of items.

- Family support, prayer, and hope—these are what got Grady through all those months in recovery.

3 A dash may be used to introduce a final element—a list of items, an explanation, or a dramatic point.

- Anne's refrigerator was packed with food for the party—trays of cold cuts, bottles of pickles, loaves of bread, and several pitchers of lemonade.
- Ravi hurriedly left work in the middle of the day—his wife was having labor pains.
- My wallet was found in a trash can—minus its cash.

Note As mentioned above, the colon can also be used to introduce a list or an explanation. A colon tends to add more formality and less drama to a sentence than a dash.

When typing, form a dash with two hyphens, leaving no space between them; do not leave spaces before or after the dash.

● Practice 5

Add **one** or **two** dashes, as needed, to each sentence.

1. A gorgeous partner, lots of money, and a great job that's all I ask of life!
2. Three babies screaming their heads off interrupted the PTA meeting.
3. My cousin Billy's behavior scared all of us tearing up his will, leaving his wife, and hopping a freight train out of town.
4. Something happened that surprised even the weather station a tornado.
5. The man on the street corner naked except for sneakers was singing a very cheerful song.

PARENTHESES ( )

Here are two common uses of **parentheses:**

1 Use parentheses to set off material that interrupts the flow of a sentence. While dashes are used to emphasize interrupting material, parentheses are generally used for material you do not wish to emphasize.

- Aunt Fern (who arrived two hours late) brought the biggest gift.

2 Place parentheses around numbers that introduce items in a list within a sentence.

- Ron's work for the evening is as follows: (1) finish a history paper, (2) read a chapter in the science text, and (3) wash a load of laundry.

● Practice 6

Add **one** set of parentheses to each sentence.

1. The tree by our front door a sycamore is home to a family of robins.
2. My mother whose maiden name is Wojcik was born in a small town in Poland.
3. The Twice Around Resale Shop it's at Fifth and Maple has wonderful clothing bargains.
4. To perform this magic trick, you need (1) a styrofoam cup, 2 a rubber band, and (3) two feet of thread.
5. Harvey Whitman and Erica Whitman they're not related will conduct a seminar on leadership for company managers.

Name ______________________________ Section ______________ Date ______________

Score: (Number right) ________ x 10 = ______________ %

Punctuation Marks: TEST 1

Place a period (.), question mark (?), or exclamation point (!) at the end of each of the following sentences.

1. I can't believe she agreed to marry me
2. There is a small post office just around the corner from here
3. Where have you been for the last three hours
4. If you don't stop driving so fast, I'm going to jump out of the car
5. Did you brush your teeth after lunch
6. I think I lost my wallet
7. I've lost my other shoe and cannot seem to find it
8. I've been wondering if I'll ever graduate from college
9. Are you going to be able to run the marathon this month
10. You can either ride with your uncle, or you can walk with me

Name ______________________ Section ____________ Date ____________

Score: (Number right) ________ x 10 = ____________ %

Punctuation Marks: TEST 2

Each of the following sentences needs one of the kinds of punctuation marks in the box. In the space provided, write the letter of the mark needed. Then add that mark to the sentence.

a Colon :	**d** Dash or dashes —
b Semicolon ;	**e** Parentheses ( )
c Hyphen -	

_____ **1.** Horrible acting, laughable dialogue, and a ridiculous plot if you like these things, you'll love this movie.

_____ **2.** The soup simmered all morning its delicious aroma filled the house.

_____ **3.** The story of Ferdinand is about a fierce looking bull who loves flowers.

_____ **4.** Groucho Marx had this to say about people, dogs, and reading "Outside of a dog, a book is a man's best friend. Inside a dog it's too dark to read."

_____ **5.** The beach was clean and inviting the water was cool and blue.

_____ **6.** There will be auditions tomorrow for three parts in the play the father, the mother, and the twelve-year-old daughter.

_____ **7.** My usually soft spoken brother began to shout angrily.

_____ **8.** Before I waded into the pond, I noticed someone else was already there a baby alligator.

_____ **9.** My grandfather actually, he's my great-grandfather will be visiting us over the holidays.

_____ **10.** Eleanor Roosevelt wrote this about courage "You gain strength, courage and confidence by every experience in which you really stop to look fear in the face. You are able to say to yourself, 'I lived through this horror. I can take the next thing that comes along.' "

18 Pronoun Forms

Basics about Pronouns

A **pronoun** is a word that can be used in place of a noun.

- Mel scrubbed the potatoes. Then **he** peeled some carrots.
  In the second sentence above, the word *he* is a pronoun that is used in place of the noun *Mel.*

For more information on pronouns, see "Parts of Speech," pages 28–30.

This chapter explains how to choose the correct pronoun to use in a sentence. It covers the following four areas:

1 Personal pronouns as subjects, objects, and possessives
2 Pronouns with *and* or *or*
3 Pronouns in comparisons
4 *Who* and *whom*

PERSONAL PRONOUNS AS SUBJECTS, OBJECTS, AND POSSESSIVES

Pronouns have different forms, or cases, depending on their use in a sentence. As explained below, they may serve as **subjects**, **objects**, or **possessives**.

Subject Pronouns

Subject pronouns act as the subjects of verbs. Here are the subject forms of personal pronouns:

	First Person	Second Person	Third Person
Singular	I	you	he, she, it
Plural	we	you	they

- **I** have an itch.
  I is the subject of the verb *have.*
- **She** always remembers her nieces' birthdays.
  She is the subject of the verb *remembers.*
- **They** agreed to the deal and shook hands.
  They is the subject of the verbs *agreed* and *shook.*

Object Pronouns

Object pronouns act as the objects of verbs or of prepositions. Here is a list of the object forms of personal pronouns:

	First Person	Second Person	Third Person
Singular	me	you	him, her, it
Plural	us	you	them

When a pronoun receives the action of a verb, an object pronoun should be used.

- Clara pinched **him.**
  Him receives the action of the verb *pinched. Him* tells who was pinched.
- Jeff is addicted to Coca-Cola. He drinks **it** for breakfast.
  It receives the action of the verb *drinks. It* tells what Jeff drinks for breakfast.

When a pronoun is the object of a preposition, an object pronoun should be used. Prepositions are words such as *to, for, with,* and *from.* (A longer list of prepositions is on page 32.)

- My sister tossed the car keys to **me**.
  Me is the object of the preposition *to.*
- Because it was her husband's birthday, Flo knitted a tie for **him**.
  Him is the object of the preposition *for.*

When the preposition *to* or *for* is understood, an object pronoun must still be used.

- My sister tossed **me** the car keys.
  The preposition *to* is implied before the pronoun *me.*
- Flo knitted **him** a tie.
  The preposition *for* is implied before the pronoun *him.*

Possessive Pronouns

Possessive pronouns show that something is owned, or possessed. Here are possessive forms of personal pronouns:

	First Person	Second Person	Third Person
Singular	my, mine	your, yours	his, her, hers, its
Plural	our, ours	your, yours	their, theirs

- If Lucille needs a sweater, she can borrow **mine**.
  Mine means *the sweater belonging to me.*
- The house lost most of **its** roof during the tornado.
  Its roof means *the roof belonging to the house.*
- Roger and Emily saw many of **their** friends at the party.
  Their friends means *the friends belonging to Roger and Emily.*

Note Possessive pronouns never contain an apostrophe.

- During the last storm, our apple tree lost all of **its** blossoms (not "it's blossoms").

Practice 1

Each sentence contains one pronoun. Underline each pronoun. Then, in the space in the margin, identify the pronoun by writing **S** for a subject pronoun, **O** for an object pronoun, and **P** for a possessive pronoun. The first item is done for you as an example.

__O__ **1.** Mary gave an envelope to her.

_____ **2.** He was not pleased with the exam results.

_____ **3.** Harry loves to give surprise gifts to her.

_____ **4.** Consequently, they returned the Christmas gifts.

_____ **5.** Our mother deserves a really nice vacation.

_____ **6.** I need to buy stamps before the next bills come out.

_____ **7.** Susie was really happy to meet your friend Julie.

_____ **8.** Matt was quite moved by Uncle Rudy's gift to us.

_____ **9.** Iris gave my car a push and the engine turned over.

_____ **10.** Ralph drew me a picture that was very realistic.

Practice 2

Fill in each blank with the appropriate pronoun in the margin. Before making your choice, decide if you need a subject, an object, or a possessive pronoun.

her, she	**1.** Over the summer, Melba changed _______ hair color, job, and boyfriend.
Me, I	**2.** _______ will treat you to lunch today.
our, us	**3.** Over the last ten years, twenty-three foster children have lived with _______.
your, you	**4.** You should iron _______ shirt before going to the job interview.
we, us	**5.** Will you join _______ at the movies Friday night?
They, Them	**6.** _______ cannot find an apartment they like in this neighorhood.
I, me	**7.** Richard must give _______ a ride to school tomorrow.
him, his	**8.** When he died at the age of ninety-six, Grandpa still had all of _______ teeth.
he, him	**9.** Jill spotted her son on the playground and brought _______ a sandwich.
We, Us	**10.** _______ held a family meeting to decide how to split up household chores.

PRONOUNS WITH *AND* AND *OR*

Deciding which pronoun to use may become confusing when there are two subjects or two objects joined by *and* or *or*. However, the rules remain the same: Use a subject pronoun for the subject of a verb; use an object pronoun for the object of a verb or preposition.

- My brother and **I** loved the *Harry Potter* books.
  I is a subject of the verb *loved. Brother* is also a subject of *loved.*
- Our parents often read to my brother and **me.**
  Me is an object of the preposition *to. Brother* is also an object of *to.*

You can figure out which pronoun to use by mentally leaving out the other word that goes with *and* or *or*. For instance, in the first example above, omitting the words *my brother and* makes it clear that *I* is the correct pronoun to use: . . . **I** loved the *Harry Potter* books. (You would never say "**Me** loved the *Harry Potter* books.")

Try mentally omitting words in the following sentences. Then fill in each blank with the correct pronoun in parentheses.

- The prom was so long ago, I can't remember all of the details. Either Gene or *(I, me)* __________ drove. Furthermore, I can't remember whether Katie Davis went with him or *(I, me)* __________.

  The correct choice for the first blank becomes clear when the words "Either Gene or" are omitted: *I drove. I* is a subject of the verb *drove.*

  The correct choice for the second blank becomes clear when the words "him or" are omitted: *I can't remember whether Katie Davis went with . . . me. Me* is an object of the preposition *with.*

Practice 3

In each sentence, a choice of a subject or an object pronoun is given in parentheses. In the blank space, write the correct pronoun.

1. Michael was not sure if Linda was going to send gifts to (*he, him*) _______ and Frank.
2. I was convinced that my friend John hated Louise and (*I, me*) _______.
3. The new house is a wedding gift for Bob and (*she, her*) _______.
4. I wonder where all the squirrels have gone, for (*they, them*) _______ should be preparing for winter hibernation.
5. The principal reprimanded my friend and (*I, me*) _______ for ditching school.
6. Solidad and (*I, me*) _______ are planning a trip around the world.
7. After the end of the month, neither Jim nor (*he, him*) _______ will be able to take vacation time.
8. Felix and (*he, him*) _______ are both helping each other with math.
9. After a few weeks, (*we, us*) _______ and our families will be going to the state fair.
10. The large grizzly bear chased the guide and (*we, us*) _______ up a tree.

PRONOUNS IN COMPARISONS

When pronouns are used in comparisons, they often follow the word *than* or *as*.

- My best friend, Matt, is a better athlete than **I**.
- Rhonda's behavior puzzled you as much as **me**.

Words are often omitted in comparisons to avoid repetition. To see whether you should use a subject or an object pronoun, mentally fill in the missing words. In the first sentence above, *I* is the subject of the understood verb *am:*

- My best friend, Matt, is a better athlete than **I** [am].

In the second sentence, *me* is the object of the verb *puzzled.* That verb is understood, but not stated, in the second part of the comparison:

- Rhonda's behavior puzzled you as much as [it puzzled] me.

Now try to fill in the correct pronouns in the following comparisons:

- Brad was my first crush. I never adored anyone as much as *(he, him)*_______.
- I had never met anyone as playful and kind as *(he, him)*_______.

In the first blank above, you should have written the object form of the pronoun, *him: I never adored anyone as much as [I adored] him. Him* is the object of the verb *adored,* which is missing but understood in the sentence.

In the second blank above, you should have written the subject form of the pronoun, *he: I had never met anyone as playful and kind as he [was]. He* is the subject of the understood verb *was.*

Practice 4

In each sentence, a choice of a subject or an object pronoun is given in parentheses. In the blank space, write the correct pronoun.

1. Della has been in the choir longer than *(we, us)* _______.
2. Our argument bothers you as much as *(I, me)* _______.
3. Omar told his teammates he runs faster than *(they, them)* _______.
4. My little brother is five inches taller than *(I, me)* _______.
5. The math final worries me more than *(she, her)* _______; she is hardly studying for it.
6. We don't give parties as often as *(them, they)* _______.
7. As a child, I had a pet collie; there was no relative I loved as much as *(he, him)* _______.
8. My family and our friends all caught the flu, but we weren't as sick as *(they, them)* _______.
9. Julius bats the ball farther than his sister, but she runs the bases faster than *(he, him)* _______.
10. That buzzing noise in the lamp annoys Dad more than *(we, us)* _______; he has to leave the room.

WHO AND *WHOM*

Who is a subject pronoun; *whom* is an object pronoun.

- The person **who** owns the expensive car won't let anybody else park it.
  Who owns the expensive car is a dependent word group. *Who* is the subject of the verb *owns*.
- The babysitter **whom** they trust cannot work tonight.
  Whom they trust is a dependent word group. *Whom* is the object of the verb *trust*. The subject of *trust* is *they*.

As a general rule, to know whether to use *who* or *whom*, find the first verb after *who* or *whom*. Decide whether that verb already has a subject. If it doesn't have a subject, use the subject pronoun *who*. If it does have a subject, use the object pronoun *whom*.

See if you can fill in the right pronoun in the following sentences.

- The arrested person is a man *(who, whom)* _______ my sister once dated.
- The man and woman *(who, whom)* _______ live next door argue constantly.

In the first sentence above, look at the verb *dated*. Does it have a subject? Yes, the subject is *sister*. Therefore the object pronoun *whom* is the correct choice: *The arrested person is a man whom my sister once dated. Whom* is the object of the verb *dated*.

In the second sentence above, look at the verb *live*. Does it have a subject? No. Therefore the subject pronoun *who* is the correct choice: *The man and woman who live next door argue constantly. Who* is the subject of the verb *live*.

Note In informal speech and writing, *who* is often substituted for *whom:*

- The babysitter who they trust cannot work tonight.

In formal writing, however, *whom* is generally used. In the practices and tests in this chapter, use the formal approach.

Practice 5

In each blank space, write the correct choice of pronoun.

1. I did not see the man *(who, whom)* _______ crossed the street in front of me.
2. Several people *(who, whom)* _______ passed the last test flunked this one.
3. To *(who, whom)* _______ are you speaking in that rude tone?
4. I fell in love with a man *(who, whom)* _______ was incapable of loving anyone other than himself.
5. The redhead was a person with *(who, whom)* _______ many women were in love.

WHO AND *WHOM* IN QUESTIONS

In questions, *who* is a subject pronoun, and *whom* is an object pronoun. You can often decide whether to use *who* or *whom* in a question in the same way you decide whether to use *who* or *whom* in a statement.

- **Who** should go?
  The verb after *who* is *should go,* which does not have another subject. Therefore use the subject form of the pronoun, *who.*
- **Whom** should I send?
  I is the subject of the verb *should send,* so use the object form of the pronoun, *whom.*

Practice 6

Fill in each blank with either *who* or *whom.*

1. *(Who, Whom)* _______ is ready to take the final exam?
2. *(Who, Whom)* _______ were you remembering when you called me by the wrong name?
3. "*(Who, Whom)* _______ will plant the wheat?" asked the farmer.
4. *(Who, Whom)* _______ did you think about last night?
5. *(Who, Whom)* _______ thought to call the police after the accident?

Name ______________________________ Section ______________ Date ______________

Score: (Number right) ________ x 10 = ____________ %

Pronoun Forms: TEST 1

Fill in each blank with the appropriate pronoun from the margin.

She, Her	**1.** __________ got the highest grade on the mid-term test.
they, their	**2.** The twins had braces on __________ teeth for three years.
we, us	**3.** We are sure that getting married is the right thing for __________.
they, them	**4.** Since my aunt and uncle enjoy basketball more than I do, I gave the tickets to __________.
I, me	**5.** She and __________ have been friends since we were little children.
he, him	**6.** I don't know whether to believe you or __________.
she, her	**7.** Hector and his sister both speak some Spanish, but Hector is more fluent than __________.
he, him	**8.** We enjoyed no teacher as much as __________; he was always interesting.
who, whom	**9.** Our mayor is a former nun __________ decided to enter politics.
who, whom	**10.** The principal is a young man __________ has earned the community's respect.

Name ______________________ Section ____________ Date ____________

Score: (Number right) ______ x 10 = ________ %

Pronoun Forms: TEST 2

Fill in each blank with the appropriate pronoun from the margin.

we, us **1.** After this is all over, James and __________ will still be friends.

we, us **2.** I am afraid that our neighbors have left without __________.

I, me **3.** My friends and __________ really want to take a trip to Europe after we graduate.

he, him **4.** After all the votes were counted, George and __________ were the new class officers.

I, me **5.** Maida was always considered a lot smarter than __________.

who, whom **6.** The truck driver, __________ is in the diner, has been in there for three hours.

he, him **7.** I have wanted to tell __________ this story for a long time.

who, whom **8.** The monkey, __________ the zoo keeper purchased from the San Diego Zoo, is very ill.

she, her **9.** I wanted to tell __________ how much the groceries cost.

they, their **10.** A few of the cowboys wanted to ride __________ horses in the parade.

19 Pronoun Problems

Three Common Pronoun Problems

This chapter explains three common problems with pronouns:

1 Pronoun shifts in number A pronoun must agree in number with the noun it refers to.

Incorrect	Each of my sisters has **their** own room.
Correct	Each of my sisters has **her** own room.

2 Pronoun shifts in person Pronouns must be consistent in person. Unnecessary shifts in person (for example, from *I* to *one*) confuse readers.

Incorrect	**One's** patience runs thin when I am faced with a slow moving line at the bank.
Correct	**My** patience runs thin when I am faced with a slow-moving line at the bank.

3 Unclear pronoun reference A pronoun must clearly refer to the noun it stands for.

Incorrect	Michael gave Arnie **his** car keys. (Does *his* refer to Michael or Arnie?)
Correct	Michael gave **his** car keys to Arnie.

PRONOUN SHIFTS IN NUMBER

A pronoun must agree in number with the noun it refers to, which is called the pronoun's **antecedent**. Singular nouns require singular pronouns; plural nouns require plural pronouns.

In the following examples, pronouns are printed in **boldface** type; the antecedents are printed in *italic* type.

- The dying *tree* lost all **its** leaves.
  The antecedent *tree* is singular, so the pronoun must be singular: *its.*
- When *Vic* moved to California, **his** little brother e-mailed **him** almost every day.
  The antecedent *Vic* is singular, so the pronouns must be singular: *his* and *him.*
- Do the *neighbors* know that **their** dog is loose?
  The antecedent *neighbors* is plural, so the pronoun must be plural: *their.*
- *Sarah and Greg* act like newlyweds, but **they** have been married for years.
  The antecedent *Sarah and Greg* is plural, so the pronoun must be plural: *they.*

Practice 1

In each blank space, write the noun or nouns that the given pronoun refers to.

Example The ridges on our fingertips have a function. They help fingers to grasp things.

They refers to ___ridges___.

1. The photographer realized she preferred film to digital cartridges.

   She refers to ______________________.

2. The cat hid its kittens in the hayloft.

   Its refers to ______________________.

3. Kate and Barry don't get along with their stepfather.

   Their refers to ______________________.

4. Martin never drinks coffee in the evening. It keeps him awake all night.

   It refers to ______________________.

5. Nora is a year older than her brother, but they are both in sixth grade.

   They refers to ______________________.

Practice 2

In the spaces provided for each sentence, write **(a)** the pronoun used and **(b)** the noun or nouns that the pronoun refers to.

1. The boy refused to eat breakfast, but now he is hungry.

   The pronoun __________ refers to ________________.

2. The book fell loudly to the ground, and it landed on the front porch step.

   The pronoun __________ refers to ________________.

3. Because the cat was out all night, he fell asleep right after coming home.

   The pronoun __________ refers to ________________.

4. Hayley and Brandon are in love, but they live far away from each other.

   The pronoun __________ refers to ________________.

5. Susie always did what her mother wanted her to do.

   The pronoun __________ refers to ________________.

Indefinite Pronouns

Most pronouns refer to one or more particular persons or things. However, **indefinite pronouns** do not refer to particular persons or things. The following indefinite pronouns are always singular:

anybody	either	neither	one
anyone	everybody	no one	somebody
anything	everyone	nobody	someone
each	everything	nothing	something

- *Something* has left **its** muddy footprints on the hood of the car.
- *One* of my sisters has lost **her** job.
- *Everybody* is entitled to change **his** or **her** mind.

The indefinite pronouns *something, one,* and *everybody* are singular. The personal pronouns that refer to them must also be singular: *its, his,* or *her.*

Note on Gender Agreement Choose a pronoun that agrees in gender with the noun it refers to. Because *one of my sisters* is clearly feminine, use *her.* But *everybody* includes males and females, so use *his or her.* If *his or her* seems awkward in a sentence, try rewriting the sentence with a plural subject:

- People are entitled to change **their** minds.

The following indefinite pronouns are always plural:

both	many	several
few	other	

- *Both* of my brothers worked **their** way through college.
  Both, the subject of this sentence, is plural, so the plural pronoun *their* is used.

The following indefinite pronouns are singular or plural, depending on their context:

all	more	none
any	most	some

- *Some* of the pie is fine, but its crust is burnt.
  Some here refers to one thing—the pie, so the singular pronoun *its* is used.
- *Some* of the students forgot their books.
  Some here refers to several students, so the plural pronoun *their* is used.

Practice 3

In the spaces provided for each sentence, write **(a)** the pronoun or pronouns needed and **(b)** the word that the pronoun or pronouns refer to.

Example Neither of the ducks has cracked out of (*his or her/their*) shell yet.

The pronoun needed is __his or her__. The word it refers to is __neither__.

1. No one needs (*their/his or her*) passport to go to Texas.

The pronoun needed is ______________. The words it refers to is ______________.

2. Either of the men could have been in (*his/their*) own car.

The pronoun needed is ______________. The word it refers to is ______________.

3. Both of the pigs wallowed in (*his or her pen/their pen*).

The pronoun needed is ______________. The word it refers to is ______________.

4. "Everything has (*its/their*) own place" is one of my mother's favorite sayings.

The pronoun needed is ______________. The word it refers to is ______________.

5. Most of my exams are over, but (*it isn't/they aren't*) graded yet.

The pronoun needed is ______________. The word it refers to is ______________.

6. Many diamond rings remain in (*its/their*) jewelry boxes, instead of being worn, for safety purposes.

The pronoun needed is ______________. The word it refers to is ______________.

7. Has everyone brought (*their textbooks/his or her textbook*) to class today?

The pronoun needed is ______________. The word it refers to is ______________.

8. When I woke up this morning, most of my makeup had worn off, and (*it is/they are*) all over the pillow.

The pronoun needed is ______________. The word it refers to is ______________.

9. I don't like any of the new movies even though reviewers think (*it is/they are*) great.

The pronoun needed is ______________. The word it refers to is ______________.

10. Anyone fool enough to take (*their/his or her*) horoscope seriously deserves to be duped.

The pronoun needed is ______________. The word it refers to is ______________.

A Note on Collective Nouns

A **collective noun** refers to a group of persons or things considered to be a unit. Collective nouns are usually singular. Following are some examples.

audience	committee	group	quartet
band	couple	herd	society
class	family	jury	team

- The *class* started late, and **it** ended early.
  Class refers to a single unit, so the singular pronoun *it* is used.

However, if a collective noun refers to the individual members of the group, a plural pronoun is used.

- The *class* handed in **their** essays before vacation.

Many writers feel it is awkward to use a collective noun as a plural. They prefer to revise the sentence.

- The class *members* handed in **their** essays before vacation.

PRONOUN SHIFTS IN PERSON

A pronoun that refers to the person who is speaking is called a **first-person pronoun**. Examples of first-person pronouns are *I, me,* and *our.* A pronoun that refers to someone being spoken to, such as *you,* is a **second-person pronoun**. And a pronoun that refers to another person or thing, such as *he, she,* or *it,* is a **third-person pronoun**.

Following are the personal pronouns in first-, second-, and third-person groupings:

	First Person	Second Person	Third Person
Singular	I, me, my, mine	you, your, yours	he, him, his; she, her, hers; it, its
Plural	we, us, our, ours	you, your, yours	they, them, their, theirs

When a writer makes unnecessary shifts in person, the writing may become less clear. The sentences below, for example, show some needless shifts in person. (The words that show the shifts are **boldfaced**.)

- The worst thing about **my** not writing letters is that **you** never get any back.
  The writer begins with the first-person pronoun *my*, but then shifts to the second-person pronoun *you.*
- Though **we** like most of **our** neighbors, there are a few **you** can't get along with.
  The writer begins with the first-person pronouns *we* and *our*, but then shifts to the second-person pronoun *you.*

These sentences can be improved by eliminating the shifts in person:

- The worst thing about **my** not writing letters is that **I** never get any back.
- Though **we** like most of **our** neighbors, there are a few **we** can't get along with.

Practice 4

Write the correct pronoun in each space provided.

they, we	**1.** Whenever students are under a great deal of stress, ____________ often stop studying.
one, you	**2.** If you want to do well in this course, ____________ should plan on doing all the assignments on time.
you, me	**3.** When I took a summer job as a waitress, I was surprised at how rude some customers were to ____________.
we, you	**4.** It's hard for us to pay for health insurance, but ____________ don't dare go without it.
you, I	**5.** When ____________ drive on the highway, I get disgusted at the amount of trash I see.
I, you	**6.** Although I like visiting my Aunt Rita, ____________ always feel as if my visit has disrupted her life.
we, you	**7.** When we answer the telephone at work, ____________ are supposed to say the company name.
I, one	**8.** I would like to go to a school where ____________ can meet many people who are different from me.
you, they	**9.** Dog owners should put tags on their dogs in case ____________ lose their pets.
we, they	**10.** People often take a first-aid course so that ____________ can learn how to help choking and heart-attack victims.

UNCLEAR PRONOUN REFERENCE

A pronoun must refer clearly to its antecedent—the word it stands for. If it is unclear which word a pronoun refers to, the sentence will be confusing. As shown below, some pronouns are unclear because they have two possible antecedents. Others are unclear because they have no antecedent.

Two Possible Antecedents

A pronoun's reference will not be clear if there are two possible antecedents.

- Eva told her mother that she had received a postcard from Alaska.
  Who received the postcard, Eva or her mother?
- I wrote a to-do list with my purple pen, and now I can't find it.
  What can't the writer find, the list or the pen?

An unclear sentence with two antecedents can sometimes be corrected by using the speaker's exact words.

- Eva told her mother, "**I** received (*or:* "**You** received) a postcard from Alaska."

For an explanation of how to use quotation marks, see pages 143–153 in "Quotation Marks."

In some cases, the best solution is to replace the pronoun with the word it was meant to refer to.

- I wrote a to-do list with my purple pen, and now I can't find **the list** (*or:* **the pen**).

No Antecedent

A pronoun's reference will not be clear if there is no antecedent.

- I just received our cable TV bill. **They** said HBO is providing a free preview next month.
  Who said there's a free preview? We don't know because *they* has no word to refer to.
- My older brother is a chemist, but **that** doesn't interest me.
  What doesn't interest the writer? The pronoun *that* doesn't refer to any word in the sentence.

To correct an unclear reference in which a pronoun has no antecedent, replace the pronoun with the word or words it is meant to refer to.

- I just received our cable TV bill. **The cable company** said HBO is providing a free preview next month.
- My older brother is a chemist, but **chemistry** doesn't interest me.

Practice 5

In each sentence below, underline the correct word or words in parentheses.

1. At a local deli, *(they / the owners)* provide each table with a free bowl of pickles.
2. Joan said the cell phone is under the red pillow, but I can't find *(it / the cell).*
3. Rita asked Paula *(if she could help with the dishes. / , "Can I help with the dishes?")*
4. In a letter from Publishers Clearing House, *(they / the contest organizers)* all but promise that I have already won ten million dollars.
5. When my cousins arrived at the picnic with the homemade pies, *(my cousins / they)* were very welcome.

Practice 6

Revise each sentence to eliminate the unclear pronoun reference.

1. When Nick questioned the repairman, he became very upset.

____

____

2. My parents are expert horseshoe players, but I've never become any good at it.

____

____

3. Mary Alice told her sister that her boyfriend was moving to another state.

____

____

4. I bought a stationary bicycle that has a timer, but I never use it.

____

____

5. I went to the hardware store for 100-watt lightbulbs, but they didn't have any.

____

____

Name ______________________ Section ____________ Date ____________

Score: (Number right) ______ x 10 = __________ %

Pronoun Problems: TEST 1

A. In each blank space, write the pronoun that agrees in number with the word or words it refers to.

his or her, their **1.** No one at the game brought __________ stadium seat.

its, their **2.** The farm has sick animals in many of __________ pens.

her, their **3.** Neither of the sisters likes to do __________ chores.

her, their **4.** Grace and Sheila often change __________ oil at the same service station.

B. For each sentence, cross out the pronoun that makes a shift in person. Then, in the space provided, write a pronoun that corrects the shift in person.

__________ **5.** We work at a store where the owners don't provide you with any health insurance.

__________ **6.** I wanted to see the movie star, but one couldn't get past her security guard.

__________ **7.** Members of that gang said they feel the gang is like your family.

C. In each sentence below, choose the correct word or words and write them in the space provided.

8. I would love to be a doctor, but I really hate __________.
- **a.** it
- **b.** blood

9. Just when I got used to the tax regulations, __________ changed them.
- **a.** they
- **b.** the IRS

10. Arletta told Susan, ______________________.
- **a.** that she was too sick to go to work
- **b.** "You are too sick to go to work"

Name ______________________ Section ____________ Date ____________

Score: (Number right) _______ x 10 = ____________ %

Pronoun Problems: TEST 2

A. In each blank space, write the pronoun that agrees in number with the word or words it refers to.

his, their **1.** Each of my brothers has ____________ own flat-screen television.

its, their **2.** Some of the businesses in town have a day-care center for the children of ____________ employees.

her, their **3.** One of the hens has laid ____________ egg on an old blanket in the shed.

his or her, their **4.** Everybody in our apartment building was told to lock ____________ door in the evening.

B. For each sentence, cross out the pronoun that makes a shift in person. Then, in the space provided, write a pronoun that corrects the shift in person.

____________ **5.** The constant ringing of my telephone often drives one crazy.

____________ **6.** If people want something from the kitchen, you have to go and get it.

____________ **7.** The newspaper carrier didn't realize that you would have to deliver papers at 5 a.m.

C. In each sentence below, choose the correct word or words and write them in the space provided.

8. Jeanine is a devoted user of coupons at the supermarket, but I can't find the time for ____________

a. it.
b. collecting coupons.

9. Ian told his father ____________

a. he was late for his doctor's appointment.
b. , "You're late for your doctor's appointment."

10. In this letter from the bank, ____________ my account is overdrawn.
a. the customer service manager says
b. they say

20 Adjectives and Adverbs

Basics about Adjectives and Adverbs

This chapter explains the following:

1 **How to identify adjectives and adverbs**

- The **circular** *(adjective)* house is **unusual** *(adjective).*
- The **extremely** *(adverb)* small boy climbed the rope **very** *(adverb)* **quickly** *(adverb).*

2 **How to use adjectives and adverbs in comparisons**

- I'm a **worse** cook than my brother, but our sister is the **worst** cook in the family.

3 **How to use two troublesome pairs: *good* and *well, bad* and *badly***

- I can usually work **well** and do a **good** job even when I don't feel **well**.
- In addition to his **bad** attitude, the outfielder has been playing **badly**.

4 **How to avoid double negatives**

Incorrect I can't hardly wait for summer vacation.
Correct I can hardly wait for summer vacation.

IDENTIFYING ADJECTIVES AND ADVERBS

Adjectives

An **adjective** describes a noun or pronoun. It generally answers such questions as What kind of? Which one? How many?

An adjective may come before the noun or pronoun it describes.

- The **weary** hikers shuffled down the **dusty** road.
  The adjective *weary* describes the noun *hikers*; it tells what kind of hikers. The adjective *dusty* describes the noun *road*; it tells what kind of road.
- The **green** car has **two** antennas.
  The adjective *green* tells which car has the antennas. The adjective *two* tells how many antennas there are.
- Don't go to the **new** movie at the mall unless you want a **good** nap.
  The adjective *new* tells which movie; the adjective *good* tells what kind of nap.

An adjective that describes the subject of a sentence may also come after a linking verb (such as *be*, *is*, *seem*, and *were*).

- That dog's skin is **wrinkled** and **dry**.
  The adjectives *wrinkled* and *dry* describe the subject, *skin*. They follow the linking verb *is*.

For more information on linking verbs, see "Subjects and Verbs," pages 38–47.

Practice 1

Complete each sentence with an appropriate adjective. Then underline the noun or pronoun that the adjective describes.

Examples My ___favorite___ sweater had shrunk in the wash.

The school principal was ___strict___.

1. This ______________ weather really bothers me.
2. I'm in the mood for a(n) ______________ movie.
3. I've never read such a(n) ______________ book.
4. A(n) ______________ person makes a poor boss.
5. My aunt has an unusually ______________ voice.
6. The dance at school last night was ______________.
7. My ______________ pants are at the cleaners.
8. It's too bad that you are so ______________.
9. ______________ bushes are growing in front of the house.
10. Sylvia wrote her sister a(n) ______________ letter.

Adverbs

An **adverb** is a word that describes a verb, an adjective, or another adverb. Many adverbs end in *-ly.* Adverbs generally answer such questions as How? When? Where? How much?

- The chef **carefully** spread raspberry frosting over the cake.
  The adverb *carefully* describes the verb *spread. Carefully* tells how the chef spread the frosting.
- The robber stood **there**.
  The adverb *there* describes the verb *stood. There* (meaning "in that place") tells where the robber stood.
- Ann was **extremely** embarrassed when she stumbled on stage.
  The adverb *extremely* describes the adjective *embarrassed.* It tells how much Ann was embarrassed.
- That lamp shines **very brightly**.
  The adverb *very* describes the adverb *brightly. Very* tells how *brightly* the lamp shines. The adverb *brightly* describes the verb *shines*; it tells how the lamp shines.

Adverbs with Action Verbs

Be careful to use an adverb—not an adjective—with an action verb. Compare the following:

Incorrect	**Correct**
The boss slept sound at his desk. *Sound* is an adjective.	The boss slept **soundly** at his desk.
The graduates marched proud. *Proud* is an adjective.	The graduates marched **proudly.**
The batter swung wild at all the pitches. *Wild* is an adjective.	The batter swung **wildly** at all the pitches.

Practice 2

Complete each sentence with the adverb form of the adjective in the margin. (Change each adjective in the margin to an adverb by adding *-ly*.)

Example ***quick*** Sandra read the book too ___quickly___.

dishonest **1.** She answered the interview questions _______________.

clear **2.** He asked her to speak more _______________.

sweet **3.** She sang the anthem very _______________.

sly **4.** Matilda _______________ asked for the latest gossip.

frantic **5.** The man ran _______________ away from the angry grizzly bear.

happy **6.** She danced _______________ along with the lively music.

bold **7.** Dan was very thirsty, so he _______________ asked the parking attendant for a sip of his drink.

sad **8.** She _______________ implored her friend to give up drinking.

angry **9.** Although Alex knew he was wrong, he still _______________ protested his innocence.

loud **10.** Though it was three in the morning, the insomniac played his music _______________.

Practice 3

Complete each sentence correctly with either the adverb or the adjective in the margin.

quick, quickly **1.** The _______________ squirrel scurried up the tall tree to safety.

quick, quickly **2.** In spite of climbing _______________, the squirrel stumbled and fell to the ground.

soft, softly **3.** The baby _______________ cooed and gurgled in her car seat.

hesitant, hesitantly **4.** The lovers spoke _______________ to each other in front of their friends.

hesitant, hesitantly	**5.** Tony and Michelle are ________________with each other.
extreme, extremely	**6.** He took ________________ measures not to be caught stealing the money.
careful, carefully	**7.** He ________________ climbed up the rickety ladder.
joyful, joyfully	**8.** She was a person who did everything ________________.
weary, wearily	**9.** After four hours of hiking, he was ________________.
weary, wearily	**10.** Mikhail ________________ trudged up six flights of stairs.

USING ADJECTIVES AND ADVERBS IN COMPARISONS

Comparing Two Things

In general, to compare two things, add *-er* to adjectives and adverbs of one syllable.

- Grilling food is **faster** than roasting.
  The adjective *faster* is used to compare two methods: grilling and roasting.
- My mother works **longer** each day than my father.
  The adverb *longer* is used to compare how long two people work each day.

For longer adjectives and adverbs, do not add *-er*. Instead, add the word *more* when comparing two things.

- My dog is **more intelligent** than my cat.
  The words *more intelligent* describe the subject *dog;* they are being used to compare two things, the dog and the cat.
- Marie sings **more sweetly** than I do.
  The words *more sweetly* describe the verb *sings*; they compare the ways two people sing.

Practice 4

Write in the correct form of the word in the margin by adding either *-er* or *more.*

Examples	***thin***	Kate is ___thinner___ than her twin sister.
	carefully	I prefer to ride with Dan. He drives ___more carefully___ than you.

full	1. This bag of potato chips is ________________ than that one.
affectionate	2. My dog is ________________ than my boyfriend.
gray	3. This shirt looks ________________ than it did before I washed it.
neat	4. The inside of my car is ________________ than the inside of my apartment.
annoying	5. There are few sounds ________________ than fingernails scratching a board.

Comparing Three Things

In general, to compare three or more things, add *-est* to adjectives and adverbs of one syllable.

- Grilling food is faster than roasting, but microwaving is **fastest** of all.
  The adjective *fastest* is used to compare three methods: grilling, roasting, and microwaving. It indicates that microwaving is faster than the other two.
- My mother works longer each day than my father, but in my family, I work **longest**.
  The adverb *longest* is used to compare how long three or more people work each day. It indicates that of the three, I work the most number of hours.

For longer adjectives and adverbs, do not add *-est.* Instead, add the word *most* when comparing three or more things.

- My dog is more intelligent than my cat, but my parrot is the **most intelligent** pet I have ever had.
  Most intelligent is used to compare three animals. It shows which one is the smartest.
- Among the couples I know, my brother and sister-in-law are the **most happily** married of all.
  Most happily is used to compare how happy many married couples are. It indicates that my brother and sister-in-law are more happily married than any of the other couples I know.

Practice 5

Write in the correct form of the word in the margin by adding either *-est* or *most.*

Examples ***cold*** The ______coldest______ it ever gets around here is about zero degrees Fahrenheit.

delightful The ______most delightful______ play of the year is now at the Morgan Theater.

young **1.** Eliza is the ______________________ of eight children.

important **2.** The ______________________ thing in Julia's life is clothes.

fresh **3.** The Metro Mart has the ______________________ vegetables in town.

artistic **4.** Of the eighteen students in my class, Juan is the ______________________.

difficult **5.** My brother enjoys playing the ______________________ video games he can find.

Notes about Comparisons

1 Do not use both an *-er* ending and *more,* or an *-est* ending and *most.*

Incorrect My uncle's hair is more curlier than my aunt's.

Correct My uncle's hair is **curlier** than my aunt's.

2 Certain short adjectives and adverbs have irregular forms:

	Comparing two	Comparing three or more
bad, **badly**	worse	worst
good, **well**	better	best
little	less	least
much, **many**	more	most

- The grape cough syrup tastes **better** than the orange syrup, but the lemon cough drops taste the **best**.
- Sid is doing **badly** in speech class, but I'm doing even **worse**.

Practice 6

Cross out the incorrect word or words of comparison in each of the following sentences. Then write the correction on the line provided.

Example ___easier___ The test was ~~more easier~~ than I expected.

______ 1. That was the baddest accident I've ever seen.

______ 2. It is gooder to try and fail than not to try at all.

______ 3. My mother is more older than my father.

______ 4. I use littler oil in my cooking than I used to.

______ 5. This grapefruit is actually more sweeter than that orange.

______ 6. This year we had the most little rain we've had in years.

______ 7. I think the peacock is the most beautifulest of all birds.

______ 8. The macaroni salad tastes worser than the potato salad.

______ 9. Cheap Charlie's is the more expensive of all the variety stores in town.

______ 10. I'm on a diet, so put more little mayonnaise on my sandwich than usual.

USING TWO TROUBLESOME PAIRS: *GOOD* AND *WELL*, *BAD* AND *BADLY*

Good is an adjective that often means "enjoyable," "talented," or "positive."

- I had a **good** day.
- Sue is a **good** skier.
- Think **good** thoughts.

As an adverb, *well* often means "skillfully" or "successfully."

- Sue skis **well**.
- The schedule worked **well**.
- Pedro interacts **well** with others.

As an adjective, *well* means "healthy."

- The patient is **well** once again.

Bad is an adjective. *Badly* is an adverb.

- I look **bad**.
  Bad is an adjective that comes after the linking verb *look*. It describes the appearance of the subject of the sentence, *I*.
- I need sleep **badly**.
  Badly is an adverb that describes the verb *need*. It explains how much the sleep is needed.

Practice 7

Complete the sentence with the correct word in the margin.

good, well 1. After being so ill, you are looking ______________ today.

good, well 2. For every ______________ day at work, I have two nasty ones!

bad, badly 3. I ______________ need to sit down and balance my checkbook before my recent checks start to bounce.

bad, badly 4. The little boy's mother often told him what a ______________ boy he was.

good, well 5. You did really ______________ on your driver's test, but it was not quite enough to pass.

good, well 6. Marie was proud of herself for doing so ______________ on her physical fitness challenge.

good, well 7. I wish you ______________ in all that you do.

bad, badly 8. That mangy dog, staggering down the street, looks really ______________.

good, well 9. My grandmother was in the hospital last week, but now she's home and doing ______________.

good, well 10. I didn't believe him, no matter how many times he told me I was doing a ______________ job.

AVOIDING DOUBLE NEGATIVES

In standard English, it is incorrect to express a negative idea by pairing one negative with another. Common negative words include *not, nothing, never, nowhere, nobody,* and *neither.* To correct a double negative, either eliminate one of the negative words or replace a negative with a positive word.

Incorrect	I **shouldn't** go **nowhere** this weekend.
Correct	I **should** go **nowhere** this weekend.
Correct	I **shouldn't** go **anywhere** this weekend.

Shouldn't means *should not,* so the first sentence above contains two negatives: *not* and *nowhere.* In the first correct sentence, *not* has been eliminated. In the second correct sentence, *nowhere* has been replaced with a positive word.

The words *hardly, scarcely,* and *barely* are also negatives. They should not be paired with other negatives such as *never* and *not.* Correct a double negative containing *hardly, scarcely,* or *barely* by eliminating the other negative word.

Incorrect	I **couldn't scarcely** recognize you.
Correct	I **could scarcely** recognize you.

● Practice 8

Correct the double negative in each sentence by crossing out one of the negative words and writing any additional correction above the line.

Example I won't ~~never~~ go to that restaurant again.

will
OR I ~~won't~~ never go to that restaurant again.

1. Don't never stick anything into an electrical outlet.
2. The two sisters don't scarcely speak to one another.
3. I won't never believe a word that Vicky says.
4. Some days I feel that I can't do nothing right.
5. Ken can't go nowhere without running into one of his ex-girlfriends.
6. It's so dark in this room that I can't scarcely read.
7. My neighbor shouldn't never have tried to fix the roof on her own.
8. Pete won't say nothing unless he's sure he's right.
9. Nobody wouldn't believe what happened to me in class today.
10. That salesperson won't never stop trying, even when a customer starts walking away.

Name ______________________ Section ____________ Date ____________

Score: (Number right) ________ x 10 = ____________ %

Adjectives and Adverbs: TEST 1

Cross out the adjective or adverb error in each sentence and write the correction in the space at the left.

Example ___sweeter___ This peach is ~~more sweeter~~ than candy.

_______________ **1.** It is always more good to try and fail than not to try at all.

_______________ **2.** Maida always spoke very serene.

_______________ **3.** I can't believe that nobody knows nothing about the car accident.

_______________ **4.** She does her homework quick.

_______________ **5.** Josh always does favors happy.

_______________ **6.** Sora was able to get a well job after college.

_______________ **7.** My health is fine, but I really do not feel good today.

_______________ **8.** They both finished the race, but Leon was more slower than Estelle.

_______________ **9.** The melted snow ran rapid down the mountainside.

_______________ **10.** Marijane was the most smartest girl I had ever met.

Name ______________________________ Section ______________ Date ______________

Score: (Number right) ______ x 10 = __________ %

Adjectives and Adverbs: TEST 2

Each short paragraph below contains **two** errors in adjective and /or adverb use. Find the errors and cross them out. Then write the correct form of each word or words in the space provided.

1. We eat three different kinds of cereal in my house. One teenager wants the most sweetest sugarcoated cereal he can find. The other doesn't like nothing sweet, so he eats shredded wheat instead. I eat hot oatmeal every morning.

a. ______________________________

b. ______________________________

2. Many people become bad depressed during the winter. Their mood improves quick when they receive natural-light therapy.

a. ______________________________

b. ______________________________

3. I can't decide which book to read for my report. *The Old Man and the Sea* is more short than *The Great Gatsby,* so at first I thought I'd read that. But now that I've glanced through *Gatsby,* it seems the most interesting book.

a. ______________________________

b. ______________________________

4. Mr. Kensington has the goodest sense of humor in his family. For instance, he'll say that his knee is stiff from a war injury. But if you ask him to explain, he'll tell you cheerful that he got old and his knee "wore out."

a. ______________________________

b. ______________________________

5. Nothing is more good on a cold day than cuddling up on the sofa with hot cocoa and a good magazine. But I've got so much studying to do lately that I haven't scarcely any time to read anything but textbooks.

a. ______________________________

b. ______________________________

21 Misplaced and Dangling Modifiers

Basics about Misplaced and Dangling Modifiers

This chapter explains two common modifier problems:

1 Misplaced modifiers

Incorrect The man bought a tie at the department store **with yellow and blue stripes.**

Correct The man bought **a tie with yellow and blue stripes** at the department store.

2 Dangling modifiers

Incorrect **Biting my lip,** not laughing was difficult.

Correct **Biting my lip, I found it difficult** not to laugh.

MODIFIERS

A **modifier** is one or more words that describe another word or word group. For example, the modifier below is **boldfaced**, and the word it modifies is underlined.

- My cousin has a cat **with all-white fur.**
  The modifier *with all-white fur* describes *cat.*

Here are a few more examples:

- The woman **behind the cash register** is the owner of the store.
- I have **nearly** a thousand baseball cards.
- He printed his name **neatly**.

MISPLACED MODIFIERS

A **misplaced modifier** is a modifier that is incorrectly separated from the word or words that it describes. Misplaced modifiers seem to describe words that the author did not intend them to describe. When modifiers are misplaced, the reader may misunderstand the sentence. Generally, the solution is to place the modifier as close as possible to the word or words it describes. Look at the following examples.

Misplaced modifier Sam bought a used car from a local dealer with a smoky tailpipe.

Corrected version Sam bought a used car **with a smoky tailpipe** from a local dealer.

In the first sentence above, the modifier *with a smoky tailpipe* is misplaced. Its unintentional meaning is that the local dealer has a smoky tailpipe. To avoid this meaning, place the modifier next to the word that it describes, *car.*

Misplaced modifier The robin built a nest at the back of our house of grass and string.

Corrected version The robin built a nest **of grass and string** at the back of our house.

In the first sentence above, the words *of grass and string* are misplaced. Because they are near the word *house,* the reader might think that the house is made of grass and string. To avoid this meaning, place the modifier next to the word that it describes, *nest.*

Misplaced modifier Take the note to Mr. Henderson's office that Kim wrote.

Corrected version Take the note **that Kim wrote** to Mr. Henderson's office.

In the first sentence above, the words *that Kim wrote* are misplaced. The words must be placed next to *note*, the word that they are clearly meant to describe.

Following is another example of a sentence with a misplaced modifier. See if you can correct it by putting the modifier in another place in the sentence. Write your revision on the lines below.

Misplaced modifier I am going to New Orleans to visit my aunt on a train.

____

____

The original version of the sentence seems to say that the speaker will visit with his aunt on the train. However, the modifier *on a train* is meant to tell how the speaker is going to New Orleans. To make that meaning clear, the modifier needs to be placed closer to the words *am going:* "I am going **on a train** to New Orleans to visit my aunt."

● Practice 1

Underline the misplaced words in each sentence. Then rewrite the sentence in the space provided, placing the modifier where its meaning will be clear.

1. She is going to e-mail her term paper at the Internet cafe, which is late.

____

____

2. The phone is sitting on the table, which has a high-pitched ringtone.

____

____

3. They ate the huge dinner with reckless abandon.

____

____

4. The man on the street corner that is homeless is asking for money.

____

____

5. The frog in the pond that is swimming is my runaway pet.

____

____

Certain Single-Word Modifiers

Certain single-word modifiers—such as *almost, only, nearly,* and *even*—limit the words they modify. Such single-word modifiers must generally be placed before the word they limit.

Misplaced modifier	Christie almost sneezed fifteen times last evening.
Corrected version	Christie sneezed **almost** fifteen times last evening.

Because the word *almost* is misplaced in the first sentence, readers might think Christie *almost sneezed fifteen times,* but in fact did not sneeze at all. To prevent this confusion, put *almost* in front of the word it modifies, *fifteen.* Then it becomes clear that Christie must have sneezed a number of times.

Practice 2

Underline the misplaced words in each sentence. Then rewrite the sentence in the space provided, placing the modifier where its meaning will be clear.

1. Carrie nearly has sixty freckles on her face.

____

____

2. Suelyn almost cried through the whole sad movie.

____

____

3. I didn't even make one mistake on the midterm test.

____

____

4. The terrible fall nearly broke every bone in the skier's body.

____

____

5. By the end of the war, twenty countries were almost involved in the fighting.

____

____

DANGLING MODIFIERS

You have learned that a misplaced modifier is incorrectly separated from the word or words it describes. In contrast, a **dangling modifier** has no word to describe in the sentence. Dangling modifiers usually begin a sentence. When a modifier begins a sentence, it must be followed right away by the word or words it is meant to describe. Look at this example:

Dangling modifier	Sitting in the dentist's chair, the sound of the drill awakened Larry's old fears.

The modifier *sitting in the dentist's chair* is followed by *the sound of the drill.* This word order suggests that the sound of the drill was sitting in the dentist's chair. Clearly, that is not what the author intended. The modifier was meant to describe the word *Larry.* Since the word *Larry* is not in the sentence (*Larry's* is a different form of the word), it is not possible to correct the dangling modifier simply by changing its position in the sentence.

Here are two common ways to correct dangling modifiers.

- **METHOD 1: Follow the dangling modifier with the word or words it is meant to modify.**

After the dangling modifier, write the word it is meant to describe, and then revise as necessary. Using this method, we could correct the sentence about Larry's experience at the dentist's office like this:

Correct version	Sitting in the dentist's chair, **Larry found that** the sound of the drill awakened **his** old fears.

Now the modifier is no longer dangling. It is followed by the word it is meant to describe, *Larry.*

Following is another dangling modifier. How could you correct it using the method described above? Write your correction on the lines below.

Dangling modifier	Depressed and disappointed, running away seemed the only thing for me to do.

____

____

The dangling modifier in the above sentence is *depressed and disappointed.* It is meant to describe the word *I,* but there is no *I* in the sentence. So you should have corrected the sentence by writing *I* after the opening modifier and then rewriting as necessary: "Depressed and disappointed, **I felt that** running away **was** the only thing for me to do."

Practice 3

Underline the dangling modifier in each sentence. Then, on the lines provided, revise the sentence, using the first method of correction.

1. Mortified by defeat, my opponent was congratulated by me.

____

____

2. After sleeping for ten hours, my alarm clock woke me up.

____

____

3. Reminded by a friend, my English paper was turned in late.

____

____

4. Swimming for six hours nonstop, my knees were severely injured.

____

____

5. Pleased and excited, the regional championships were won.

____

____

● Method 2: Add a subject and a verb to the opening word group.

The second method of correcting a dangling modifier is to add a subject and a verb to the opening word group and revise as necessary. We could use this method to correct the sentence about Larry's experience at the dentist's office.

Dangling modifier	Sitting in the dentist's chair, the sound of the drill awakened Larry's old fears.
Correct version	**As Larry was** sitting in the dentist's chair, the sound of the drill awakened **his** old fears.

In this revision, the subject *Larry* and the verb *was* have been added to the opening word group.

Following is the dangling modifier that you revised using the first method of correction. How could you correct it using the second method? Write your revision on the lines below.

Dangling modifier	Depressed and disappointed, running away seemed the only thing for me to do.

____

____

You should have revised the sentence so that *I* and the appropriate verb are in the opening word group: "**Because I was** depressed and disappointed, running away seemed the only thing for me to do."

● Practice 4

Underline the dangling modifier in each sentence. Then, on the lines provided, revise the sentence using the second method of correction.

1. While waiting for an important call, Peg's phone began making weird noises.

2. After being shampooed, Trish was surprised by the carpet's new look.

3. Touched by the movie, tears came to my eyes.

4. After eating one too many corn dogs, Stella's stomach rebelled.

5. Born on the Fourth of July, Rob's birthday cake was always red, white, and blue.

Name ______________________ Section __________ Date __________

Score: (Number right) ______ x 10 = ______ %

Misplaced and Dangling Modifiers: TEST 1

In each sentence, underline the **one** misplaced or dangling modifier. (The first five sentences contain misplaced modifiers; the second five sentences contain dangling modifiers.) Then rewrite each sentence so that its intended meaning is clear.

1. The customer demanded that the waiter take her order rudely.

____

____

2. I peeled the potatoes before I cooked them with a paring knife.

____

____

3. In one week, the cat nearly had caught every mouse in the house.

____

____

4. The child playing on the jungle gym with fuzzy orange hair is my nephew.

____

____

5. We discovered an Italian bakery a few miles from our house that had just opened.

____

____

6. After visiting the bakery, the aroma of freshly baked bread filled our car.

____

____

7. Lying on the sunny beach, thoughts of skin cancer began to enter my mind.

____

____

Name ______________________ Section ____________ Date ____________

Score: (Number right) ________ x 10 = ____________ %

8. Not meaning to be cruel, George's careless remark hurt Jackie's feelings.

____

____

9. Though not a fan of science fiction, the new *Star Trek* movie, to my surprise, was very enjoyable.

____

____

10. Exhausted by his first day at school, Sam's eyes closed in the middle of his favorite TV show.

____

____

Name ______________________ Section ____________ Date ____________

Score: (Number right) ________ x 10 = ____________ %

Misplaced and Dangling Modifiers: TEST 2

Each group of sentences contains **one** misplaced modifier and **one** dangling modifier. Underline the two errors. Then, on the lines provided, rewrite the sentences that contain the errors so that the intended meanings are clear.

1. I thought my cousin would arrive by train that is on my mother's side of the family. Confused, the bus was his mode of transportation.

____

____

2. John wanted to work on the senator's campaign badly. Shyly asking to be part of the campaign, John's reluctance was obvious.

____

____

3. All of the shop employees were running late. Stalled in traffic, their tardiness could be excused. They almost were late by two hours.

____

____

4. The gambler's tension was palpable. Feeling unlucky, the next hand was dealt. He nearly lost all of his money.

____

____

5. The farmer's chickens were nervously pacing around their pen. The ten chickens had laid six eggs only that week. Clucking loudly, the farmer wondered what was bothering the chickens.

____

____

22 Word Choice

Basics about Word Choice

Not all writing problems involve grammar. A sentence may be grammatically correct, yet fail to communicate well because of the words that the writer has chosen. This chapter explains three common types of ineffective word choice:

1 Slang

Slang My sister is **something else**.

Revised My sister is a very special person.

2 Clichés

Cliché This semester, I have **bitten off more than I can chew**.

Revised This semester, I have taken on more work than I can manage.

3 Wordiness

Wordy It is **absolutely essential and necessary** that you borrow some folding chairs for the party.

Revised It is essential that you borrow some folding chairs for the party.

SLANG

Slang expressions are lively and fun to use, but they should be avoided in formal writing. One problem with slang is that it's not always understood by all readers. Slang used by members of a particular group (such as teenagers or science-fiction fans) may be unfamiliar to people outside of the group. Also, slang tends to change rapidly. What was *cool* for one generation is *awesome* for another. Finally, slang is by nature informal. So while it adds color to our everyday speech, it is generally out of place in writing for school or work. Use slang only when you have a specific purpose in mind, such as being humorous or communicating the flavor of an informal conversation.

Slang After a bummer of a movie, we pigged out on a pizza.

Revised After a **disappointing** movie, we **devoured** a pizza.

● Practice 1

Rewrite the slang expression (printed in *italic type*) in each sentence.

1. Tiffany did not *have a clue* about what was being taught in her science class.

____

2. When my parents see my final grades, I will be *dead meat.*

____

3. Everyone was *grossed out* when the cat brought home a dead rat.

____

4. Exhausted by their trip, the twins *sacked out* as soon as they got home.

____

5. Freddie is really *in la-la land* if he thinks he can make a living as a juggler.

____

CLICHÉS

A cliché is an expression that was once lively and colorful. However, because it has been used too often, it has become dull and boring. Try to use fresh wording in place of predictable expressions. Following are a few of the clichés to avoid in your writing:

Common Clichés

avoid like the plague	last but not least	sick and tired
better late than never	light as a feather	sigh of relief
bored to tears	make ends meet	time and time again
easy as pie	pie in the sky	tried and true
in the nick of time	pretty as a picture	under the weather
in this day and age	sad but true	without a doubt

Cliché Our new family doctor is as sharp as a tack.

Revised Our new family doctor is **very insightful**.

Practice 2

Rewrite the cliché (printed in *italic type*) in each sentence.

1. *For all intents and purposes,* my job is over.

____

2. The new math placement test is *easy as pie.*

____

3. I am going to *cut a few corners* by using a cake mix for the birthday cake.

____

4. My new neighbor really *rubs me the wrong way.*

____

5. I am going to buy a new car right now because I am tired of *beating around the bush.*

____

WORDINESS

Some writers think that using more words than necessary makes their writing sound important. Actually, wordiness just annoys and confuses your reader. Try to edit your writing carefully.

First of all, remove words that mean the same as other words in the sentence, as in the following example.

Wordy Though huge in size and blood red in color, the cartoon monster had a sweet personality.

Revised Though **huge** and **blood red**, the cartoon monster had a sweet personality.

Huge refers to size, so the words *in size* can be removed with no loss of meaning. *Red* is a color, so the words *in color* are also unnecessary. Following is another example of wordiness resulting from repetition. The author has said the same thing twice.

Wordy Scott finally made up his mind and decided to look for a new job.

Revised Scott finally **decided** to look for a new job.

Secondly, avoid puffed-up phrases that can be expressed in a word or two instead.

Wordy Due to the fact that the printer was out of paper, Renee went to a store for the purpose of buying some.

Revised **Because** the printer was out of paper, Renee went to a store **to buy** some.

In general, express your thoughts in the fewest words that are still complete and clear. Notice, for example, how easily the wordy expressions in the box below can be replaced by one or two words. The wordy expressions in the box on the next page can be made concise by eliminating repetitive words.

Wordy Expression	Concise Replacement
a large number of	many
at an earlier point in time	before
at this point in time	now
be in possession of	have
due to the fact that	because
during the time that	while
each and every day	daily
in order to	to
in the event that	if
in the near future	soon
in this day and time	today
made the decision to	decided

Examples of Wordiness due to Repetition

few ~~in number~~
green ~~in color~~
postponed ~~until later~~
small ~~in size~~
listened ~~with his ears~~
punched ~~with his fist~~
~~the feeling of~~ sadness
~~hurriedly~~ rushed
the first paragraph ~~at the beginning~~ of the chapter

See if you can revise the following wordy sentence by

1 replacing one group of words and
2 eliminating two unnecessary words.

- Owing to the fact that I was depressed, I postponed my guitar lesson until later.

____

The wordy expression *owing to the fact that* can be replaced by the single word *because* or *since.* The words *until later* can be eliminated with no loss of meaning. Here's a concise version of the wordy sentence: "Because I was depressed, I postponed my guitar lesson."

Practice 3

Underline the **one** example of wordiness in each sentence that follows. Then rewrite the sentence as clearly and concisely as possible.

Example I suddenly realized that my date was not going to show up and had stood me up.
I suddenly realized that my date was not going to show up.

1. Due to the fact that Lionel won the lottery, he won't be coming to work today.

____

____

2. My sister went ahead and made the decision to take a job in Maryland.

____

____

3. Jeff hid his extra house key and has forgotten the location where it is.

____

____

4. I do not know at this point in time if I will be going to this school next year.

____

____

5. Daily exercise every day of the week gives my mother more energy.

____

____

Name ______________________________ Section ______________ Date ______________

Score: (Number right) ________ x 10 = ______________ %

Word Choice: TEST 1

A. Each sentence below contains **one** example of slang or clichés. Underline the error and then rewrite it, using more effective language.

1. Get off my case, or I will quit this job!

____

2. He gave me a bum steer about those stock options.

____

3. You think the world revolves around you, but it doesn't!

____

4. If I hear that hackneyed expression one more time, I will lose my marbles.

____

5. I told that pushy salesman to take a hike.

____

B. Underline the **one** example of wordiness in each sentence that follows. Then rewrite the sentence as concisely as possible.

6. Due to the fact that my mother is visiting, we will be going out to a nice restaurant.

____

7. I neglected to remember to call you last night.

____

8. In the event that we are late to the movie, we can choose another.

____

9. I'm glad that I made the decision to return the library books today.

____

10. At this time, I regret to inform you that you have flunked your final exam.

____

Name ______________________ Section ____________ Date ____________
Score: (Number right) ________ x 10 = ____________ %

Word Choice: TEST 2

Each item below contains **two** examples of ineffective word choice: slang, clichés, or wordiness. Underline the errors. Then rewrite each underlined part as clearly and concisely as possible.

1. In the event that I get the part-time job, I will heave a sigh of relief.

a. ______________________

b. ______________________

2. Thirty-seven students signed up for the creative-writing class, but only twenty-four could be accepted. The other thirteen were really bummed out. They asked the teacher to consider opening a second section of the class, but he gave them the cold shoulder.

a. ______________________

b. ______________________

3. Wally assembled the big circular track for his son's model train. Then he connected the cars, hooking them up together. Finally, he threw the switch and watched the train glide around the track. He was as pleased as punch that it all worked perfectly.

a. ______________________

b. ______________________

4. The microwave oven I bought from your store is a loser. Although I have followed the manufacturer's instructions, the oven has never worked properly. I expect you to replace the oven in the very near future. If that is not possible, please return my money.

a. ______________________

b. ______________________

5. The movie I saw last night was advertised as a comedy, but I didn't laugh once. Instead, it weirded me out. It showed married people who hated one another and parents who shouted at their children. Why do people in this day and age think it is funny for people to mistreat one another?

a. ______________________

b. ______________________

23 Numbers and Abbreviations

Basics about Numbers and Abbreviations

This chapter explains the following:

1. **When to write out numbers (*one, two*) and when to use numerals (*1, 2*)**
2. **When to use abbreviations and which ones to use**

NUMBERS

Here are guidelines to follow when using numbers.

1. **Spell out any number that can be written in one or two words. Otherwise, use numerals.**

   - When my grandmother turned **sixty-nine**, she went on a **fifteen**-day trip across **nine** states.
   - The YouTube video received **10,450** hits in one day.

   Note When written out, numbers twenty-one through ninety-nine are hyphenated.

2. **Spell out any number that begins a sentence.**

   - **Eight hundred and seventy-one** dollars was found in the briefcase.

   To avoid writing out a long number, you can rewrite the sentence:

   - The briefcase contained **$871**.

3. **If one or more numbers in a series need to be written as numerals, write all the numbers as numerals.**

   - The movie theater sold **137** tickets to a horror movie, **64** to a comedy, and **17** to a romance.

4. **Use numerals to write the following.**

   a. **Dates**

   - My grandfather was born on July **4, 1949**.

   b. **Times of the day**

   - The last guest left at **1:45** a.m.

   But when the word *o'clock* is used, the time is spelled out:

   - I got home at **six o'clock**.

   Also spell out the numbers when describing amounts of time:

   - Marian worked **fifty** hours last week.

   c. **Addresses**

   - The bookstore is located at **1216** North **48th** Street.

d Percentages

- Nearly **70** percent of the class volunteered for the experiment.

e Pages and sections of a book

- Jeff read pages **40–97** of the novel, which includes chapters **2** and **3**.

f Exact amounts of money that include change

- My restaurant bill was **$8.49**.

g Scores

- The Sacramento Kings beat the Los Angeles Lakers **94–90**.
- People with an IQ between **20** and **35** are considered severely retarded.

5 When writing numerals, use commas to indicate thousands.

- Angie has **1,243** pennies in a jar.
- The number that comes after **999,999** is **1,000,000**.

BUT Do not use commas in telephone numbers (1-800-555-1234), zip codes (08043), street numbers (3244 Oak Street), Social Security numbers (372-45-0985), or years (2004).

Practice 1

Cross out the **one** number mistake in each sentence. Then write the correction in the space provided.

________________ **1.** In a search engine, the words "identity theft" yielded twenty five thousand thirteen hits.

________________ **2.** If ninety percent of people are in favor of changing the Electoral College, why doesn't it happen?

________________ **3.** Page sixty in chapter 10 is where you will find the answer to the essay question.

________________ **4.** At the last minute, thirty turkeys, 640 chickens, and 941 ducks were ordered for Thanksgiving.

________________ **5.** When the little girl turned 6, she began first grade.

________________ **6.** There are more than fifty quarters and 40 nickels on my bedside table.

________________ **7.** I will see you at the back gate at 10 o'clock.

________________ **8.** 340 cartons of nails spilled onto the busy highway.

________________ **9.** Please wake me at six nineteen exactly.

________________ **10.** I cannot believe we have lived at this address since nineteen eighty seven.

ABBREVIATIONS

Abbreviations can save you time when you are taking notes. However, you should avoid abbreviations in papers you write for classes. The following are among the few that are acceptable in formal writing.

1 Titles that are used before and after people's names

- **Ms.** Glenda Oaks
- **Dr.** Huang
- Keith Rodham, **Sr.**

2 Initials in a person's name

- Daphne **A.** Miller
- **T.** Martin Sawyer

3 Time and date references

- The exam ended at 4:45 **p.m.**
- Cleopatra lived from about 69 to 30 **B.C.**

4 Organizations, agencies, technical words, countries, or corporations known by their initials. They are usually written in all capital letters and without periods.

- YMCA
- FBI
- DVD
- AIDS
- USA
- NBC

Practice 2

Cross out the **one** abbreviation mistake in each sentence. Then write the correction in the space provided.

______________________ **1.** Buddhism was founded in the sixth cent. B.C. by Buddha.

______________________ **2.** Dr. Diamond works for the YMCA in Phila.

______________________ **3.** Mr. Ostrow emigrated from Russia to Can. in 1995.

______________________ **4.** On Mon., I have an appointment at the Google headquarters with Ms. Janice Grant.

______________________ **5.** Dwight D. Eisenhower was born in Abilene, Kan., in 1890.

______________________ **6.** My brother Wm. tried to get his VCR to record a show at 5:30 p.m.

______________________ **7.** When my grandfather retd., he volunteered to work with a local AIDS group.

______________________ **8.** In 1970, the FBI expanded the nmbr. of criminals on its most-wanted list from ten to sixteen.

______________________ **9.** My cousin is getting married at 9:30 a.m. on the beach in Santa Cruz, Calif.

______________________ **10.** According to an NBC reporter, many of today's coll. students drink in binges.

Name ______________________________ Section ______________ Date ____________

Score: (Number right) ______ x 10 = __________ %

Numbers and Abbreviations: TEST 1

Cross out the one number or abbreviation mistake in each of the following sentences. Then write the correction on the line provided.

____________ **1.** On October thirty first, it will be the baby's first Halloween.

____________ **2.** You are late; you should have been here by 7 o'clock.

____________ **3.** I only brought a few dollars with me, but the admission charge is six dollars and fifty cents.

____________ **4.** I love Mar. because it is my birthday month.

____________ **5.** My house on Studebaker Rd. is ten miles from the nearest store.

____________ **6.** I've been waiting for you for over 50 minutes.

____________ **7.** I really want to go to Fla. on spring break.

____________ **8.** I hate the advertisements of that co. and I will never buy its products.

____________ **9.** The little girl counted out her life's savings of ten pennies, 145 quarters, and 25 nickels.

____________ **10.** Please, try to take Route 66 through AZ.

Name ______________________ Section ____________ Date ____________

Score: (Number right) ______ x 10 = ________ %

Numbers and Abbreviations: TEST 2

Cross out the one number or abbreviation mistake in each of the following sentences. Then write the correction on the line provided.

__________ **1.** Ms. Bradley begins her day at 5 o'clock.

__________ **2.** An officer of the NAACP will speak on campus in Jan.

__________ **3.** Shelly watched a program on PBS for 30 minutes before going to work.

__________ **4.** I listed Dr. Keenan as a ref. on my résumé.

__________ **5.** The vendors sold eighty soft pretzels, 145 soft drinks, and 106 hot dogs.

__________ **6.** While in San Fran., we were part of a six-car accident on the Golden Gate Bridge.

__________ **7.** The twenty-seven students in Mrs. Greene's class are learning about South Amer.

__________ **8.** The YWCA on Waverly Blvd. is having an open house in two weeks.

__________ **9.** Since the meal was about ten dollars, the tip should be at least one dollar and fifty cents.

__________ **10.** On May first, 2011, U.S. Navy Seals, under the direction of President Obama, killed Osama bin Laden.

24 More about Subjects and Verbs

More about Subjects

THE SUBJECT AND DESCRIPTIVE WORDS

A subject is often accompanied by one or more words that describe it. See if you can find the subjects of the following sentences and the words that describe them.

- A very large truck stalled on the bridge.
- Some tomatoes are yellow.
- Two young boys were playing catch in the alley.

In the first sentence, *truck* is the subject. The words *a, very,* and *large* describe the word *truck.* In the second sentence, *tomatoes* is the subject, and *some* describes it. In the third sentence, the subject is *boys*; the words describing that subject are *two* and *young.*

For more information on descriptive words (also known as adjectives and adverbs), see "Adjectives and Adverbs," pages 215–224, and "Parts of Speech," pages 27–37.

Practice 1

Add an appropriate word to each blank. The word that you insert will be the subject of the sentence. It will tell who or what the sentence is about.

1. All the ______________ at the construction site were temporary workers.
2. The ______________ was pacing in his cage and growling at the onlookers.
3. There are dangerous ______________ in the desert.
4. Ryan's ______________ resembled him so much even their mother could not tell them apart.
5. Susan is a cheerful person. ______________ just always sees events in a positive light.
6. Many ______________ are on the honor roll this term.
7. ______________ is a person known for her superior intelligence.
8. Outside of his house, the ______________ paced up and down.
9. Nine ______________ were required to fell the large oak tree.
10. Many ______________ border the city of Charleston.

THE SUBJECT AND PREPOSITIONAL PHRASES

The subject of a sentence is never part of a prepositional phrase. As explained on page 32, a **prepositional phrase** is a group of words that begins with a preposition (a word like *in, from, of,* or *with*) and ends with a noun or pronoun (the object of the preposition). Following are some common prepositions:

about	before	down	like	to
above	behind	during	of	toward
across	below	except	off	under
after	beneath	for	on	up
among	beside	from	over	with
around	between	in	since	without
at	by	into	through	

Here are a few examples of prepositional phrases:

- in the house
- from the bakery
- of the world
- with your permission

Now look at the sentence below. What is the subject? Write your answer here: __________

- A bunch of green grapes fell onto the supermarket floor.
  The answer is *bunch*, but many people would be tempted to choose *grapes*. In this case, however, *grapes* is part of the prepositional phrase *of green grapes*, so it cannot be the subject.

As you look for the subject of a sentence, it may help to cross out the prepositional phrases. For example, look at the following sentences. In each sentence, find the prepositions and cross out the prepositional phrases. Then underline the subject. After finding each subject, read the explanation that follows.

- The sick man, with shaking hands, poured the pills from the brown bottle.
  The prepositions are *with* and *from*. Cross out *with shaking hands* and *from the brown bottle*, and you are left with the sentence *The sick man poured the pills*. Ask yourself, "Who poured the pills?" The answer, *man*, is the subject of the sentence.
- A student in the class fell asleep during the long lecture.
  In and *during* are prepositions. You should have crossed out the prepositional phrases *in the class* and *during the long lecture*. When you do this, you are left with the sentence *A student fell asleep*. Ask yourself, "Who fell asleep?" The answer, *student*, is the subject of the sentence.

For more information on prepositions, see "Parts of Speech," pages 32–33.

● Practice 2

Cross out the **one** prepositional phrase in each sentence. Then underline the subject of the sentence.

Example The pack ~~of cookies~~ disappeared quickly.

1. The blueberries in this pie are bitter.
2. On weekends, Troy works overtime.
3. The woman with a pierced nose is my hairdresser.
4. Leaves from our neighbor's tree covered our lawn.
5. During the school play, the lead actress lost her voice.
6. Some of the roof shingles are loose.
7. Like her father, Abby adores baseball.
8. The dust under your bed contains tiny creatures.
9. One of my best friends is a computer programmer.
10. From my bedroom window, I can watch my neighbor's TV.

A Note on Singular and Plural Subjects

In addition to finding subjects, you should note whether a subject is **singular** (one) or **plural** (more than one). Most plural subjects simply end in *s*:

Singular The **car** in front of us is speeding.
Plural The **cars** in front of us are speeding.

Some plural subjects are irregular:

Singular The **child** was crying.
Plural The **children** were crying.

A **compound subject** is two or more subjects connected by a joining word such as *and.* Compound subjects are usually plural.

Compound The **car** and the **truck** in front of us are speeding.

For more information on compound subjects, see "Subject-Verb Agreement," pages 60–69.

Practice 3

Underline the subject or subjects of each sentence. Then in the space on the left, write **S** if the subject is singular and **P** if the subject is plural.

Example __P__ Love and hate are closely related emotions.

_____ 1. The people around the corner have just moved in.

_____ 2. Monkeys often exhibit similar mannerisms to humans.

_____ 3. The sound of the drums kept me awake all night.

_____ 4. My Aunt Sue and Uncle Phil are getting a divorce.

_____ 5. The speed of the race cars was unbelievably fast.

_____ 6. Six children in the preschool came down with the flu at the same time.

_____ 7. The watch belonged to my grandfather.

_____ 8. The sink and the bathtub both need to be cleaned with bleach.

_____ 9. The front of her dress was torn and dirty.

_____ 10. For some time, the grass and the flowers had needed tending.

More about Verbs

Every complete sentence contains a verb. In general, as explained briefly on pages 30–31, there are two types of verbs: **action verbs** and **linking verbs**.

FINDING ACTION VERBS

See if you can double-underline the action verb in the following two sentences. Then read the explanations.

- The moon disappeared behind the clouds.
- The impatient customer tapped her fingers on the counter.

In looking for the verb in the first sentence, you can eliminate the prepositional phrase *behind the clouds.* That leaves the words *the moon disappeared.* The *moon* is what did something, so it is the subject of the sentence. What did the moon do? It *disappeared.* So *disappeared* is the action verb.

In the second sentence, you can also eliminate a prepositional phrase: *on the counter.* That leaves *The impatient customer tapped her fingers.* The subject is *customer*—that's who did something. What did the customer do? She *tapped.* So *tapped* is the action verb in that sentence.

Just as a sentence can contain a compound subject, a sentence can contain a **compound verb**: two or more verbs that have the same subject or subjects. For example, here's another version of one of the sentences above:

- The impatient customer tapped her fingers on the counter and cleared her throat.

In this version, the customer did two things: *tapped* (her fingers) and *cleared* (her throat). Therefore, the subject *customer* has a compound verb: *tapped* and *cleared.*

In case you have trouble finding the verb of a sentence, here is one other way to identify a verb: Try putting a pronoun such as *I, you, he, she, it,* or *they* in front of the word you suspect is a verb. If the word is a verb, the resulting sentence will make sense. Notice, for instance, that for the sentences on the previous page, *it disappeared* and *she tapped* make sense.

Practice 4

Double-underline the action verb or verbs in each sentence. You may find it helpful to first identify and underline the subject and to cross out any prepositional phrases.

1. Members of the audience applauded loudly.
2. Before the party, I took a short nap.
3. Without warning, the can of red paint slid off the ladder.
4. Wesley tripped on the steps.
5. The huge tree on the front lawn shades our front porch in the afternoon.
6. Aunt Lois opened the package and gasped in delight.
7. A German shepherd waited patiently for his owner to return.
8. The angry bull snorted loudly and charged at the red blanket.
9. Without a word, Paul raced out of the house and into the front yard.
10. By 7 a.m., impatient shoppers were gathering at the front entrance of the mall for a special sale.

LINKING VERBS

Linking verbs do not show action. **Linking verbs** join (or link) the subject to one or more words that describe the subject. Look at the following examples.

- Before the race, the runners were anxious.

  The subject of this sentence is *runners.* The sentence has no action verb—the runners did not **do** anything. Instead, the verb *were* links the subject to a word that describes it: *anxious.* (*Before the race* is a prepositional phrase, and so it cannot contain the subject or the verb.)

- Cara's boyfriend is a good mechanic.
  The subject of this sentence is *boyfriend.* The linking verb *is* joins that subject with words that describe it: *a good mechanic.*

Most linking verbs are forms of the verb *be.* Here are forms of *be,* which is the most used verb in the English language:	am	were	had been
	is	will be	will have been
	are	have been	
	was	has been	

Here are other common words that can be linking verbs.	appear	feel	seem	sound
	become	look	smell	taste

Now see if you can double-underline the linking verbs in the following two sentences.

- George looks uncomfortable in a suit and tie.
- Sometimes anger is a healthy emotion.

If you underlined *looks* in the first sentence, you were right. *Looks* links the subject, *George,* to words that describe him: *uncomfortable in a suit and tie.*

If you underlined *is* in the second sentence, you were right. *Is* links the subject, *anger,* to words that describe it: *a healthy emotion.*

Practice 5

Double-underline the **one** word that is a linking verb in each sentence. You may find it helpful to first identify and underline the subject and to cross out any prepositional phrases.

1. That nurse was kind.
2. The kitchen smells spicy.
3. Trisha and I are roommates.
4. Velvet feels soft and silky.
5. The chocolate cookies taste salty and dry.
6. After jogging, I am always hungry.
7. Those dishes from the dishwasher still look dirty.
8. Since his divorce, Nate seems unhappy.
9. The cashier at our supermarket is a student at Jefferson High School.
10. During the hot, dry summer, the farmers were uneasy about their crops.

MAIN VERBS AND HELPING VERBS

Most of the verbs you have looked at so far have been just one word—*wrote, drifted, is, look,* and so on. But many verbs consist of a main verb plus one or more **helping verbs**. Look at the following two sentences and explanations.

- My sister is joining a book club.

Sister is the subject of this sentence. She is the person who is doing something. What is she doing? She *is joining* (a book club). In this sentence, *is* is a helping verb, and *joining* is the main verb.

Joining by itself would not make sense as a verb. It would be incorrect to say, "My sister joining a book club." Words that end in *-ing* cannot be the verb of a sentence unless they are accompanied by a helping verb.

- Mikey should have given his dog a bath before the pet contest.

In this sentence, *Mikey* is the subject. What should he have done? He *should have given* (his dog a bath). *Should* and *have* are helping verbs. The last verb in the word group, *given,* is the main verb.

Given by itself could not be the verb. It would not be correct to say, "Mikey given his dog a bath . . ."

The helping verbs are listed in the box below.

Forms of *be*:	be, am, is, are, was, were, being, been
Forms of *have*:	have, has, had
Forms of *do*:	do, does, did
Special verbs:	can, could, may, might, must, ought (to), shall, should, will, would These special verbs are also known as ***modals***.

The **modals**, unlike the other helping verbs, do not change form to indicate tense. In other words, they do not take such endings as *-ed, -s,* and *-ing.* After the modals, always use the basic form of a verb, the form in which a verb is listed in the dictionary (*go, see, work,* and so on).

- You *can* turn in the paper tomorrow.
- We *should* visit Dee in the hospital.

Now see if you can underline the main verbs and the helping verbs in the following two sentences. Then read the explanations.

- Gwen has visited the learning skills lab.
- I will be running in the school's five-mile race.

In the first sentence, *Gwen* is the subject. She is the one who has done something. To find the verb, we can ask, "What did Gwen do?" The answer is *has visited. Has* is the helping verb, and *visited* is the main verb.

In the second sentence, *I* is the subject. What will that subject be doing? He or she *will be running.* So in this sentence, *will* and *be* are helping verbs, and *running* is the main verb.

Practice 6

Fill in the blanks under each sentence.

1. He should have started his English paper sooner.

   Helping verb[s]: __________________ *Main verb:* __________________

2. Muriel has dedicated her life to the poor and homeless.

   Helping verb[s]: __________________ *Main verb:* __________________

3. I really do think you are beautiful and intelligent.

   Helping verb[s]: __________________ *Main verb:* __________________

4. Mark should be here soon.

   Helping verb[s]: __________________ *Main verb:* __________________

5. They will cheer the team to victory.

   Helping verb[s]: __________________ *Main verb:* __________________

6. She was laughing hysterically at everything John said last night.

   Helping verb[s]: __________________ *Main verb:* __________________

7. The main character in the play might have forgotten his lines.

   Helping verb[s]: __________________ *Main verb:* __________________

8. The little boy must have left his truck on the stairs last night.

   Helping verb[s]: __________________ *Main verb:* __________________

9. You could have done your homework yesterday.

   Helping verb[s]: __________________ *Main verb:* __________________

10. You will appear in court on the tenth of July on the charges against you.

    Helping verb[s]: __________________ *Main verb:* __________________

WORDS THAT ARE NOT VERBS

Here is some added information that will help when you look for verbs in a sentence.

1 The verb of a sentence never begins with the word *to.*

- The instructor **agreed** to provide ten minutes for study before the quiz.
  Although *provide* is a verb, *to provide* cannot be the verb of a sentence. The verb of this sentence is *agreed.*

2 Certain words—such as *always, just, never, not,* and *only*—may appear between the main verb and the helping verb. Such words are **adverbs**. They describe the verb, but they are never part of it.

- Our canary **does** not **sing** in front of visitors.
- We **will** never **eat** at that restaurant again.
- You **should** always **wear** your seat belt in a moving vehicle.

For more information on adverbs, see "Adjectives and Adverbs," pages 215–224, and "Parts of Speech," pages 33–34.

Practice 7

In the space provided, write the complete verb in each sentence.

1. My uncle is not wearing his toupee anymore.

   Complete verb: ______________________

2. The children hurried to finish their art projects by the end of the class.

   Complete verb: ______________________

3. The noodles should not be boiled more than seven minutes.

   Complete verb: ______________________

4. The teacher has promised to return the papers by Friday.

   Complete verb: ______________________

5. Reba will always love her ex-husband.

   Complete verb: ______________________

Name ______________________ Section ____________ Date ____________

Score: (Number right) ______ x 5 = ____________ %

More about Subjects and Verbs: TEST 1

For each sentence, cross out any prepositional phrases. Then, on the lines provided, write the subject(s) and verb(s), including any helping verb(s).

1. Fred and John ran the race and finished in the top ten.

   Subject(s): ____________ *Verb(s):* ____________

2. The cleaner should have been finished with the room by now.

   Subject(s): ____________ *Verb(s):* ____________

3. Knives and forks did not belong in the top drawer.

   Subject(s): ____________ *Verb(s):* ____________

4. Around the corner, my cousin is working at a new job.

   Subject(s): ____________ *Verb(s):* ____________

5. The railway station at the end of the block is being torn down soon.

   Subject(s): ____________ *Verb(s):* ____________

6. The reindeer on the neighbors' house are grazing on their roof tiles.

   Subject(s): ____________ *Verb(s):* ____________

7. My last class for this school year is the day after tomorrow.

   Subject(s): ____________ *Verb(s):* ____________

8. For every wealthy person in this city, there are two homeless people.

   Subject(s): ____________ *Verb(s):* ____________

9. The red pants in the corner of the room need to be put in the wash now.

   Subject(s): ____________ *Verb(s):* ____________

10. The sombrero on the man's head is too big for him.

    Subject(s): ____________ *Verb(s):* ____________

Name ______________________ Section ____________ Date ____________
Score: (Number right) ________ x 5 = ____________ %

More about Subjects and Verbs: TEST 2

In each of the ten sentences in this paragraph, cross out any prepositional phrases. Then, underline all the subjects once and the verbs twice. Remember to include any helping verb(s) and also all parts of compound subjects and verbs.

[1]Sharks, with their pointed snouts and fearsome teeth, terrify most people. [2]However, of the 375 or so different types of sharks, few have attacked people. [3]Most sharks will attack only when in danger. [4]The great white shark is one of the most dangerous sharks to humans. [5]Many people know and fear this shark from its role in the movie *Jaws.* [6]It can grow to over twenty feet in length. [7]The coloring of the great white shark is a camouflage in the water. [8]The color of its belly is white. [9]From underneath, the white belly blends with the bright sky overhead. [10]Seals, smaller fish, and people often do not see the great white shark in time.

25 More about Subject-Verb Agreement

You have already reviewed (on pages 60–69) two situations that affect subject-verb agreement:

1 **Words between the subject and the verb**

2 **Compound subjects**

This section will cover five other situations that affect subject-verb agreement:

3 **Verb coming before the subject**

4 **More about compound subjects**

5 **Collective nouns**

6 **Indefinite pronoun subjects**

7 **Relative pronoun subjects: *who, which, that***

VERB COMING BEFORE THE SUBJECT

The verb follows the subject in most sentences:

- *Hector* **passed** the course.
- A *rabbit* **lives** in my backyard.
- The *plane* **roared** overhead.

However, in some sentences, the verb comes *before* the subject. To make the subject and verb agree in such cases, look for the subject after the verb. Then decide if the verb should be singular or plural. Sentences in which the verb comes first include questions.

- What **was** your *score* on the test?
  The verb *was* is singular. It agrees with the singular subject *score. On the test* is a prepositional phrase. The subject of a sentence is never in a prepositional phrase. (See page 246.)

The verb also comes first in sentences that begin with such words as *there is* or *here are.*

- There **are** *ants* in the sugar jar.
  The verb of this sentence is the plural verb *are,* so the subject should be plural as well. You can find the subject by asking, "What are in the sugar jar?" The answer, *ants,* is the subject.
- Here **is** the *menu.*
  The subject of this sentence is *menu,* which needs a singular verb.

The verb may also come before the subject in sentences that begin with a prepositional phrase.

- On that shelf **are** the *reports* for this year.
  The sentence begins with the prepositional phrase *on that shelf,* which is followed by the plural verb *are.* You can find the subject by asking, "What are on that shelf?" The answer is the subject of the sentence: *reports.* The subject and verb agree—they are both plural.

Here's another helpful way to find the subject when the verb comes first: Try to rearrange the sentence so that the subject comes first. The subject may be easier to find when the sentence is in the normal order. For the sentences on the previous page, you would then get:

- Your *score* on the test **was** what?
- *Ants* **are** in the sugar jar.
- The *menu* **is** here.
- The *reports* for this year **are** on that shelf.

Practice 1

Underline the subject of each sentence. Then, in the space provided, write the form of the verb that agrees with the subject. (If you have trouble finding the subject, try crossing out any prepositional phrases.)

is, are	**1.** Here _______________ some messages for you.
is, are	**2.** What _______________ your middle name?
stands, stand	**3.** Beside the stream _______________ a low wooden fence.
grows, grow	**4.** In that little garden _______________ twenty herbs.
was, were	**5.** There _______________ black clouds in the sky this morning.
is, are	**6.** Where _______________ the box for these crayons?
lies, lie	**7.** On the table in the dining room _______________ a letter for you.
is, are	**8.** There _______________ good reasons to hire older workers.
is, are	**9.** Why _______________ Jamie sitting outside in the car?
rests, rest	**10.** On the bench outside of the mall _______________ two tired shoppers.

MORE ABOUT COMPOUND SUBJECTS

As explained on pages 60 and 247, a **compound subject** is made up of two nouns connected by a joining word. Subjects joined by *and* generally take a plural verb.

However, when a compound subject is connected by *or, nor, either ... or,* or *neither ... nor,* the verb must agree with the part of the subject that is closer to it.

- My *aunts* or my *mother* usually **hosts** our family gatherings.
  The singular noun *mother* is closer to the verb, so the singular verb *hosts* is used.
- Either *he* or *his parents* were home that night.
- Either *his parents* or *he* was home that night.
  In the first sentence, the plural noun *parents* is closer to the verb, so the verb is plural. In the second sentence, the singular noun *he* is closer to the verb, so the verb must be singular.
- Neither the *teacher* nor the *students* **are** to blame for the shortage of textbooks.
  The plural noun *students* is closer to the verb, so the verb is plural.

Practice 2

In each sentence, underline the compound subject. Then, in the space provided, write the correct form of the verb in the margin.

needs, need 1. "After you do the dishes," Rene said, "either you or your brother __________ to feed the dog."

wants, want 2. Neither John nor his roommates __________ to mow the lawn.

pays, pay 3. His cousins or he __________ for dinner this time.

seems, seem 4. Neither the cat nor the dogs __________ energetic today.

takes, take 5. Either Susie or her sisters usually __________ their mother to church.

COLLECTIVE NOUNS

A **collective noun** refers to a group of persons or things that are thought of as one unit. Collective nouns are usually considered singular. Following are some examples.

- The **family** *lives* on Russell Avenue.
  Family refers to a single unit, so the singular verb *lives* is used. However, if a collective noun refers to the individual members of the group, a plural verb is used.
- The **family** *are* Republicans, Democrats, and Independents.
  Since one unit cannot have three different political views, *family* in this sentence clearly refers to the individual members of the group, so the plural verb *are* is used. To emphasize the individuals, some writers would use a subject that is clearly plural:
- The **members** of the family *are* Republicans, Democrats, and Independents.

Practice 3

In each sentence, underline the subject and decide if it needs a singular or plural verb. Then fill in the correct form of the verb in the margin.

sings, sing 1. Every Sunday, the family ______________ together in church.

wears, wear 2. The twins ______________ completely different clothing.

is, are 3. The quartet ______________ in perfect harmony today.

is, are 4. The company's board ______________ unanimous in its choice of the new president.

plays, play 5. The orchestra ______________ Handel's *Messiah* every Easter.

INDEFINITE PRONOUN SUBJECTS

Indefinite pronouns are pronouns that do not refer to a specific person or thing. The ones in the box below are always singular:

anybody	either	neither	one
anyone	everybody	no one	somebody
anything	everyone	nobody	someone
each	everything	nothing	something

In the following sentences, the subjects are singular indefinite pronouns. Each of the verbs is therefore also singular.

- *Each* of the puppies **is** cute in its own way.
- *Neither* of the boys **wants** to walk the dog.
- Despite the rules, nearly *everyone* in my apartment building **owns** a pet.

Note that the indefinite pronoun *both* is always plural:

- *Both* of the puppies **are** cute in their own ways.

The definite pronoun *most* is singular or plural, depending on its context:

- *Most* of his outfit **is** white.
  Most here refers to one thing—the outfit, so the singular verb *is* is used.
- *Most* of the salespeople **are** friendly.
  Most here refers to several salespeople, so the plural verb *are* is used.

Practice 4

Underline the subject of each sentence. Then, in the space provided, write the form of the verb that agrees with the subject.

is, are **1.** Everybody at my new school _______________ friendly.

feels, feel **2.** Neither of those mattresses _______________ comfortable.

knows, know **3.** Nobody in my family _______________ how to swim.

is, are **4.** Both of my parents _______________ allergic to peanuts.

has, have **5.** Most of the house _______________ been painted.

needs, need **6.** Each of the children _______________ some attention.

seem, seems **7.** Either Monday or Friday _______________ like a good day for the meeting.

goes, go **8.** Everything in that box _______________ to the neighborhood garage sale.

is, are **9.** Both of my best friends _______________ older than I.

has, have **10.** Most of the wedding invitations _______________ been addressed and mailed.

RELATIVE PRONOUN SUBJECTS: *WHO, WHICH, THAT*

The relative pronouns *who, which,* and *that* are singular when they refer to a singular noun. They are plural when they refer to a plural noun.

- I met a woman *who* **is** from China.
- I met two women *who* **are** from China.
  In the first sentence above, *who* refers to the singular word *woman,* so the verb is singular too. In the second sentence, *who* refers to the plural word *women,* so the verb must be plural.
- Our car, *which* **is** only a year old, already needs a new battery.
  Which refers to *car,* a singular noun, so the singular verb *is* is used.
- My boss collects old wind-up toys *that* still **work**.
  That refers to the plural noun *toys,* so the plural verb *work* is used.

For more information on relative pronouns, see "Parts of Speech," page 29.

Practice 5

In each sentence, underline the noun that the relative pronoun refers to. Then fill in the correct form of the verb in the margin.

is, are 1. Michael loves his new toys, which ____________ very expensive.

is, are 2. Michael loves his new toy, which ____________ very expensive.

is, are 3. Sarah plays a musical instrument that ____________ several hundred years old.

is, are 4. Sarah plays musical instruments that ____________ several hundred years old.

is, are 5. The new neighbor, who ____________ from Puerto Rico, just left.

is, are 6. The new neighbors, who ____________ from Puerto Rico, just left.

digs, dig 7. We have adopted a new dog who ____________ holes in our backyard.

digs, dig 8. We have adopted two new dogs who ____________ holes in our backyard.

blooms, bloom 9. They love their garden, which ____________ profusely each spring.

blooms, bloom 10. They love their flowers, which ____________ profusely each spring.

Name ______________________ Section ____________ Date ____________

Score: (Number right) ______ x 10 = ________ %

More about Subject-Verb Agreement: TEST 1

For each section, fill in the correct form of the verb in the margin.

needs, need	**1.** The house or the barn ______________ to be painted this year.
is, are	**2.** Also, both buildings, which ______________ very old, need repairs.
itches, itch	**3.** Each of these sweaters ______________.
gets, get	**4.** Our group ______________ together every Friday night to read and discuss fiction.
was, were	**5.** There ______________ sad expressions on the students' faces.
is, are	**6.** In my English class, either a novel or short stories ______________ assigned every week.
hurries, hurry	**7.** Through the airport ______________ travelers from all over the world.
likes, like	**8.** My neighbors are people who ______________ their privacy.
is, are	**9.** Why ______________ the lights off?
knows, know	**10.** No one ______________ how long the rain delay will continue.

Name ______________________ Section ____________ Date ____________

Score: (Number right) ________ x 10 = ____________ %

More about Subject-Verb Agreement: TEST 2

For each sentence, fill in the correct form of the verb in the margin.

was, were **1.** Neither Phillip nor Henry ____________ in the mood to go to the movies.

loves, love **2.** The pilot is a person who ____________ to fly her own plane.

is, are **3.** There ____________ too many weeds in my neglected garden.

was, were **4.** The landfill and the surrounding areas ____________ covered over last year.

has, have **5.** The school boards ____________ argued about that issue for ten years.

was, were **6.** After many ballots, there ____________ a unanimous decision.

was, were **7.** It has not been determined whether many drivers or just one ____________ responsible for the traffic fatality.

donates, donate **8.** No one in the surrounding counties ____________ blood on a regular basis.

is, are **9.** What ____________ the calories in this yummy chocolate bar?

plays, play **10.** The jukebox on the table ____________ some very old songs.

26 More about Verbs

Verb Tenses

All verbs have various **tenses**—forms that indicate the time the sentence is referring to. This chapter explains the following about verb tenses:

1 **The four principal verb parts that are the basis for all of the tenses**

2 **The most common verb tenses in English**

Six main tenses	present, past, future present perfect, past perfect, future perfect
Three progressive tenses	present progressive, past progressive, future progressive

THE FOUR PRINCIPAL PARTS OF VERBS

Each verb tense is based on one of the four principal parts of verbs. Following are explanations of each of those verb parts.

1 **Basic Form** The basic form is the form in which verbs are listed in the dictionary. It is used for the present tense for all subjects except third-person singular subjects.

- I **ask** questions in class.

Third-person singular verbs are formed by adding *-s* to the basic form.

- Sue **asks** questions in class.

2 **Past Tense Form** The past tense of most verbs is formed by adding *-ed* or *-d* to the basic form.

- We **asked** the teacher to postpone the test.
- I **amused** the children by doing magic tricks.

3 **Present Participle** The present participle is the *-ing* form of a verb. It is used in the progressive tenses, which you will learn about later in the chapter.

- Jack is **asking** the teacher something in the hallway.
- I am **amusing** the children while their mother does errands.

4 **Past Participle** The past participle of a verb is usually the same as its past tense form. The past participle is the form that is used with the helping verbs *have, has,* and *had* and with *am, is, are, was,* or *were.*

- The teachers have **asked** us to study in groups.
- I was **amused** when the children asked if I could stay forever.

Here are the principal parts of three regular verbs:

Basic Form	Past Tense Form	Present Participle	Past Participle
work	worked	working	worked
smile	smiled	smiling	smiled
wonder	wondered	wondering	wondered

SIX MAIN TENSES

There are six main tenses in English. They are **present**, **past**, **future**, **present perfect**, **past perfect**, and **future perfect**.

Look at the following chart. It shows the six basic tenses of the verb *work.*

Tense	Example
Present	I **work.**
Past	I **worked.**
Future	I **will work.**
Present Perfect	I **have worked.**
Past Perfect	I **had worked.**
Future Perfect	I **will have worked.**

These tenses are explained in more detail below and on the pages that follow.

Present Tense

Verbs in the **present tense** express present action or habitual action. (A habitual action is one that is often repeated.)

- Our dog **smells** the neighbor's barbecue.
  Smells expresses a present action.
- Jay **works** as a waiter on weekends.
  Works expresses a habitual action.

The forms of present tense verbs are shown with the verb *work* in the box below. Notice the difference between the singular third-person form and the other present tense forms.

	Singular	Plural
First person	I work	we work
Second person	you work	you work
Third person	he, she, it works	they work

Present tense verbs for the third-person singular end with an *s*. Here are some other sentences in the present tense with subjects that are third-person singular:

- She **reads** a book a week on her new Kindle.
- It **takes** me a month to read a book.
- Dan **drives** an hour to school every day.
- His old car **averages** only ten miles a gallon.

Note A third-person subject is he, she, it, or any single person or thing other than the speaker (first person) or the person spoken to (second person).

Practice 1

A. Fill in the present tense of *smile* for each of the following:

	Singular	Plural
First person	I ________	we ________
Second person	you ________	you ________
Third person	he, she, it ________	they ________

B. Fill in each space with the present tense form of the verb shown in the margin.

drill	**1.** The dentist ____________ the cavity as his assistant watches.
practice	**2.** Ling ____________ her typing every day.
ring	**3.** Those church bells ____________ on the hour.
make	**4.** He suddenly ____________ a U-turn.
dig	**5.** Some workers ____________ through the stones and rubble.
trim	**6.** I ____________ my fingernails before playing the piano.
clean	**7.** Dinah ____________ her apartment every Saturday.
tell	**8.** The nurse ____________ the patient to make a fist.
discover	**9.** My sister often ____________ loose change in her coat pockets.
remember	**10.** Children often ____________ the fights their parents used to have.

Past Tense

Verbs in the **past tense** express actions that took place in the past.

- Last year, Jay **worked** as a messenger.
- One day our dog **chased** a raccoon.

The past tense is usually formed by adding *-ed* or *-d* to the end of the basic form of the verb. In the above sentences, the *-ed* and *-d* endings are added to the basic forms of the verbs *work* and *chase*.

Note People sometimes drop the -ed or -d ending in their everyday speech. They then tend to omit those endings in their writing as well. For example, someone might say

- I finish the paper an hour before class.

instead of

- I **finished** the paper an hour before class.

In written English, however, the *-ed* or *-d* ending is essential.

Practice 2

Fill in each space with the past tense form of the verb shown in the margin.

love **1.** Laughton ____________ his new puppy Fergie.

swat **2.** The first night of camping they ____________ mosquitoes all night long.

ask **3.** She ____________ everyone to call her by her nickname.

sail **4.** Last summer, the men ____________ their boat to Catalina Island.

rub **5.** Mattie ____________ the magic lamp and a genie popped out.

graze **6.** The cows ____________ all day in the beautiful green field.

lock **7.** My cousin Phoebe ____________ her keys in the trunk of her new car.

derail **8.** The speeding trains ____________ within a mile of each other.

appear **9.** Ghosts ____________ in the haunted house shortly after the guests arrived.

strum **10.** The man on the street corner ____________ his guitar lazily.

Future Tense

Verbs in the **future tense** describe future actions.

- Next summer, Jay **will work** at a camp.

The future tense is formed by adding the word *will* or *shall* to the basic form of the verb.

Practice 3

Fill in the space with the future tense form of the verb shown in the margin.

run **1.** I ____________ in the next Boston Marathon.

succeed **2.** She ____________ her sister as president of their sorority.

sell **3.** The scalpers ____________ the concert tickets for double their original price.

arrive **4.** We ____________ early to help you with the party preparations.

grade **5.** Monty ____________ the exams after he has his morning coffee.

Present Perfect Tense (*have* or *has* + past participle)

The **present perfect** tense describes an action that began in the past and either has been finished or is continuing at the present time.

- I **have written** five pages of notes on the textbook chapter.
- Jay **has worked** at a number of jobs over the years.

The present perfect tense is formed by adding the correct form of the helping verb *have* to the past participle of the verb. Here are the present tense forms of *have*:

	Singular	Plural
First person	I have	we have
Second person	you have	you have
Third person	he, she, it has	they have

Practice 4

Fill in each space with the present perfect tense form of the verb shown in the margin. One is done for you as an example.

complete **1.** Shauna has completed over forty half-marathons since beginning running.

decide **2.** Although Ralph will be thirty next week, he ______________ to stay twenty-nine forever.

talk **3.** The people in the back of the bus ______________ nonstop since they got on in Phoenix.

cook **4.** I ______________ dinner for over ninety people on several occasions.

move **5.** They ______________ to another state to avoid their creditors.

Past Perfect Tense (*had* + past participle)

The **past perfect** tense describes an action that was completed in the past before another past action.

- Jay **had worked** as a messenger before he located a better job as a waiter.

The past perfect tense is formed by adding *had* to the past participle of a verb.

Practice 5

Fill in the space with the past perfect tense form of the verb shown in the margin. Add *had* to the past participle of the verb. One is done for you as an example.

mix **1.** Laurie had mixed up the recipes for lemon cake and lemon pie and ended up with a delicious new dessert.

wish **2.** I ______________ for a million dollars for most of my life until I realized there were far more important things to wish for.

gamble **3.** She _______________ away most of her money before she joined Gamblers Anonymous.

bought **4.** My brother already _______________ the bright green jacket, but regretted the purchase when he later saw himself in a mirror.

struggle **5.** She _______________ through four marriages and divorces before realizing being single wasn't so bad after all.

Future Perfect Tense (*will have* + past participle)

The **future perfect** tense describes an action that will be completed before some time in the future.

- Jay **will have worked** at a half dozen different jobs before college graduation.

The future perfect tense is formed by adding *will have* to the past participle of a verb.

Practice 6

Fill in the space with the future perfect tense form of the verb shown in the margin. Add *will have* to the past participle of the verb. One is done for you as an example.

complete **1.** I __will have completed__ five exams by the end of finals week.

attend **2.** By graduation day, I _______________ five parties.

finish **3.** You eat so slowly that I _______________ my ice cream before you begin your spaghetti.

hire **4.** The company _______________ several new employees by May.

design **5.** By the end of the summer, my mother _______________ and sewed my sister's wedding dress.

THE PROGRESSIVE TENSES

As their names suggest, the **progressive tenses** express actions still in progress at a particular time. They are made by adding a form of the helping verb *be* to the *-ing* form of the verb, the present participle.

Present Progressive Tense (*am*, *are*, or *is* + present participle)

The **present progressive** tense expresses an action taking place at this moment or that will occur sometime in the future.

- Jay **is working** at the restaurant today.
- I **am going** to get home late tonight.

The present progressive tense is formed by adding the correct present tense form of the helping verb *be* to the *-ing* form of the verb.

Present Tense Forms of the Verb *Be*

	Singular	Plural
First person	I am	we are
Second person	you are	you are
Third person	he, she, it is	they are

Practice 7

Below are five sentences with verbs in the present tense. Cross out each verb and change it to the present progressive in the space provided. One is done for you as an example.

1. The child ~~plays~~ with the puppy. is playing
2. The microwave beeps loudly. ______
3. The roses in the garden bloom. ______
4. I practice my speech tonight. ______
5. The visitors pace in the hospital lobby. ______

Past Progressive Tense (*was* or *were* + present participle)

The **past progressive** tense expresses an action that was in progress at a certain time in the past.

- Jay **was working** yesterday.

The past progressive tense is formed by adding the correct past tense form of *be* to the *-ing* form of the verb.

Past Tense Forms of the Verb *Be*

	Singular	Plural
First person	I was	we were
Second person	you were	you were
Third person	he, she, it was	they were

Practice 8

Below are five sentences with verbs in the past tense. Cross out each verb and change it to the past progressive in the space provided. One is done for you as an example.

1. The child ~~played~~ with the puppy. was playing
2. The microwave beeped loudly. ______
3. The roses in the garden bloomed. ______
4. I practiced my speech last night. ______
5. The visitors paced in the hospital lobby. ______

Future Progressive Tense (*will be* + present participle)

The **future progressive** tense expresses an action that will be in progress at a certain time in the future.

- Jay **will be working** tomorrow.

The future progressive tense is formed by adding *will be* to the *-ing* form of the verb.

Practice 9

Below are five sentences with verbs in the future tense. Cross out each verb and change it to the future progressive in the space provided. One is done for you as an example.

1. The child ~~will play~~ with the puppy. will be playing
2. The microwave will beep loudly. ____________
3. The roses in the garden will bloom. ____________
4. I will practice my speech tonight. ____________
5. The visitors will pace in the hospital lobby. ____________

A Note on *-ing* Verbs

Look at the following word groups:

- Jay working tonight.
- The visitors pacing in the hospital lobby.

The above word groups express incomplete thoughts because their verbs are incomplete. The *-ing* form of a verb cannot stand by itself as the verb of a sentence—it must be accompanied by a helping verb:

- Jay **is working** tonight.
- The visitors **were pacing** in the hospital lobby.

Practice 10

The verb in each of the following sentences is incomplete. Correct each incomplete thought by adding *is, are, was,* or *were* in the space provided.

1. The farm workers ____________ picking lettuce from dawn to dusk for very little pay.
2. After the last rain, the storefronts ____________ dripping for hours.
3. Six men ____________ waiting for the ten o'clock bus.
4. She ____________ knitting and crocheting items for the church fair.
5. Alsace ____________ studying for his final exams.

A SUMMARY OF THE NINE MOST COMMON VERB TENSES

Using the regular verb *call*, the chart below illustrates the nine most common tenses in English.

The Nine Most Common Verb Tenses

Present	I **call** my grandmother Nana. My mother **calls** her Babe.
Past	A number of employees **called** in sick today.
Future	Because the flu is going around, more **will** probably **call** in sick tomorrow.
Present perfect	Rebecca **has called** the radio station at least ten times to request her favorite song.
Past perfect	No one **had called** Mitchell "Shorty" for years until he attended his grade-school reunion.
Future perfect	When you finish your first day as a telemarketer, you **will have called** forty potential customers.
Present progressive	Ken **is calling** the restaurant right now to make a reservation for dinner.
Past progressive	He **was calling** a different restaurant when I came in, but I urged him to call my favorite one.
Future progressive	Mom **will be calling** when she arrives at work and realizes she left her purse here.

Name ______________________ Section ____________ Date ____________

Score: (Number right) ______ x 10 = ________ %

More about Verbs: TEST 1

A. In each space, write the **present tense** form of the verb in the margin.

Examples *plan* Carl ___plans___ to enter the contest.

attend The students ___attend___ a meeting on the new dress code.

rise **1.** The airplane ____________ slowly from the runway.

swim **2.** The whales ____________ effortlessly in their large tanks.

remember **3.** Hector ____________ to brush his teeth each day.

B. In each space, write the **past tense** form of the verb in the margin.

Example *promise* My brother ___promised___ to wash our car on Saturday.

pull **4.** The girls ____________ each other's hair and screamed loudly.

twinkle **5.** The reindeer ____________ their eyes at the small children.

scurry **6.** Nine mice ____________ across the slippery floor.

trudge **7.** The climbers ____________ up the steep mountain toward the summit.

C. In each space, write the **future tense** form of the verb in the margin.

Example *check* The nurse ___will check___ your blood pressure each day.

laugh **8.** Those men ____________ at anything that comedian says.

sit **9.** The teacher said, "You ____________ down or go to the principal's office."

knock **10.** I predict that Maurice ____________ on our door within the next ten minutes.

Name ______________________________ Section ______________ Date ______________

Score: (Number right) ________ x 10 = ____________ %

More about Verbs: TEST 2

A. In each space, write the **present perfect tense** form of the verb in the margin.

Examples *walk* Bernice has walked over twenty miles this week.

look I have looked all over for my glasses.

wash **1.** The students ______________ nearly seventy cars to raise money for their class trip.

learn **2.** We ______________ about the civil rights movement in our history class this semester.

gain **3.** Rodney ______________ ten pounds in his first year of college.

notice **4.** I ______________ changes in you since you started going to the gym.

B. In each space, write the **past perfect tense** form of the verb in the margin.

Example *walk* Before her heart attack, Bernice seldom had walked for exercise.

argue **5.** Fritz ______________ with a friend before the car accident.

warn **6.** Before she left for her hair appointment, Jenna ______________ us that she would soon be looking very different.

manage **7.** Chelsea ______________ to clean the entire house by the time her parents got home last evening.

C. In each space, write the **future perfect tense** form of the verb in the margin.

Example *walk* By the end of this month, Bernice will have walked over one-hundred miles.

work **8.** Paco ______________ fifty-five hours by the end of the week.

interview **9.** By the time she writes her paper, Jodi ______________ six nurses.

watch **10.** By the end of the day, the children ______________ five hours of television.

27 Even More about Verbs

More about Verb Tenses

This chapter explains three other things you should know about verb tense:

1 Consistent verb tense

Inconsistent verb tense	We **parked** the car and **head** toward the movie theater.
Consistent verb tense	We **parked** the car and **headed** toward the movie theater.

2 The passive and active voices

Passive voice	I **was visited** last week by a former neighbor.
Active voice	A former neighbor **visited** me last week.

3 Nonstandard and standard verbs

Nonstandard verbs	Every week, Mandy **volunteer** at a nursing home near her apartment. She often **read** to residents there.
Standard verbs	Every week, Mandy **volunteers** at a nursing home near her apartment. She often **reads** to residents there.

CONSISTENT VERB TENSE

In your writing, avoid illogical or needless shifts in tense. For example, if you are writing a paper with the action in the past tense, don't shift suddenly to the present for no reason. Look at the examples below:

Inconsistent verb tense — In my nightmare, a hairy spider **crawled** up the side of my bed and **races** quickly onto my pillow.

There is no reason for the writer to shift suddenly from the past tense (*crawled*) to the present tense (*races*). The inconsistency can be corrected by using the same tense for both verbs:

Consistent verb tense — In my nightmare, a hairy spider **crawled** up the side of my bed and **raced** quickly onto my pillow.

● Practice 1

In each short passage, there is **one** illogical change in verb tense. Cross out the incorrect verb. Then write the correct form of that verb on the line provided.

_______________ **1.** The ice skater moved smoothly through her routine. On her last jump, however, she lost her balance and crashes to the ice with a thud.

_______________ **2.** On many farms, machines milk the cows. The farmers then send the fresh milk to a processing plant. Workers there heated the milk at high temperatures. The intense heat removes bacteria.

_______________ **3.** When Tina saw flames and smoke coming from her kitchen, she reacted quickly. She picks up her kitten and her purse. Then she rushed out into the fresh air.

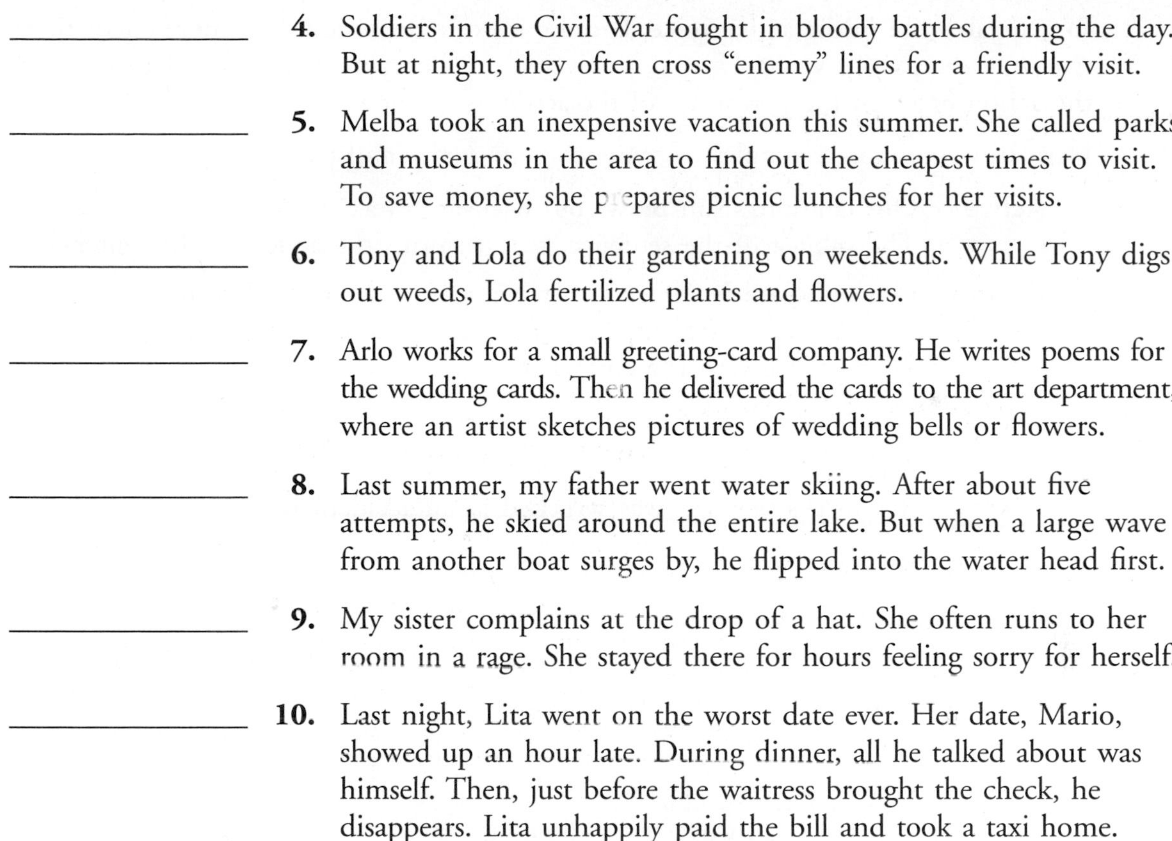

_______________ **4.** Soldiers in the Civil War fought in bloody battles during the day. But at night, they often cross "enemy" lines for a friendly visit.

_______________ **5.** Melba took an inexpensive vacation this summer. She called parks and museums in the area to find out the cheapest times to visit. To save money, she prepares picnic lunches for her visits.

_______________ **6.** Tony and Lola do their gardening on weekends. While Tony digs out weeds, Lola fertilized plants and flowers.

_______________ **7.** Arlo works for a small greeting-card company. He writes poems for the wedding cards. Then he delivered the cards to the art department, where an artist sketches pictures of wedding bells or flowers.

_______________ **8.** Last summer, my father went water skiing. After about five attempts, he skied around the entire lake. But when a large wave from another boat surges by, he flipped into the water head first.

_______________ **9.** My sister complains at the drop of a hat. She often runs to her room in a rage. She stayed there for hours feeling sorry for herself.

_______________ **10.** Last night, Lita went on the worst date ever. Her date, Mario, showed up an hour late. During dinner, all he talked about was himself. Then, just before the waitress brought the check, he disappears. Lita unhappily paid the bill and took a taxi home.

THE PASSIVE AND ACTIVE VOICES

The subject of a sentence usually performs the action of the verb. In such cases, the verb is in the **active voice**. For example, look at the following sentence:

- My father **planted** the Japanese maple tree in the front yard.

  The verb in this sentence is *planted.* Who performed that action? The answer is *father*, the subject of the sentence. Therefore, the verb is in the **active voice**.

Now look at this version of that sentence:

- The Japanese maple tree in the front yard **was planted** by my father.

  The verb in this sentence is *was planted.* The subject of the sentence, *tree*, did not perform the action. It received the action; the tree was acted upon by the father. When the subject of a sentence is acted upon, the verb is in the **passive voice**.

Passive verbs are formed by combining a form of *to be* (*am, is, are, was, were*) with the past participle of a verb (which is usually the same as its past tense form). For example, in the sentence above, *was* plus the past participle of *plant* results in the passive verb *was planted.*

Here are some other passive verbs:

Form of *to be*	+	past participle	=	passive verb
am	+	pushed	=	am pushed
is	+	surprised	=	is surprised
was	+	delayed	=	was delayed

In general, write in the active voice. Because it expresses action, it is more energetic and effective than the passive voice. Use the passive voice when you wish to emphasize the receiver of the action or when the performer of the action is unknown.

Here are some more examples of sentences with active and passive verbs:

Active Our landlord's son **mows** our backyard every week.
The subject of the sentence, *son*, performs the action of the sentence, *mows*.

Passive Our backyard **is mowed** every week by our landlord's son.
The subject of the sentence—*backyard*—does not act. Instead, it is acted upon. (The passive verb is a combination of *is* plus the past participle of *mow*.)

Active My sister **wrecked** her new car in an accident last night.
The subject of the sentence, *sister*, is the one who acted—she *wrecked* the car.

Passive My sister's new car **was wrecked** in an accident last night.
The subject of this sentence, *car*, does not do anything. Something is done to it.

● Practice 2

Underline the verb in each sentence. Then circle the **A** in the margin if the verb is active. Circle the **P** in the margin if the verb is passive.

Example A (P) The car window was shattered by a poorly aimed baseball.

A P 1. Mary was run over by a speeding car.

A P 2. John deflated the tires on his bike to store it for the winter.

A P 3. The company was taken over by a giant corporation.

A P 4. The men pushed the stalled car down the block to the gas station.

A P 5. Stuart tightened the screws on the lawn mower.

A P 6. The children were led across the street by their mother.

A P 7. The papers were scattered all over the floor.

A P 8. The bells of the church were rung for twenty minutes on Easter Day.

A P 9. He wrote an entire book in less than three weeks.

A P 10. They jogged almost ten miles last Saturday.

Rewriting from the Passive to the Active Voice

Keep in mind that in the active voice, the subject performs the action. Here's a sentence with a passive verb. See if you can rewrite the sentence using the active voice.

Passive voice Our roof was damaged by the storm.

Active voice ______________________________

In the passive version of the sentence, the subject (*roof*) was acted upon by the storm. The storm is what did the action. To write an active version of the sentence, you should have made *storm* the subject: *The storm damaged our roof.*

Practice 3

The following sentences are written in the passive voice. For each sentence, underline the verb. Then rewrite the sentence in the active voice, changing the wording as necessary.

Example Fruits and vegetables are painted often by artists.
Artists often paint fruits and vegetables.

1. The cat was named Leo by my brother.

2. Soccer is played by children all over the world.

3. The book report was prepared hastily by Sean.

4. Some students were pushed around by the gym teacher.

5. Shipping labels are printed quickly by the computer.

6. A nest was constructed in our mailbox by some robins.

7. The alarm clock was invented by an American.

8. The pizza restaurant was closed by the health inspector.

9. My telephone was used for a long-distance call by Jana without permission.

10. Many annoying insects, such as mosquitoes, are consumed by spiders.

NONSTANDARD AND STANDARD VERBS

Nonstandard expressions such as *they ain't, we has, I be,* or *he don't* are often part of successful communication among family members and friends. In both college and the working world, however, standard English is widely accepted as the norm for speaking and writing.

The chart below shows both nonstandard and standard forms of the regular verb *like.* Practice using the standard forms in your speech and writing.

	Nonstandard Forms		Standard Forms	
Present Tense	I likes	we likes	I like	we like
	you likes	you likes	you like	you like
	he, she, it like	they likes	he, she, it like**s**	they like
Past Tense	I like	we like	I like**d**	we like**d**
	you like	you like	you like**d**	you like**d**
	he, she, it like	they like	he, she, it like**d**	they like**d**

Notes

1 In standard English, always add *-s* or *-es* to a third-person singular verb in the present tense.

Nonstandard Rex dislike his new job in Utah, and he miss his San Diego friends.

Standard Rex **dislikes** his new job in Utah, and he **misses** his San Diego friends.

2 Always add the ending *-ed* or *-d* to a regular verb to show it is past tense.

Nonstandard As children, Mona and her brother enjoy their piano lessons but hate practicing.

Standard As children, Mona and her brother **enjoyed** their piano lessons but **hated** practicing.

Practice 4

In each blank below, write the standard form of the verb in parentheses.

1. The insects (*swarms, swarm*) ____________ around their heads every time they go to the park.
2. As soon as Sue returned onstage, everyone (*applaud, applauded*) ____________.
3. Sometimes, John (*sleep, sleeps*) ____________ for nine or ten hours at a time.
4. A long time ago, pioneers (*leave, left*) ____________ their homes to cross the frontier.
5. After it rained last week, the sidewalks (*glisten, glistened*) ____________.
6. In spite of the pesky mosquitoes, Dad (*vows, vow*) ____________ to attend every outdoor classical concert the park offers.
7. At dawn, the rooster (*crows, crow*) ____________ and wakes everyone up.
8. Last week, Hannah (*delivers, delivered*) ____________ some beautiful flowers to her mother.
9. Every Saturday, the Tuckers (*makes, make*) ____________ popcorn for their late night snack.
10. Fred (*shuffles, shuffle*) ____________ cards faster than anyone I know.

Name ______________________ Section ____________ Date ____________

Score: (Number right) ______ x 10 = ____________ %

Even More about Verbs: TEST 1

A. In each short passage, there is one illogical shift in verb tense. Cross out the incorrect verb. Then write the correct form of that verb on the line provided.

______________ **1.** All the children love playground time. They go on the merry-go-round, climbed the jungle gym, and play in the sandbox.

______________ **2.** Susanna went to New York last week. She shopped on Fifth Avenue. She saw three different plays on Broadway. She eats at several fine restaurants. Exhausted, she came home at three in the morning happy and broke.

______________ **3.** Lynette wanted the perfect wedding dress. She decided to make it herself. It takes four months from start to finish. She looked lovely on her wedding day.

______________ **4.** Jim started his 10-K race strongly, sailed through the first five miles, and collapses at the finish line.

B. The following sentences are written in the passive voice. In each sentence, underline the verb. Then rewrite the sentence in the active voice, changing the wording as necessary.

5. The soldier was decorated for bravery by his commanding officer.

____

6. Her coffin was lowered slowly into the ground by grandma's eight grandsons.

____

7. The little girl was scolded by her mother.

____

C. In each blank below, write the standard form of the verb in parentheses.

8. The ants (*carries/carried*) ______________ a cube of sugar into the anthill in our backyard.

9. Sara (*frowns/frown*) ______________ a lot, but she really is a happy person overall.

10. After a bad accident, my grandfather (*decide/decided*) ______________ to give up his motorcycle.

Name ______________________________ Section ____________ Date ____________

Score: (Number right) ______ x 10 = __________ %

Even More about Verbs: TEST 2

A. In each short passage, there is **one** illogical shift in verb tense. Cross out the incorrect verb. Then write the correct form of that verb on the line provided.

______________ **1.** As we walked into the department store, a well-dressed woman from the cosmetics department approached us. Before we could protest, she sprays a cloud of musky-smelling perfume in our direction.

______________ **2.** My friends worked at odd jobs this past summer. Carlos worked at a zoo, cleaning out the bird cages. Jenny worked at Pizza Hut. She delivers pizzas every night of the week.

______________ **3.** White flowers blossom on the apple trees every spring. Then tiny green apples appeared. Finally, the apples turn into sweet red fruit.

______________ **4.** On the first Thanksgiving, pilgrims celebrated their survival through the winter. They served many foods, but turkey was not one of them. The menu includes duck, goose, seafood, and eels.

B. Each of the following sentences is written in the passive voice. Rewrite each in the active voice, changing the wording as necessary.

5. Directions to the hotel were provided by a taxi driver.

____

6. The dinner table was always cleared by the children.

____

7. Much air pollution is caused by cars and factories.

____

C. In each blank below, write the standard form of the verb in parentheses.

8. Before he leaves for work each morning, Duncan (*make/makes*) ______________ coffee and pours it into a thermos.

9. When they were teenagers, Kate and Nellie often (*trade/traded*) ______________ secrets.

10. My cat (*know/knows*) ______________ which bedroom window is mine, and he scratches at it to get my attention.

28 More about Run-Ons and Comma Splices

You have already reviewed (on pages 102 and 112) the most common ways of correcting run-on sentences and comma splices:

1 **Use a period and a capital letter.**

2 **Use a comma and a joining word.**

3 **Use a dependent word.**

This section will describe one other method of correction:

ANOTHER METHOD OF CORRECTING A RUN-ON: USE A SEMICOLON

Run-on sentences and comma splices may be corrected by putting a **semicolon (;)** between the two complete thoughts. A semicolon is made up of a period and a comma. It is used between two closely related complete thoughts.

Run-on	The fish was served with its head still on Fred quickly lost his appetite.
Comma splice	The fish was served with its head still on, Fred quickly lost his appetite.
Correct version	The fish was served with its head still on; Fred quickly lost his appetite.

● Practice 1

Draw a line (|) between the two complete thoughts in each run-on or comma splice that follows. Then rewrite the item, using a semicolon to connect the two complete thoughts. Note the example below.

Example The exam was not easy|there were two-hundred multiple-choice items.

The exam was not easy; there were two-hundred multiple-choice items.

1. My friend Jose loves the ocean he really needs to learn to swim.

____

2. Alex fell off the ladder he is very accident-prone.

____

3. I was alone in a dark alley the sound of approaching footsteps made my heart skip a beat.

____

____

4. The neighbor's dog howled all night I didn't get any sleep.

____

5. Noah is the oldest of five children he is even a godfather to his youngest brother.

____

Semicolon with a Transitional Word or Words

A semicolon is sometimes used with a transitional word (or words) and a comma to join two complete thoughts.

Run-on	The fish was served with its head still on as a result, Fred quickly lost his appetite.
Comma splice	The fish was served with its head still on, as a result, Fred quickly lost his appetite.
Correct version	The fish was served with its head still on**; as a result,** Fred quickly lost his appetite.

Below are some common transitional words that may be used when correcting a run-on or comma splice.

Common Transitional Words

afterwards	however	moreover
also	in addition	nevertheless
as a result	in fact	on the other hand
consequently	instead	otherwise
furthermore	meanwhile	therefore

Practice 2

Draw a line between the two complete thoughts in each item. Then write out each sentence using a semicolon to connect the two thoughts.

Example The air is very stale in the library|moreover, the lighting is poor.

The air is very stale in the library; moreover, the lighting is poor.

1. I don't usually like desserts however, this pumpkin pie is delicious.

____

____

2. Our dog barks all the time, as a result, the landlord has refused to renew our lease.

____

____

3. The house needs a new septic system, in addition, it should have a new roof.

____

____

4. I almost never write to my brother however, I call him several times a month.

____

____

5. You should eat a good breakfast otherwise, you'll be out of energy before noon.

____

____

Name ______________________ Section ____________ Date ____________

Score: (Number right) ______ x 20 = ________ %

More about Run-Ons and Comma Splices: TEST 1

Draw a line (|) between the two complete thoughts in each run-on or comma splice. Then rewrite each sentence using a semicolon to connect the two complete thoughts.

1. The cat slept on the windowsill she was wrapped in warm sunlight.

   ____

2. Larry is not a good babysitter he treats his little brother like an insect.

   ____

3. The wind knocked over a ladder the ladder then broke a window.

   ____

4. We decided to leave the restaurant the food was too expensive.

   ____

5. The hammer and saw began to rust, they had been left out in the rain.

   ____

Name ______________________________ Section ______________ Date ______________

Score: (Number right) ________ x 20 = ______________ %

More about Run-Ons and Comma Splices: TEST 2

Draw a line (|) between the two complete thoughts in each run-on or comma splice. Then rewrite each sentence using a semicolon to connect the two complete thoughts. Note that a transitional word or phrase is part of each sentence.

1. I really like Charlie consequently, I want him to be my best man.

   ____

2. I have finished my final exams in addition, I just handed in my last ever research paper.

   ____

3. The light is green therefore, you can cross the street now.

   ____

4. My stomach aches nevertheless, I am not going to the doctor.

   ____

5. Jim just lost his job as a result, he applied for unemployment benefits.

   ____

29 More about Commas

A comma often marks a slight pause, or break, in a sentence. These pauses or breaks occur at the point where one of the six main comma rules applies. When you read a sentence aloud, you can often hear the points where slight pauses occur.

In general, use a comma only when a comma rule applies or when a comma is otherwise needed to help a sentence read clearly.

You have already reviewed (on page 122) three main uses of the comma:

1 **The comma is used to separate three or more items in a series.**

2 **The comma is used to separate introductory material from the rest of the sentence.**

3 **The comma is used between two complete thoughts connected by the joining words** *and, but,* **or** *so.* **(***Or, nor, for,* **and** *yet* **are also joining words.)**

This chapter will consider three other uses of the comma:

4 **Around words that interrupt the flow of a sentence**

5 **For words of direct address and short expressions**

6 **In dates, addresses, and letters**

AROUND WORDS THAT INTERRUPT THE FLOW OF A SENTENCE

Sentences sometimes contain material that interrupts the flow of thought. Such words and word groups should be set off from the rest of the sentence by commas. For example:

- Our minivan, **which has stickers from every state we've visited**, seems like part of the family.

If you read this sentence out loud, you can hear that the words *which has stickers from every state we've visited* interrupt the flow of thought.

Here are some other examples of sentences with interrupters:

- Liza, **who was wearing a new dress**, yelled at the waiter who spilled wine on her.
- The waiter, **however**, was not very apologetic.
- The restaurant manager, **afraid that Liza might cause a scene**, rushed to help.

More about Interrupters

A word group that identifies another word in the sentence is not an interrupter. It is needed for the full meaning of the sentence and should not be set off with commas.* For instance, consider the boldfaced words in the following sentences:

- The man **who came to the party with Joy** says he was kidnapped by aliens.
- Harvey, **who came to the party with Joy,** says he was kidnapped by aliens.

*Grammar books sometimes refer to interrupters as "nonrestrictive elements" and essential descriptions as "restrictive elements."

In the first sentence, the boldfaced words are needed to identify the man. Without them, we would not know who said he was kidnapped by aliens. Such essential words are not interrupters and should not be set off with commas. In the second sentence, however, we know who said he was kidnapped by aliens even without the boldfaced words. (It was Harvey.) In that case, the boldfaced words are not essential to the main message of the sentence. So in the second sentence, *who came to the party with Joy* is an interrupter and should be set off by commas.

To find out whether a word group is an interrupter, try reading the sentence without it. The first sentence above would then read: "The man says he was kidnapped by aliens." This version makes us ask, "Which man?" The boldfaced words are essential to answer that question. If we read the second sentence without the boldfaced words, we would not be omitting essential information: "Harvey says he was kidnapped by aliens."

Practice 1

Four of the following five sentences contain interrupters. Insert commas around the interrupting word groups. One sentence includes a word group that provides essential information and should not be enclosed by commas.

1. Penguins' wings which are short and thick are not designed for flight.
2. King Arthur according to legend will return some day to rule Britain.
3. Our basketball coach it is rumored is about to be fired.
4. The woman who sat in front of me at the concert was wearing strong perfume.
5. Grandfather likes to joke that his hometown which has only one traffic light and two gas stations could be missed if a traveler blinked.

Practice 2

Write three sentences using the suggested interrupters. Add words both before and after the interrupting words. Then add the necessary commas.

1. Use the words *who borrowed my car last fall* in the middle of a sentence.

2. Use the words *now sagging in the middle* in the middle of a sentence.

3. Use the words *which is not on my diet* in the middle of a sentence.

FOR WORDS OF DIRECT ADDRESS AND SHORT EXPRESSIONS

For words of direct address: Use commas to set off names or other words used to address directly the person or people being spoken to.

- You, Mr. Gimble, are the lucky winner of a ballpoint pen.
- Ladies and gentlemen, the sword-swallower is unable to perform tonight due to a bad sore throat.

For short expressions: Use commas to set off words such as *well, yes, no,* and *oh.*

- No, you cannot have a raise.
- Well, I thought I would at least ask.

IN DATES, ADDRESSES, AND LETTERS

Within a date: Place commas after the day of the week (if used), the date, and the year.

- Friday, October 13, 2003, was the date of the wedding.
- On March 7, 1876, Alexander Graham Bell received a patent for the telephone.

In an address within a sentence: Place a comma after each part of the address except between the state and the ZIP code.

- Send your comments about *English Essentials: What Everyone Needs to Know about Grammar, Punctuation, and Usage* to Townsend Press, 1038 Industrial Drive, West Berlin, NJ 08091-9164.

In informal letters: Place a comma after the opening and closing.

- Dear Grandma,
- With love,
- Fondly,

Note In business letters, a colon is used after the opening, but a comma is still used after the closing.

- Dear Mr. Cramer:
- Dear Homeowner:
- Yours truly,

Practice 3

Insert commas where needed **(a)** to set off words of direct address and short expressions and **(b)** in dates and addresses.

1. I was married on August 29, 2005, in New Mexico.
2. Susie, where have you been?
3. You know how to dance, Fred, and how to play the ukulele.
4. Darn, the rain has started.
5. He used to live at 20 Parks Lane, Phoenix, Arizona 09090.

Practice 4

Complete each sentence as indicated, inserting commas where needed.

1. ____ is my home address.
   (Fill in your address.)

2. ____ is the date that I was born.
   (Fill in your complete date of birth.)

3. Dear ________________________
   Meet me at the fountain in the mall tomorrow.

   ____
   Marco

   (Complete the heading of the above letter with the word *Susan,* and add as a closing the word *Sincerely.*)

Another use of the comma is to set off direct quotations from the rest of a sentence, as explained in "Quotation Marks" on page 143.

Name ______________________________ Section ______________ Date ______________

Score: (Number right) ________ x 10 = ____________ %

More about Commas: TEST 1

On the lines provided, write the word or words in each sentence that need to be followed by a comma. Include each missing comma as well.

1. The monkeys languishing on the rocks were falling asleep.

   ____

2. The last man in line fidgeting and sighing was finally able to get his blood test.

   ____

3. In spite of your explanation Marge I am still angry with you.

   ____

4. When you send the letter to 1733 Wilson Avenue Cheyenne WY 82009 an answer should come within four days.

   ____

5. Yuck the vegetables are burned.

   ____

6. Oh I have forgotten my appointment with Mr. Leonard.

   ____

7. My plane will arrive on March 27 2008 in London.

   ____

8. Chuck and Louise who were married in 2003 are a lovely couple.

   ____

9. I am so sorry Ernie for my rude remarks yesterday.

   ____

10. It is wrong my fellow Americans to disparage your country.

   ____

Name ______________________ Section ____________ Date ____________

Score: (Number right) ______ x 10 = ________ %

More about Commas: TEST 2

In each space, write the letter of the **one** comma rule that applies to the sentence. Then insert one or more commas where they belong in the sentence.

a Around interrupting words
b To set off words of direct address and short expressions
c In dates, addresses, and letters

_____ **1.** I'm sorry sir but the diner is now closing.

_____ **2.** This coffee shop my friends is a nonsmoking area.

_____ **3.** I'm already planning my fiftieth birthday party for Friday March 6 2035 at Disney World.

_____ **4.** No you may not have a third piece of chocolate cake.

_____ **5.** The campers unused to the silence of the forest found it hard to sleep.

_____ **6.** Eric jokingly gave his address as 25 Main Street Elmhurst Illinois North America Planet Earth.

_____ **7.** Our final exam will be given on Wednesday June 2.

_____ **8.** Yes I have dated both Louise and her sister.

_____ **9.** Diamonds the most expensive jewels on Earth are closely related to lumps of coal.

_____ **10.** Many visitors take the tour of the NBC Studios at 3000 Alameda Avenue Burbank California.

30 More about Apostrophes

REVIEW OF THE APOSTROPHE IN POSSESSIVES

To show that something belongs to someone, we could say, for example, the iPad owned by Rita. But it's much simpler to say:

- *Rita's iPad*

To make most nouns possessive, add an apostrophe plus an *s*. To help you decide which word to make possessive, ask yourself the following:

1 What is owned?

2 Who is the owner?

Then put the apostrophe plus an *s* after the name of the owner. **Here's an example:**

What is owned? *The iPad*
Who is the owner? *Rita*

When an apostrophe plus an *s* is added to the name of the owner, the result is the possessive form of the word: *Rita's*. That word is then followed by what is owned: *Rita's iPad.*

Here is another example:

- the waiting room belonging to the doctor

Again, ask yourself, "What is owned?" The answer is *waiting room.* Then ask, "Who is the owner?" The answer is *the doctor.* So add an apostrophe plus *s* after the name of the owner and add what is owned: *the doctor's waiting room.* The apostrophe plus *s* shows that the waiting room belongs to the doctor.

Here is a third example:

- the hopes of everyone

Again, ask yourself, "What is owned?" The answer is *hopes.* Then ask, "Who is the owner?" The answer is *everyone.* So add an apostrophe plus *s* after the name of the owner and add what is owned: *everyone's hopes.* The apostrophe plus *s* shows that the hopes belong to everyone.

Practice 1

Rewrite the items below as possessives with an apostrophe plus *s.* In the first column, write the name of the owner. In the second column, write the possessive form plus what is owned.

	Who is the owner?	*Possessive form plus what is owned*
1. the hand belonging to Soren	______________	________________________
2. the pain of Louise	______________	________________________
3. the knees of our neighbors	______________	________________________
4. the claws of the lion	______________	________________________
5. the mother of the child	______________	________________________

Practice 2

Underline the word in each sentence that needs an apostrophe plus *s*. That word is the owner. Then write the word correctly, along with what is owned, in the space provided.

1. I found my brother car keys. ______________________
2. Philadelphia Liberty Bell is seen by millions each year. ______________________
3. The king crown weighs over ten pounds. ______________________
4. The child blocks were scattered all over the floor. ______________________
5. The family house was demolished by a hurricane. ______________________

Practice 3

Write three sentences that include words ending in an apostrophe plus *s*.

1. ____

____

2. ____

____

3. ____

____

Showing Possession with Singular and Plural Nouns That End in *s*

An apostrophe plus *s* is used to show possession even with a singular noun that already ends in *s:*

- Gus'**s** computer (the computer belonging to Gus)
- The boss'**s** secretary (the secretary belonging to the boss)

However, an apostrophe alone is used to show possession with a plural noun that ends in s:

- the contestants**'** answers (the answers of a number of contestants)
- the three lawyers**'** office (the office belonging to three lawyers)

Practice 4

Underline the word that needs an apostrophe in each sentence below. Then write that word, adding the **'** or the **'s** in the space provided.

______________ 1. Adam carefully removed the fishhook from the bass mouth.

______________ 2. The lions keeper has worked with them from birth.

______________ 3. Otis story about being kidnapped by a flying saucer is hard to believe.

______________ 4. The twins mother was a twin herself.

______________ 5. The Olsons home has a secret passageway.

WHEN *NOT* TO USE AN APOSTROPHE

Do *NOT* Use an Apostrophe in Plurals and with Verbs

People sometimes confuse possessive and plural forms of nouns. Remember that a plural is formed simply by adding an *s* to a noun; no apostrophe is used. Look at the sentence below to see which words are plural and which word is possessive:

- Lola's necklace has pearls and diamond chips.

The words *pearls* and *chips* are plurals—there is more than one pearl, and there is more than one diamond chip. But *Lola's*, the word with the apostrophe plus *s*, is possessive. Lola owns the necklace.

Also, many verbs end with an *s*. Do not use an apostrophe in a verb.

- Jenny **plays** poker once a week.
- She often **wins**.

Practice 5

In the spaces provided under each sentence, correctly write the one word that needs an apostrophe. Also, explain why the other word or words ending in *s* do not get apostrophes.

Example The patients eyes opened slowly after surgery.

patients: patient's, meaning "belonging to the patient"

eyes: eyes, meaning "more than one eye"

1. The reindeers noses sniff the cookies left for Santa Claus.

   reindeers: ______________________

   noses: ______________________

   cookies: ______________________

2. The ladders were left at the work site by the companys crew.

   ladders: ______________________

   companys ______________________

3. Ron knows his mothers passwords for her computer.

   knows: ______________________

   mothers: ______________________

   passwords: ______________________

4. Toys and clothes were needed for the churchs fundraiser.

   Toys: ______________________

   clothes: ______________________

   churchs: ______________________

5. Trends are affected by young peoples thoughts, actions, and desires.

   Trends: ______________________________

   peoples: ______________________________

   thoughts: ______________________________

   actions: ______________________________

   desires: ______________________________

Do *NOT* Use an Apostrophe with Possessive Pronouns

Do not use an apostrophe in the possessive pronouns *his, hers, its, yours, ours, theirs,* and *whose.*

- Those seats are **ours**.
- **His** car is purple.

People often confuse certain possessive pronouns with contractions. For instance, *its* is often confused with *it's*. The following sentence includes both words:

- **It's** sad that our old tree is losing **its** leaves.

The word *it's* is a contraction meaning *it is.* Contractions, of course, do have apostrophes. *Its* means *belonging to it*—the leaves belong to it (the tree). *Its* is a possessive pronoun and does not have an apostrophe.

Following are examples of other possessive pronouns and the contractions they are confused with.

- The Pratts rarely mow **their** lawn. **They're** not concerned about the looks of the neighborhood.
  Their means *belonging to them* (the lawn belongs to them). *They're* is a contraction that means *they are.*
- **You're** going to fall if you do not tie **your** shoelaces.
  You're is a contraction that means *you are. Your* means *belonging to you* (the shoelaces belong to you).
- **Who's** the person **whose** car is blocking ours?
  Who's is a contraction meaning *who is. Whose* means *belonging to whom* (the car belonging to whom).

Practice 6

Underline the correct word within each pair of parentheses.

1. We arranged with two neighborhood boys to mow our lawn, but now (*they're/their*) father tells me (*they're/their*) going to camp for a month.
2. Darryl told his son, "If (*you're/your*) homework is not done by seven o'clock, (*you're/your*) not going to watch the movie."
3. (*Who's/Whose*) turn is it to wash the dishes, and (*who's/whose*) going to dry them?
4. (*It's/Its*) difficult, if not impossible, to get toothpaste back into (*it's/its*) tube.
5. The fruit salad on the table is (*hers'/hers*), and the freshly baked bread is (*ours'/ours*).

Name ______________________ Section ____________ Date ____________

Score: (Number right) ______ x 10 = ________ %

More about Apostrophes: TEST 1

Each of the sentences below contains **one** word that needs an apostrophe. Write the word, with its apostrophe, in the space provided.

1. She doesnt want to go to the park today.

____

2. Where is Mollys missing jacket?

____

3. The cars screeching brakes could be heard from two blocks away.

____

4. Some patients were waiting for over two hours in the doctors office.

____

5. The old computers monitor was too heavy to carry.

____

6. Sundays television schedule is published on Friday.

____

7. Frank plays cards every night, but he swears hes not an addict.

____

8. Who is in charge of the committees schedule?

____

9. "Shell be coming round the mountain when she comes" is a famous song lyric.

____

10. Rays temper caused him to lose someone who loved him very much.

____

Name ______________________________ Section ____________ Date ____________

Score: (Number right) ______ x 10 = ____________ %

More about Apostrophes: TEST 2

Each of the sentences below contains **one** word that needs an apostrophe. Write the word, with its apostrophe, in the space provided.

1. We didnt recognize our teacher at first without his beard.

   ____

2. Both of Janes husbands were named Andrew.

   ____

3. Half-finished paintings filled the artists studio.

   ____

4. Someone will be taking in our mail while were away on vacation.

   ____

5. Floridas neighbors are Alabama and Georgia.

   ____

6. The snowflakes glittered in the flashlights glare.

   ____

7. The farmers may lose their entire wheat crop if it doesnt rain soon.

   ____

8. Someday Ill tell you about the day Uncle Harry was chased by some mad chickens.

   ____

9. The two brothers relationship has remained strong through the years.

   ____

10. The film reviewers were careful not to give away the movies surprise ending.

    ____

31 More about Quotation Marks

REVIEW OF QUOTATIONS WITH SPLIT SENTENCES

In a direct quotation, one sentence may be split into two parts:

- "Add the eggs to the sauce," said the TV chef, "blending them together."

Note that the chef's exact words are set off by two sets of quotation marks. The words *said the TV chef* are not included in the quotation marks since they were not spoken by the chef.

The words *blending them together* begin with a small letter because they are a continuation of a sentence, not a new sentence. (The full sentence spoken by the chef is "Add the eggs to the sauce, blending them together.")

Commas are used to set off the quoted parts from the rest of the sentence:

- "Add the eggs to the sauce," said the TV chef, "blending them together."

QUOTATIONS OF MORE THAN ONE SENTENCE

A direct quotation can be divided into separate sentences:

- "I really hate my job," Stan told his wife. "I think I'd better start looking for a new one."

The words *Stan told his wife* are not part of the direct quotation.

At times, a direct quotation will be more than one sentence:

- Our minister always says, "It's every citizen's responsibility to vote. If you don't vote, you shouldn't complain."

Note that only one pair of quotation marks is used. Do not use quotation marks for each new sentence as long as the quotation is not interrupted.

Practice 1

Insert quotation marks where needed in the following sentences.

1. The wait for a table, said the restaurant hostess, will be about forty minutes.
2. I don't mind if you borrow my new sweater, said my sister, but I don't expect to find it rolled up in a ball under your bed.
3. The newspaper editor said to the new reporter, I'm sorry to have to tell you this. I can't use the article that you spent two weeks writing.
4. Why don't you go to the grocery store, suggested Sara, and pick up some steaks for us to grill tonight.
5. Our math teacher is unfair, complained James. He assigns four hours of homework for each class. Does he think we have nothing else to do?

QUOTATIONS WITH QUESTION MARKS AND EXCLAMATION POINTS

If a direct quotation is a question, place the question mark within the quotation marks:

- "Where are my red shoes?" asked Lana.

  After a question mark, no comma is used to set off the direct quotation.

If the entire sentence is a question, place the question mark after the quotation marks:

- Did you say "Thank you"?

An exclamation point also goes within quotation marks unless it applies to the whole sentence.

- The kids shouted, "Let's go to the pool!"

INDIRECT QUOTATIONS

Often we express someone's spoken or written thoughts without repeating the exact words used. When we use an **indirect quotation**, we put the message into our own words. Indirect quotations do not require quotation marks.

The following example shows how the same material could be handled as either a direct or an indirect quotation.

Direct Quotation

- The baker said, **"I forgot** to put yeast in the dough."

  The words *I forgot* tell us that the baker's exact words are being used—he's referring to himself. Since his exact words are being used, they must be put in quotation marks.

Indirect Quotation

- The baker said **that he had forgotten** to put yeast in the dough.

  The sentence refers to the baker as *he,* so we know that the baker's exact words are not being quoted. Quotation marks are not used for indirect quotations. The word *that* often signals an indirect quotation.

Here are a few more examples of indirect quotations:

- The boss said that workers could have a day off on their birthdays.
- Mom told us not to answer the front door.
- The park rangers warned us to keep our windows closed.

Practice 2

Rewrite each of the following indirect quotations as a direct quotation. The direct quotation will include the words that someone actually spoke.

Note that you will have to change some of the words as well as add capital letters, quotation marks, and any other punctuation needed.

1. The man asked me if I knew the way to regent's park.

____

____

2. The man cautioned us that a hurricane was on its way.

____

____

3. The manager of the team warned his players that the game could be lost if they did not play their best.

____

____

4. My brother said that he would loan me his car if I brought it back by ten o'clock.

____

____

5. The store clerk asked if I wanted any help.

____

____

QUOTATION MARKS FOR TITLES OF SHORT WORKS

Use quotation marks to set off the titles of short stories, newspaper or magazine articles, songs, poems, episodes of TV series, book chapters, and other parts of longer works.

- Our teacher assigned the short story "The Open Boat" by Stephen Crane.
- The familiar song "For He's a Jolly Good Fellow" is over two hundred years old.
- The witty poet Ogden Nash wrote a poem titled "Never Mind the Overcoat, Button Up That Lip."

Note The titles of longer works, such as books, newspapers, magazines, plays, movies, TV series, and record albums, should be underlined when handwritten. When typed on a computer, such titles should appear in *italic type.*

- Our assignment was to read the chapter titled "The Traits of Happy People" in a book by David Meyers, The Pursuit of Happiness.
- "Three Words That Can Change Your Life" was the first article I turned to in the current issue of Reader's Digest.

Practice 3

Insert quotation marks or underlines where needed in the sentences below.

1. The chapter titled Extrasensory Perception in the textbook Psychology Today says there is no evidence that ESP actually exists.
2. The article Policing the Police in Newsweek magazine is about good cops who go bad.
3. The beloved song Over the Rainbow was first heard in the movie The Wizard of Oz.
4. The editor of the Daily Tribune has received many letters supporting and opposing her editorial Let's Ban Proms in Schools.

Name ______________________ Section ____________ Date ____________

Score: (Number right) ______ x 10 = ____________ %

More about Quotation Marks: TEST 1

Add opening and closing quotation marks where needed. One sentence does not need quotation marks.

1. Somebody has stuck gum all over my computer keyboard, Coco said angrily.
2. One lucky caller wins a trip to Disneyland, the radio announcer promised.
3. I bought a truck, Julie stated, because I sit higher and feel safer.
4. When you see me next, laughed the brunette, I'll be a blonde.
5. The racecar driver said he wanted a quart of milk waiting for him at the finish line.
6. More Children Alone is the title of a recent article in the New York Times.
7. An hour after lunch, Rudy said, I'm starving. I hope dinner will be ready soon.
8. The park ranger said, Watch out for ticks.
9. I need to move back home, said Wally to his parents.
10. The Monopoly card that I drew said, Do not pass Go. Do not collect $200.

Name ______________________ Section ____________ Date ____________

Score: (Number right) ______ x 10 = ________ %

More about Quotation Marks: TEST 2

On the lines provided, rewrite the following sentences, adding quotation marks as needed. One sentence does not need quotation marks.

1. The billboard had a very stern message that read, You will die an early death if you continue to smoke. Worse yet, your loved ones might die.

   ____

   ____

2. After you finish your writing assignment, the teacher stated, you must do silent reading for one half hour.

   ____

   ____

3. I'd love to come to your party, Cheryl told her neighbor, but I have made previous plans.

   ____

   ____

4. Alfred, Lord Tennyson, once said, I am part of all that I have met.

   ____

   ____

5. I am tired of reality TV, my friend Casey said. I would love to watch a good documentary.

   ____

   ____

6. I once read an anonymous quotation that said Choose hope. I have tried to live by that idea ever since.

   ____

   ____

7. Everyone at the party asked me if I was all right after my painful breakup.

   ____

   ____

Name ______________________ Section ____________ Date ____________

Score: (Number right) ______ x 10 = ________ %

8. I want us to be together forever. Will you marry me? replied my boyfriend when I asked him if he loved me.

____

____

9. Celebrity Divorce Battles is the name of a recent tabloid article.

____

____

10. My mother always said to me, If you aren't beautiful, you just have to smile a little harder.

____

____

32 More about Homonyms

You have already reviewed a number of common homonyms (words that sound alike). This section describes some other homonyms as well as other confusing words.

OTHER HOMONYMS

buy to purchase
by (1) close to; (2) no later than; (3) through the action of

- **Buy** furniture from Sofas Inc. **by** the end of the year, and you won't have to pay until March.

Spelling hint I'd like to b**u**y something for **U**.

Fill in each blank with either *buy* or *by.*

1. Why must you ____________ such expensive designer jeans?
2. The beautiful mural in the lobby was painted ____________ a student.
3. An old dog was sleeping on the front porch ____________ the screen door.
4. We have to turn in our research papers ____________ the end of the month.
5. My sister is hoping to ____________ a home of her own this year.

passed (the past tense of *pass*) (1) handed to; (2) went by; (3) completed successfully
past (1) the time before the present; (2) by

- In the **past,** I have **passed** all my courses, but I may not pass them all this semester.

Spelling hint If you need a verb, use ***passed.*** The *-ed* at its end shows it is the past tense of the verb *pass.*

Fill in each blank with either *passed* or *past.*

1. Only five minutes have ____________ since I last looked at the clock.
2. A bumblebee just flew ____________ my head.
3. Mick ____________ his driver's test on the third try.
4. Unfortunately, one of the cars that Marylou ____________ on the highway was a police car.
5. Life was not always as carefree in the ____________ as some people would like to believe.

principal (1) main; (2) the person in charge of a school
principle a guideline or rule

- Our **principal** believes in the **principle** of giving teachers a great deal of freedom.

Spelling hint Ideally, a school princi**pal** should be a **pal**.

Fill in each blank with either *principal* or *principle.*

1. My aunt is the _______________ owner of a beauty shop on Mill Avenue.
2. I try to live by the _______________ of treating others as I want to be treated.
3. Mr. Larson became _______________ of Coles High School after teaching there for years.
4. The _______________ reason the Butlers are moving to California is to be near their grandchildren.
5. Our basketball coach taught us to follow the _______________ of being gracious in defeat as well as in victory.

OTHER CONFUSING WORDS

Here are some words that are not homonyms but are still confusing words. In most cases, they have similar sounds and are often misused and misspelled.

a used before words that begin with a consonant sound

an used before words that begin with a vowel or a silent *h* (as in *an hour*).

- Would you like **an** ice-cream cone or **a** shake?

Fill in each blank with either *a* or *an.*

1. __________ insect has six legs and a three-part body.
2. I left __________ note on the kitchen counter saying when I'd be back.
3. Is that __________ alligator you are petting in that photograph?
4. A hush fell over the circus audience when __________ tightrope walker fell.
5. Although she worked hard, Louise was shocked to receive such __________ honor as "Worker of the Year."

accept (1) to receive; (2) to agree to take; (3) to believe in

except (1) excluding or leaving out; (2) but

- All the employees **except** the part-timers were willing to **accept** the new contract.

Fill in each blank with either *accept* or *except.*

1. Mrs. Carlotti says she will ____________ an appointment to the school board.
2. My daughter likes all types of food ____________ meat, fish, dairy products, and vegetables.
3. Whatever your decision is, I will ____________ it.
4. All of my relatives attended our family reunion ____________ for an elderly aunt.
5. At the company dinner, Meredith will ____________ the award on behalf of her department.

advice opinion meant to be helpful
advise to give an opinion meant to be helpful

● Never take the **advice** of someone who **advises** you to act against your conscience.

Fill in each blank with either *advice* or *advise.*

1. "I ____________ you to replace your fan belt," the gas station attendant said.
2. Don't seek ____________ from anybody you don't admire.
3. Employment experts ____________ people to get training throughout their lives.
4. There's so much conflicting ____________ about diet that it's no wonder people are confused about what they should eat.
5. My son's kindergarten teacher said the best ____________ she could give parents is to read regularly to their children.

affect to influence
effect a result

● Divorce **affects** an entire family, and its **effects**—both good and bad—last for years.

Fill in each blank with either *affect* or *effect.*

1. Your actions ____________ those around you, whether you're aware of it or not.
2. The child spattered red paint on the paper and then stepped back to admire the ____________.
3. According to psychologists, the colors of the clothes we wear ____________ our moods.
4. What will be the economic ____________s if the factory closes?
5. The referees did not allow the obnoxious behavior of some fans to ____________ their decisions.

desert (1) a verb meaning "to leave or abandon"; (2) a noun meaning "a dry region with little or no plant growth"
dessert a sweet course eaten at the end of a meal

● The children were willing to **desert** the TV set only when **dessert** was served.

Fill in each blank with either *desert* or *dessert.*

1. For me, a real ____________ must contain chocolate.
2. As a result of irrigation, this area is now farmland instead of ____________.
3. What causes a parent to ____________ his or her children?
4. If I'm not very hungry, I skip the meal and eat ____________.
5. Certain medications can make your mouth feel as dry as a ____________.

fewer used for items that can be counted
less used for general amounts

● As our congregation ages, our church is left with **fewer** members and **less** financial support.

Fill in each blank with either *fewer* or *less.*

1. By the 1920s, there were ____________ horses and more cars on the road.
2. When I get too little sleep, I have ____________ patience than usual.
3. Whose car had ____________ miles on it, yours or Carl's?
4. Two-percent milk has ____________ fat in it than whole milk.
5. Two-percent milk also contains ____________ calories.

loose (1) not tight; (2) free; not confined
lose (1) to misplace; (2) to not win; (3) to be deprived of something one has had

● If you don't fix that **loose** steering wheel, you could **lose** control of your car.

Fill in each blank with either *loose* or *lose.*

1. I ____________ my keys at least once a week.
2. A ____________ shutter was banging against the side of the house.
3. I always ____________ when I play chess against my computer.
4. Clyde was warned that he would ____________ his job if he were late to work one more time.
5. In our town, it's illegal to allow cats and dogs to run ____________.

quiet (1) silent; (2) relaxing and peaceful
quite (1) truly; (2) very; (3) completely
quit (1) to stop doing something; (2) to resign from one's job

● Giselle was **quiet** after saying she might want to **quit** her job but that she wasn't **quite** sure.

Fill in each blank with either *quiet, quite,* or *quit.*

1. The rain had frozen, and the roads were ____________ slippery.
2. Let's spend a ____________ evening at home tonight.
3. The waitress began to take my dish, but I wasn't ____________ finished.
4. My speech teacher told me to ____________ saying the word *like* so much, but, like, what's wrong with that word?
5. We had enjoyed the glitter and noisy excitement of Las Vegas, but we were glad to be back home in our ____________ little town.

than a word used in comparisons
then (1) at that time; (2) next

- First Dad proved he was a better wrestler **than** I am; **then** he helped me improve.

Fill in each blank with either *than* or *then.*

1. I scrubbed the potatoes, and ____________ I poked fork holes in them.
2. Crossword puzzles are more difficult ____________ word searches.
3. My parents were born in the 1960s. There were no cell phones or Web sites ____________.
4. Every eligible voter should learn about the candidates and ____________ go and vote.
5. The tiny family-owned shop is always more crowded ____________ the huge supermarket.

use to make use of
used (to) accustomed to or in the habit of

- I am **used to** very spicy food, but when I cook for others, I **use** much less hot pepper.

Spelling hint Do not forget to include the *d* with *used to.*

Fill in each blank with either *use* or *used.*

1. After spending six years in Alaska, I am ____________ to cold weather.
2. Should I ____________ a paste or liquid wax on the car?
3. After you get married, will you ____________ your husband's last name?
4. Since she is the youngest of four girls, Elaine is ____________ to wearing hand-me-downs.
5. Because you ____________ the cell phone all day, you should recharge the battery.

were the past tense of *are*
we're contraction of *we are*

- **We're** going to visit the town in Florida where my grandparents **were** born.

Fill in each blank with either *were* or *we're.*

1. Where ____________ you when I needed you?
2. ____________ having a quiz on Friday.
3. Our relatives ____________ not surprised to hear of my brother's divorce.
4. I don't think ____________ going to have to wait more than five minutes to get seated.
5. The Beatles ____________ once known as Long John and the Silver Beatles.

Name ______________________ Section ____________ Date ____________

Score: (Number right) ______ x 5 = ____________ %

More about Homonyms: TEST 1

In the space provided, write the word that correctly fits each sentence.

use, used ***than, then***	**1.** I am more ______________ to eating healthily ______________ when my children were at home.
loose, lose ***than, then***	**2.** I prefer wearing ______________, comfortable clothing during the day, ______________ tight, sexy clothes at night.
principal, principle ***a, an***	**3.** The ______________ of our school is ______________ former professional football player.
we're, were ***a, an***	**4.** We ______________ very sad to have ______________ family friend die unexpectedly last week.
past, passed ***quiet, quite, quit***	**5.** Our friend drank too much at a party, ______________ out, and vowed, the next day, to ______________ forever.
less, fewer ***less, fewer***	**6.** I have ______________ headaches now that I drink ______________ coffee.
effects, affects ***loose, lose***	**7.** A thunderstorm really ______________ my mood, especially when I ______________ sleep during one.
principal, principle ***quiet, quite, quit***	**8.** The ______________ payment is ______________ higher than the later installments.
advice, advise ***except, accept***	**9.** Experts ______________ people to pay down their credit card balances, ______________ when they cannot pay their basic living expenses.
by, buy ***use, used***	**10.** I wanted to ______________ a new car, but I was not sure I would ______________ it enough to make it worthwhile.

Name ______________________ Section ____________ Date ____________

Score: (Number right) ________ x 5 = ____________ %

More about Homonyms: TEST 2

In the space provided, write the word that correctly fits each sentence.

were, we're ***a, an***	**1.** Tomorrow ______________ going to buy ______________ computer for Mom.
dessert, desert ***than, then***	**2.** Gina would rather hike in the ______________ ______________ in the mountains.
advice, advise ***lose, loose***	**3.** Some of the best ______________ I ever got was this: "When you ______________ your temper, count to ten before you speak."
then, than ***desert, dessert***	**4.** First we'll have salad, ______________ a main course, and finally ______________.
were, we're ***loose, lose***	**5.** Because ______________ going to be traveling in a hot climate, I packed clothes that were ______________ and cool.
quite, quit, quiet ***affects, effects***	**6.** Some medications, unfortunately, have ______________ a few unpleasant side ______________.
fewer, less ***passed, past***	**7.** More than half of today's college students are female; far ______________ women went to college in the ______________.
quit, quiet, quiet ***lose, loose***	**8.** The boy was a poor sport who would ______________ the game early if he saw he was going to ______________.
advise, advice ***accept, except***	**9.** Even though the job doesn't pay much now, I strongly ______________ you to ______________ it. It's a wonderful opportunity.
principal, principle ***than, then***	**10.** Until my graduation, I had never seen our ______________ wearing anything other ______________ a suit and tie.

33 More about Capital Letters

Other Rules for Capital Letters

You have already reviewed (on page 163) the following uses of capital letters:

1. **The first word in a sentence or direct quotation**
2. **The word "I" and people's names**
3. **Names of specific places, institutions, and languages**
4. **Product names**
5. **Calendar items**
6. **Titles**

This chapter will consider other uses of capitals:

7. **Capitalize a word that is used as a substitute for the name of a family member. Also, capitalize words like *aunt*, *uncle*, and *cousin* when they are used as part of people's names.**

- My biggest fan at the dirt-bike competitions was Mom.
- Go help Grandfather carry those heavy bags.
- Phil is staying at Uncle Raymond's house for the holidays.

BUT Do not capitalize words such as *mom* or *grandfather* when they come after possessive words such as *my*, *her*, or *our*.

- My grandmother lives next door to my parents.
- Phil and his uncle are both recovered alcoholics.

8. **Capitalize the names of specific groups: races, religions, nationalities, companies, clubs, and other organizations.**

- Edward, who is Polish American, sometimes cooks Chinese dishes for his Northside Chess Club meetings.
- Arlene, the local president of Mothers Against Drunk Driving, is a part-time real estate agent for Century 21.

9. **Capitalize the names of specific school courses.**

- This semester, Jody has Dance 101, General Psychology, and Economics 235.

BUT The names of general subject areas are not capitalized.

- This semester, Jody has a gym class, a psychology course, and a business course.

10 **Capitalize the names of specific periods and famous events in history.**

- During the Middle Ages, only the nobility and the clergy could read and write.
- The act of protest in which 342 tea chests were thrown into the ocean came to be known as the Boston Tea Party.

11 **Capitalize the opening and closing of a letter.**

Capitalize words in the salutation of a letter.

- Dear Ms. Axelrod:
- Dear Sir or Madam:

Capitalize only the first word of the closing of a letter.

- Sincerely yours,
- Yours truly,

12 **Capitalize common abbreviations made up of the first letters of the words they represent:**

- IBM
- ABC
- FBI
- AIDS
- UFO
- NASA
- NAACP

Name ______________________ Section ____________ Date ____________

Score: (Number right) ______ x 5 = ____________ %

More about Capital Letters: TEST 1

Underline the **two** words that need capitalizing in each sentence. Then write those words correctly in the spaces provided.

1. Dear sir: Please tell me who played the character aunt Bea on the old *Andy Griffith Show.*
Sincerely yours,
Clint Hart

______________ ______________

2. In today's history 201 class, we learned about the founding of the naacp.

______________ ______________

3. All Vietnam war veterans are invited to this Friday's ceremony at the vfw hall.

______________ ______________

4. During the period known as the dark ages, the rate of literacy fell in Europe.

______________ ______________

5. My mother is Mexican and a baptist, while my dad is italian and a Catholic.

______________ ______________

6. When grandma retired from Blooming valley Nursery, her employers gave her a dozen rose bushes.

______________ ______________

7. Dear aunt Sally,
Thank you so much for your generous birthday check. I can certainly put it to good use!
with love,
Rachel

______________ ______________

8. Uncle Leonardo is active in the local sons of italy social club.

______________ ______________

9. In our offices at townsend Press, we have Internet service through aol.

______________ ______________

10. The Art league of Middletown is sponsoring a show of paintings by the artist known as grandma Moses.

______________ ______________

Name ______________________ Section ______________ Date ______________

Score: (Number right) ______ x 5 = ______________ %

More about Capital Letters: TEST 2

Underline the **two** words that need capitalizing in each sentence. Then write those words correctly in the spaces provided.

1. The civil war was a great tragedy because Americans were killing each other.

______________ ______________

2. My english writing class and my chemistry 101 class both have very strict teachers.

______________ ______________

3. The harlem renaissance produced some great poets.

______________ ______________

4. Dear madam:
I regret to inform you that your lease will not be renewed.
best,
Luke Rielding

______________ ______________

5. He joined the Bull moose party, originally founded by Theodore Roosevelt.

______________ ______________

6. The United auto workers became a union before my grandfather John was born.

______________ ______________

7. Our german shepherd is very gentle, but dad just does not like her.

______________ ______________

8. Martin Luther King's I have a dream speech has been heard and read by millions of people all around the world.

______________ ______________

9. The Cooper River bridge run is the first Saturday in April in Charleston, South Carolina.

______________ ______________

10. The state of California has a large population of mexican americans.

____

PART THREE Proofreading

PART THREE
Proofreading

PREVIEW

Part Three describes how to proofread and includes ten practice tests:

34 Proofreading

Basics about Proofreading

An important step in becoming a good writer is learning to proofread. When you proofread, you check the next-to-final draft of a paper for grammar, punctuation, and other mistakes. Such mistakes are ones you did not find and fix in earlier drafts of a paper because you were working on content.

All too often, students skip the key step of proofreading in their rush to hand in a paper. As a result, their writing may contain careless errors that leave a bad impression and result in a lower grade. This chapter explains how to proofread effectively and suggests a sequence to follow when proofreading. The chapter also provides a series of practices to improve your proofreading skills.

HOW TO PROOFREAD

1 Proofreading is a special kind of reading that should not be rushed. Don't try to proofread a paper minutes before it is due. If you do, you are likely to see what you intended to write, not what is actually on the page. Instead, do one of the following:

- Read your writing out loud.
- Alternatively, do the reading "aloud" in your head, perhaps moving your lips as you read.

In either case, listen for spots that do not read smoothly and clearly. You will probably be able to hear where your sentences should begin and end. You will then be more likely to find any fragments and run-ons that are present. Other spots that do not read smoothly may reveal other grammar or punctuation errors. Take the time needed to check such spots closely.

2 Read through your paper several times, looking for different types of errors in each reading. Here is a good sequence to follow:

- Look for sentence fragments, run-ons, and comma splices.
- Look for verb mistakes.
- Look for capital letter and punctuation mistakes.
- Look for missing words or missing *-s* endings.
- Look for spelling mistakes, including errors in homonyms.

This chapter will give you practice in proofreading for the above mistakes. In addition, as you proofread your work, you should watch for problems with pronoun and modifier use, word choice, and parallelism.

SENTENCE FRAGMENTS, RUN-ONS, AND COMMA SPLICES

Sentence Fragments

When proofreading for sentence fragments, remember to look for the following:

- Dependent-word fragments
- Fragments without subjects
- Fragments without a subject and a verb (*-ing* and *to* fragments, example fragments)

In general, correct a fragment by doing one of the following:

1. Connect the fragment to the sentence that comes before or after it.
2. Create a completely new sentence by adding a subject and/or a verb.

To further refresh your memory about fragments, turn to pages 81–101.

Run-On Sentences and Comma Splices

When proofreading for run-on sentences and comma splices, keep the following definitions in mind:

- A **run-on sentence** results when one complete thought is immediately followed by another, with nothing between them.
- A **comma splice** is made up of two complete thoughts that are incorrectly joined by only a comma.

To correct run-on sentences and comma splices, do one of the following:

1. Use a period and a capital letter to create separate sentences.
2. Use a comma plus a joining word (such as *and, but,* or *so*) to connect the two complete thoughts into one compound sentence.
3. Use a dependent word (see page 112) to make one of the complete thoughts dependent upon the other one.
4. Use a semicolon to connect the two complete thoughts.

To further refresh your memory about run-on sentences and comma splices, turn to pages 102–111 and 112–121.

Practice 1

Read each of the following short passages either aloud or to yourself. Each passage contains a sentence fragment, a run-on, or a comma splice. Find and underline the error. Then correct it in the space provided.

1. That bookcase is too heavy on top it could fall over. Take some of the big books off the highest shelf and put them on the bottom one.

   ____

   ____

2. The detective asked everyone to gather in the library. He announced that he had solved the mystery. And would soon reveal the name of the murderer. Suddenly the lights went out.

   ____

   ____

3. That rocking chair is very old. It belonged to my great-grandfather, he brought it to the United States from Norway. I like to think about all the people who have sat in it over the years.

   ____

   ____

4. Before you leave the house. Please close all the windows in case it rains. I don't want the carpet to get soaked.

   ____

   ____

5. Midori is from Taiwan, she uses the English name Shirley, which is easier for her American friends to say. Everyone in her family has both a Chinese and an English name.

   ____

   ____

6. My aunt took a trip on a boat off the coast of California. She wanted to see whales. Whales are always sighted there. At a certain time of the year.

   ____

   ____

7. For vacation this year, we are going to rent a cabin. It is on a lake in the mountains we can swim, fish, and sunbathe there. Everyone in the family is looking forward to that week.

   ____

   ____

8. Rosalie went to the hair salon on Friday. To get her long hair trimmed just a little. However, she changed her mind and had it cut very short.

____

____

9. The Webbs put a white carpet in their living room. Now they feel that was a foolish choice. Every bit of dirt or spilled food shows on the white surface. And is nearly impossible to get rid of.

____

____

10. That waiter is quick and hard working, he is not friendly with customers. For that reason, he doesn't get very good tips. His boss tells him to smile and be more pleasant, but he doesn't seem to listen.

____

____

COMMON VERB MISTAKES

When proofreading, look for the following common verb mistakes:

- The wrong past or past participle forms of irregular verbs (pages 48–59)
- Lack of subject-verb agreement (pages 60–69; 256–262)
- Needless shifts of verb tense (pages 274–280)

Practice 2

Read each of the following sentences either aloud or to yourself. Each contains a verb mistake. Find and cross out the error. Then correct it in the space provided.

_______ 1. Suzette loves to eat, but complained that she is always twenty pounds overweight.

_______ 2. There are a reason I haven't started my essay yet.

_______ 3. The frog leaps out of the pond and hopped into the bushes.

_______ 4. The lawnmowers is not on sale yet.

_______ 5. The man scratched his head after he bangs it on the pillar.

_______ 6. Neither of the books are worth reading.

_______ 7. The bird flied around the church steeple three times.

_______ 8. After the building burned to the ground, the city planners build another on the same spot.

_______ 9. The shrimp fishermen works seven days a week.

_______ 10. The old man breaked his leg after tripping on a loose rug.

CAPITAL LETTER AND PUNCTUATION MISTAKES

When proofreading, be sure the following begin with **capital letters**:

- The first word in a sentence or direct quotation
- The word *I* and people's names
- Family names
- Names of specific places and languages
- Names of specific groups
- Names of days of the week, months, and holidays (but not the seasons)
- Brand names
- Titles
- Names of specific school courses
- Names of historical periods and well-known events
- Opening and closing of a letter

When proofreading, look for **commas** in the following places:

- Between items in a series
- After introductory material
- Around words that interrupt the flow of a sentence
- Between complete thoughts connected by a joining word
- Before and/or after words of direct address and short expressions
- In dates, addresses, and letters

When proofreading, be sure **apostrophes** are used in the following:

- Contractions
- Possessives (but not in plurals or verbs)

When proofreading, look for quotation marks around direct quotations. Eliminate any quotation marks around indirect quotations.

Finally, remember to also watch for problems with colons, semicolons, hyphens, dashes, and parentheses.

To further refresh your memory, turn to "Capital Letters," pages 163–172; "The Comma," pages 122–132; "The Apostrophe," pages 133–142; "Quotation Marks," pages 143–153; and "Punctuation Marks," pages 189–195.

Practice 3

Read each of the following sentences either aloud or to yourself. Each sentence contains an error in capitalization, an error in comma or apostrophe use, or two missing quotation marks. Find the mistake, and correct it in the space provided.

______________ 1. "Where are the sunflower seeds? the man asked the store clerk. Also, do you have any whole wheat flour?"

______________ 2. All of these book's are overdue.

______________ 3. Even though I love sweets they do not always love me in return.

______________ 4. I havent seen my mother in over a year.

______________ 5. In the Winter, we love to go skiing.

______________ 6. Don't forget your raincoat, my mother reminded me.

______________ 7. We love charleston because there are so many things to do.

______________ 8. The waffle iron is hot, replied my brother.

______________ 9. I forgot to put the dogs collar on him, so he won't get lost.

______________ 10. My knapsack held books, pencils, paper and lunch.

MISSING *-S* ENDINGS AND MISSING WORDS

Since you know what you meant when you wrote something, it is easy for you not to notice when a word ending or even a whole word is missing. The following two sections will give you practice in proofreading for such omissions.

Missing *-s* Endings

When you proofread, remember the following about noun and verb endings:

- The plural form of most nouns ends in *s* (for example, two *cups* of coffee).
- Present tense verbs for the singular third-person subjects end with an *s*.

To further refresh your memory about the present tense, turn to pages 264–265.

Practice 4

Read each of the following sentences either aloud or to yourself. In each case an *-s* ending is needed on one of the nouns or verbs in the sentence. Find and cross out the error. Then correct it in the space provided, being sure to add the *s* to the word.

______________ 1. All of the pay telephone are gone.

______________ 2. You should check your front left tire because it look a little flat.

______________ 3. My uncle is always telling terrible joke.

______________ 4. Most barn are painted a dark red color.

_______________ **5.** Ella make new friends quite easily.

_______________ **6.** Luis got his job because he speak Spanish and English equally well.

_______________ **7.** The drugstore close at nine o'clock, but the other mall stores stay open till ten.

_______________ **8.** The grass always grow faster whenever we have a heavy summer rain.

_______________ **9.** There are two can of soda hidden on the shelf of the refrigerator.

_______________ **10.** Many red-haired people have freckle on their skin and also get sunburned quickly.

Missing Words

When you proofread, look for places where you may have omitted such short words as *a*, *of*, *the*, or *to*.

● Practice 5

Read each of the following sentences either aloud or to yourself. In each sentence, one of the following little words has been omitted:

a **and** **by** **of** **the** **to** **with**

Add a caret (‸) at the spot where the word is missing. Then write the missing word in the space provided.

Example ___of___ My new pair‸jeans is too tight.

_______________ **1.** Several pieces this puzzle are missing.

_______________ **2.** When she went to the grocery store, Louise forgot buy bread.

_______________ **3.** Some the programs on TV are too violent for children.

_______________ **4.** That orange shirt looks great the black pants.

_______________ **5.** I didn't think I had a chance of winning prize in the contest.

_______________ **6.** Paul plays both the piano the bass guitar.

_______________ **7.** Sandra became tired climbing up steep hill.

_______________ **8.** Everyone was surprised the school principal's announcement.

_______________ **9.** Do you drink your coffee cream or just sugar?

_______________ **10.** It's hard pay attention to a boring speaker.

HOMONYM MISTAKES

When proofreading, pay special attention to the spelling of words that are easily confused with other words.

To refresh your memory of the homonyms listed in this book, turn to pages 154–162 and 304–310.

● Practice 6

Read each of the following sentences either aloud or to yourself. Each sentence contains a mistake in a commonly confused word. Find and cross out the error. Then correct it in the space provided.

________ **1.** My cousin's dreams tormented him because they were always about his painful passed.

________ **2.** The dog continued to wag it's tail long after the petting had stopped.

________ **3.** I looked over their but could not figure out what my sister was pointing to.

________ **4.** I am going too the next level in this exercise routine if it kills me!

________ **5.** I am so tired of hearing they're sad stories that I wish my cousins would not phone so often.

________ **6.** Its a shame that the leftover restaurant food cannot always be given to the poor.

________ **7.** Please pick up you're dirty clothes off the bedroom floor.

________ **8.** Whose going to run the marathon next month?

________ **9.** If your going to continue skipping classes, you will flunk out of school.

________ **10.** John loved too cook all day but hated to clean up the kitchen.

A Note on Making Corrections in Your Papers

You can add minor corrections to the final draft of a paper and still hand it in. Just make the corrections neatly. Add missing punctuation marks right in the text, exactly where they belong. Draw a straight line through any words or punctuation you wish to eliminate or correct. Add new material by inserting a caret (^) at the point where the addition should be. Then write the new word or words above the line at that point. Here's an example of a sentence that was corrected during proofreading:

● Some Hondas are made in ~~japan~~ Japan, but others are made ^in this country.

Retype or recopy a paper if you discover a number of errors.

Practice 7

Here are five sentences, each of which contains **two** of the types of errors covered in this chapter. Correct the errors by crossing out or adding words or punctuation marks, as in the example above.

1. Helena is taking two english course in school this semester.

2. I feel sorry for Donnas dog, it lost a leg in a car accident.

3. Rusty cans, plastic bags, and scraps of wood washed up on deserted beach.

4. My mother take night classes at college, wear she is learning to use a computer.

5. When the power came back on. All the digital clocks in the house began to blink, the refrigerator motor started to hum.

35 Ten Proofreading Tests

Name ______________________________ Section ______________ Date ______________

Score: (Number right) _______ x 20 = ____________ %

Proofreading: TEST 1

Read the following passage either aloud or to yourself, looking for the following **five** mistakes:

- **1 fragment**
- **1 missing apostrophe**
- **1 missing word**
- **1 missing comma**
- **1 verb mistake**

Correct the mistakes, crossing out or adding words or punctuation marks as needed.

[1]When we moved our cat had a hard time. [2]She became agitated as soon as we began packing our boxes. [3]When the movers came, she hid and refused to come to us. [4]We locked her in empty room with food, water, and her bedding while the movers put our things in their truck. [5]We checked on her every so often, but she clearly was not a happy cat. [6]By the time we placed her in her carrier and in the car for the five-mile ride to the new house, shed begun to howl. [7]Unfortunately, escaping from the new room we placed her in on our arrival. [8]She shot out the door and was missing for two days. [9]By the time we found her, she is so glad to see us that she seemed to have decided that home was where her people were and settled right in.

Name ______________________ Section ____________ Date ____________

Score: (Number right) ________ x 20 = ____________ %

Proofreading: TEST 2

Read the following passage either aloud or to yourself, looking for the following **Five** mistakes:

1 comma splice
2 verb mistakes
1 missing word
1 homonym mistake

Correct the mistakes, crossing out or adding words or punctuation marks as needed.

[1]My aunt is the thriftiest person I have ever known. [2]She will do just about anything to save a penny. [3]For example, she never throws away old socks, she uses them as dust rags. [4]Instead of using a sandwich bag once and disposing of it, she wash and reuses it. [5]When she receives a gift, she carefully unwraps it without tearing the wrapping paper. [6]She'll use that paper to wrap next gift she gives. [7]Her old milk cartons become bird feeders. [8]Her tin cans become flowerpots. [9]Plastic bags from the grocery store becomes liners for her wastebaskets. [10]When her family's blue jeans are too worn out to where, she recycles them into cozy quilts for the beds. [11]She really is a model of thriftiness.

Name ______________________________ Section ____________ Date ____________

Score: (Number right) ______ x 20 = __________ %

Proofreading: TEST 3

Read the following passage either aloud or to yourself, looking for the following **five** mistakes:

2 fragments
1 comma splice
1 missing quotation mark
1 homonym mistake

Correct the mistakes, crossing out or adding words or punctuation marks as needed.

[1]My aunt bakes all of her family's bread. [2]She makes her own flour tortillas, pizza crusts, whole wheat bread, and even sourdough muffins. [3]She bakes her own bread for fun, for its superior nutritional content, and for thrift. [4]She has been making bread for so long that she does not use any recipes. [5]Instead, going by the "feel" of the dough. [6]Because of this approach, sometimes my aunt has too add additional ingredients to the dough to make sure the bread rises. [7]The bread will not rise properly if there is too much or too little flour in the dough. [8]So, most recipes call for adding flour during the kneading process, however, my aunt often has to do the reverse—knead in water to fix a too dry dough. [9]This is a step not included in standard recipes, but one that she herself has created through much experimentation. [10]In addition, experimenting with the process or ingredients each time so as not to be bored. [11]This results in no bread product from my aunt's kitchen ever being quite the same as another. [12]The problem with this creative process is that sometimes the bread is a great success, sometimes not. [13]My aunt, however, is very philosophical. [14]She says, "Food is foremost fuel for your body; eating bread that might be a little flat or chewy is just the price one pays for creativity.

Name ______________________________ Section ______________ Date ______________

Score: (Number right) ________ x 20 = ______________ %

Proofreading: TEST 4

Read the following passage either aloud or to yourself, looking for the following **six** mistakes:

1 fragment
1 missing comma
1 missing capital letter
1 missing apostrophe
2 verb mistakes

Correct the mistakes, crossing out or adding words or punctuation marks as needed.

[1]It was the first time I had visited the southern city, charleston, South Carolina. [2]I enjoyed walking through the historic areas and viewing the beautiful old mansions. [3]In addition, taking long walks along the waterfronts. [4]Civil War locations were abundant including Fort Sumter and Fort Moultrie. [5]What I also wanted to experience was authentic southern food. [6]Charleston is known for its fine food, and many of its restaurants signature dishes are centered around seafood. [7]However, as I am a vegetarian, I knew it might be more difficult for me to experience true southern cuisine. [8]Having done quite a bit of traveling to places, such as Germany and Poland, where meat is central to meals, I knew how to be creative. [9]By choosing several side dishes, appetizers, or extras, a vegetarian can usually had a lovely meal. [10]As I perused the menu in a popular Charleston seafood restaurant, I will notice several authentic southern dishes. [11]I felt full and satisfied after enjoying a meal of cheese grits, sweet iced tea, fried green tomatoes, and tomato and pimiento pie—all vegetarian and all authentically southern.

Name ______________________________ Section ______________ Date ______________

Score: (Number right) ________ x 20 = ______________ %

Proofreading: TEST 5

Read the following passage either aloud or to yourself, looking for the following **five** mistakes:

1 fragment
1 run-on sentence
1 missing comma
1 missing apostrophe
1 verb mistake

Correct the mistakes, crossing out or adding words or punctuation marks as needed.

[1]When a group of rare white lions arrived at the Philadelphia Zoo. [2]it was an exciting event. [3]The lions were the only ones of their kind in North America they soon became the zoo's most popular exhibit. [4]The lions are native to southern Africa. [5]They are so rare because of a problem caused by their unusual color. [6]Most lions, with their golden-brown color, can sneak through grass and trees without being detected. [7]But the moonlight shining on the white lions' coats make it difficult for them to hunt at night. [8]Its too easy for other animals to see them. [9]Therefore, most white lions in the wild starve to death. [10]Although all the white lions in Philadelphia are female the zoo is hoping to get a white male soon and raise a family of white lion cubs.

Name ______________________ Section ____________ Date ____________

Score: (Number right) ______ x 20 = __________ %

Proofreading: TEST 6

Read the following passage either aloud or to yourself, looking for the following **eleven** mistakes:

1 run-on sentence
1 missing *-s* ending
3 missing capital letters
1 missing quotation mark
2 verb mistakes
1 homonym mistake
1 spelling error
1 punctuation mistake

Correct the mistakes, crossing out or adding words or punctuation marks as needed.

[1]Ella and Stefan were on vacation in bali, indonesia. [2]They both love traveling to different countries. [3]They were also excited to learn how to surf. [4]When their plain landed and they took a taxi to their hotel, they decide to rest on the beach for a few hour. [5]Because of the 17-hour plane ride, they were very tired. [6]They slept on the beach until the stars and full moon came out when they awoke, they thought they were dreaming. [7]Ella said, "Let's go eat some delicious dinner! [8]Stefan agreed and added, "Are we really on the other side of the world." [9]The next day they hired a surfing instructer. [10]It was clear that Ella was the better surfer, but Stefan was lighthearted about it and made up a nickname for her. [11]He called her Surfella. [12]At the end of their week in bali, both Ella and Stefan agree it was the most beautiful place they had ever been.

Name ______________________________ Section ______________ Date ______________

Score: (Number right) ________ x 10 = ____________ %

Proofreading: TEST 7

Read the following passage either aloud or to yourself, looking for the following **ten** mistakes:

- **2 fragments**
- **2 comma splices**
- **2 missing apostrophes**
- **1 missing comma**
- **1 missing word**
- **1 homonym mistake**
- **1 verb mistake**

Correct the mistakes, crossing out or adding words or punctuation marks as needed.

[1]On TV, people who sleepwalk generally act like zombies, they stagger along with their arms held stiffly in front of them. [2]In fact (as you know if youve ever seen one), most sleepwalkers walk around quite normally. [3]They may even perform routine tasks. [4]Such as getting dressed or brushing their teeth. [5]Sometimes they talk, although there conversation may not make a lot of sense. [6]Sleepwalking is a fairly common behavior. [7]Especially among children. [8]It occurs during periods of very deep sleep. [9]In most cases, a person sleepwalks just a few times, then the sleepwalking stops forever. [10]If sleepwalking becomes a frequent problem the sleepwalker may need a doctors help. [11]What should you do if you see someone sleepwalking? [12]Leading the sleepwalker back bed is usually all that is necessary. [13]But if the sleepwalker be in danger of injury, gently wake him or her up.

Name ______________________ Section ____________ Date ____________

Score: (Number right) ______ x 10 = ________ %

Proofreading: TEST 8

Read the following passage either aloud or to yourself, looking for the following **ten** mistakes:

- **1 missing capital letter**
- **2 verb mistakes**
- **2 missing apostrophes**
- **2 homonym mistakes**
- **2 comma splices**
- **1 missing comma**

Correct the mistakes, crossing out or adding words or punctuation marks as needed.

[1]Normandy, France is a beautiful place. [2]Normandys beaches and surrounding areas are peaceful and breathtakingly lovely. [3]The city today could make anyone forget what transpired their over sixty years ago. [4]I visit Normandy on the sixtieth anniversary of the Normandy Invasion. [5]I stand in the american cemetery on a hill above the beach, thousands of American soldiers perished just below this hill. [6]Many were buried within a short distance of wear they fell. [7]Their gravestones reveal their extreme youth, they lived such short lives, some only eighteen or nineteen when they died. [8]The graves in neat rows, the green grass, and the beautiful flowers belie the chaos that transpired during the Normandy Invasion. [9]To stand there in the peacefulness and beauty now makes the soldiers sacrifice all the more poignant and profound.

Name ______________________________ Section ______________ Date ______________

Score: (Number right) _______ x 10 = ____________ %

Proofreading: TEST 9

Read the following passage either aloud or to yourself, looking for the following **ten** mistakes:

- **2 fragments**
- **2 run-on sentences**
- **1 comma splice**
- **2 missing apostrophes**
- **1 capital letter mistake**
- **2 verb mistakes**

Correct the mistakes, crossing out or adding words or punctuation marks as needed.

[1]Why would a lifelong meat eater become a vegetarian? [2]I became a vegetarian during a very gradual process. [3]I have always liked vegetables, grains, nuts, and beans, but they were, for years, secondary to meat. [4]I had gradually over a long period of time learned that I actually preferred meatless meals to those centered on animal products. [5]Sometimes, I would go a couple of months without having any meat or poultry at all. [6]I would, however, occasionally craved meat, have some, and then not crave it again for several months.

[7]My philosophy about meat also underwent a change. [8]Reading about animal rights groups and others who supported a vegetarian lifestyle. [9]I even start feeling sad when I saw pictures of lambs, cows, or pigs being sent for slaughter. [10]Then one day in response to a friend asking me if I wanted a ham sandwich, I said, “No thanks; I am a vegetarian.” [11]Previously, I had always had fried chicken for my birthday, even though I did not have meat other times. [12]A tradition to have fried chicken, mashed potatoes, coleslaw, and biscuits every March 16. [13]My last birthday, I had all of those other foods, but I had soy chicken patties instead of the fried chicken. [14]A famous celebrity and

Name ______________________ Section ____________ Date ____________

Score: (Number right) ______ x 10 = __________ %

vegetarian once said, "No one has to die for my lunch" I agree with that sentiment. [15]Former beatle Paul McCartney embraced being a vegetarian by saying it was one of the best choices an individual could make for the planet.

[16]There are so many reasons to be a vegetarian, including creating really healthy dishes from nonanimal-based sources. [17]Additionally, Ive lost twenty pounds and never felt better physically and mentally. [18]The process of becoming a vegetarian was gradual and life changing. [19]I believe the world would be a finer and more peaceful place if no one killed any fellow beings, but that is just my theory, the rest of the world might take some time to reach the same conclusion.

Name ______________________________ Section ____________ Date ____________

Score: (Number right) ______ x 10 = __________ %

Proofreading: TEST 10

Read the following passage either aloud or to yourself, looking for the following **ten** mistakes:

1 fragment
1 run-on
1 missing capital
3 missing commas
2 missing apostrophes
1 verb mistake
1 homonym mistake

Correct the mistakes, crossing out or adding words or punctuation marks as needed.

[1]One of the most amazing things about the Internet is the way it makes a hole world of facts available to you. [2]Have you ever wondered for instance what that little bump of flesh just in front of your ear canal is called? [3]Go to the Internet and type in the name "Google," which is a good search engine. [4]In the Google search field, type "What is the bump in front of the ear called?" [5]In less than a second, youve learned that little bump is called the "tragus." [6]And by the way, the pale half-moon at the base of your fingernail is the "lunula." [7]You dont even have to search for weird, interesting facts. [8]Just go to one of the hundreds of trivia sites online and read the items collected there. [9]Thanks to such sites, I now know that Murphy's Oil Soap is what most zookeepers use to wash their elephants. [10]Believe it or not, the people of Des Moines, Iowa, eats more Jell-O than the people of any other city. [11]Another interesting fact is that more films have been made about dracula than about any other fictional character. [12]Getting weird facts off the Internet can be habit-forming you may find it very hard to stop with just one . . . or two . . . or ten. [13]Before you know it you have spent an hour at the computer. [14]And completely forgotten what you wanted to look up in the first place.

PART FOUR Related Matters

PART FOUR
Related Matters

PREVIEW

Part Four includes two chapters that will further strengthen your English skills:

36 Spelling Improvement

This chapter explains the following ways to improve your spelling:

1 Use the dictionary and other spelling aids
2 Keep a personal spelling list
3 Learn commonly confused words
4 Learn some helpful spelling rules
   a *I* before *E* rule
   b Silent *E* rule
   c *Y* rule
   d Doubling rule
   e Rules for adding *-es* to nouns and verbs that end in *s, sh, ch,* or *x*
   f Rules for adding *-es* to nouns and verbs ending in a consonant plus *y*

USE THE DICTIONARY AND OTHER SPELLING AIDS

The single most important way to improve your spelling is to get into the habit of checking words in a dictionary. But you may at times have trouble locating a given word. "If I can't spell a word," you might ask, "how can I find it in the dictionary?" The answer is that you have to guess what the letters might be.

Here are some hints to help you make informed guesses.

Hint 1

If you're not sure about the vowels in a word, you will have to experiment. Vowels often sound the same. So try an *i* in place of an *a*, an *e* in place of an *i*, and so on.

Hint 2

Consonants are sometimes doubled in a word. If you can't find your word with single consonants, try doubling them.

Hint 3

In the box on the following page are groups of letters or letter combinations that often sound alike. If your word isn't spelled with one of the letters in a pair or group shown in the box on the following page, it might be spelled with another in the same pair or group. For example, if it isn't spelled with a *k*, it may be spelled with a *c*.

Vowels					
ai / ay	**au / aw**	**ee / ea**	**ou / ow**	**oo / u**	
Consonants					
c / k	**c / s**	**f / ph**	**g / j**	**sch / sc / sk**	**s / z**
Combinations					
re / ri	**able / ible**	**ent / ant**	**er / or**	**tion / sion**	

Practice 1

Use your dictionary and the above hints to find the correct spelling of the following words.

1. divelop ________________
2. diferent ________________
3. sertain ________________
4. chearful ________________
5. sergery ________________
6. skedule ________________
7. fony ________________
8. comfortible ________________
9. mayer ________________
10. paiment ________________
11. aukward ________________
12. photografy ________________
13. asemble ________________
14. seazon ________________
15. dependant ________________
16. terrable ________________
17. dezign ________________
18. rilease ________________
19. funcsion ________________
20. awthor ________________

In addition to a dictionary, take advantage of a spelling checker on your computer. Also, pocket-size electronic spelling checkers are widely available.

KEEP A PERSONAL SPELLING LIST

In a special place, write down every word you misspell. Include its correct spelling, underline the difficult part of the word, and add any hints you can use to remember how to spell it. If spelling is a particular problem for you, you might even want to start a spelling notebook that has a separate page for each letter of the alphabet.

Here's one format you might use:

	How I spelled it	*Correct spelling*	*Hints*
	recieve	*receive*	*I before E except after C*
	seperate	*separate*	*There's A RAT in sepARATe*
	alot	*a lot*	*Two words (like "a little")*
	alright	*all right*	*Two words (like "all wrong")*

Study your list regularly, and refer to it whenever you write and proofread a paper.

LEARN COMMONLY CONFUSED WORDS

Many spelling errors result from words that sound alike or almost alike but that are spelled differently, such as *break* and *brake*, *wear* and *where*, or *right* and *write*. To avoid such errors, study carefully the list of words on pages 154–162 and 304–310.

LEARN SOME HELPFUL SPELLING RULES

Even poor spellers can improve by following a few spelling rules.
Following are **six** rules that apply to many words.

RULE #1
I before E rule

I** before **E** except after **C
Or when sounded like *A*, as in *neighbor* and *weigh*.

	I before E	*Except after C*	*Or when sounded like A*
Examples	belief, chief field	receive, ceiling	vein, eight

Exceptions to the above rule include: either, leisure, foreign, science, society

Practice 2

A. Complete each word with either *ie* or *ei*.

1. dec_____ve
2. bel_____ve
3. br_____f
4. fr_____ght
5. c_____ling
6. pr_____st
7. cash_____r
8. w_____gh
9. p_____ce
10. r_____ndeer

B. In each sentence, fill in the blank with either ***ie*** or ***ei***.

11. I rec_____ved some interesting junk mail today.

12. Many of the people in my n_____ghborhood are retired.

13. Norma never gave up her bel_____f in her husband's innocence.

14. What do you like to do in your l_____sure time?

15. There's a lot of traffic now, so don't ignore this y_____ld sign.

16. The r_____gn of Queen Victoria of Great Britain lasted over sixty years.

17. My parents are working hard to ach_____ve their retirement goals.

18. I have never traveled to any for_____gn countries.

19. My _____ghty-year-old grandfather still does a daily twenty pushups.

20. A th_____f broke into Parker's Bakery last night and stole all the dough.

RULE #2
Silent *E* rule

If a word ends in a silent (unpronounced) *e*, drop the *e* before adding an ending that starts with a vowel. Keep the *e* when adding an ending that begins with a consonant.

	Drop the e with endings that start with a vowel	*Keep the e with endings that start with a consonant*
Examples	like + ed = liked	love + ly = lovely
	confuse + ing = confusing	shame + ful = shameful
	fame + ous = famous	hope + less = hopeless
	guide + ance = guidance	manage + ment = management

Exceptions include: noticeable, argument, judgment, truly

Practice 3

A. Write out each word shown.

1. abuse + ing = ________________

2. hope + ed = ________________

3. have + ing = ________________

4. desire + able = ________________

5. ridicule + ous = ________________

6. sincere + ity = ________________

B. Write out each word shown.

7. sincere + ly = ________________

8. peace + ful = ________________

9. advance + ment = ________________

10. noise + less = ________________

11. large + ness = ________________

12. grace + ful = ________________

13. bare + ly = ________________

C. Write out each word shown.

14. write + ing = ________________

15. care + ful = ________________

16. safe + ly = ________________

17. hire + ed = ________________

18. serve + ing = ________________

19. notice + able = ________________

20. excite + ment = ________________

RULE #3
Y rule

Change the final *y* of a word to *i* when both of the following are present:

a the last two letters of the word are a consonant plus *y*. (Keep a *y* that follows a vowel.)

b the ending being added begins with a vowel or is *-ful*, *-ly*, or *-ness*.

Exception Keep the *y* if the ending being added is *-ing*.

	Change the y to i	*Keep the y*
Examples	happy + ness = happiness	destroy + s = destroys
	lucky + ly = luckily	display + ed = displayed
	beauty + ful = beautiful	gray + ed = grayed
	try + ed = tried	try + ing = trying
	carry + er = carrier	carry + ing = carrying

Practice 4

A. Write out each word shown.

1. rely + ed = ____________________
2. holy + ness = ____________________
3. play + ful = ____________________
4. cry + ing = ____________________
5. cry + ed = ____________________
6. plenty + ful = ____________________
7. lazy + ness = ____________________
8. fly + ing = ____________________
9. angry + ly = ____________________
10. betray + ed = ____________________

B. Write out each word shown.

11. stay + ing = ________________ stay + ed = ________________
12. busy + est = ________________ busy + ly = ________________
13. silly + er = ________________ silly + ness = ________________
14. employ + ed = ________________ employ + er = ________________
15. bury + ing = ________________ bury + ed = ________________
16. dry + ing = ________________ dry + ed = ________________
17. happy + ly = ________________ happy + er = ________________
18. funny + er = ________________ funny + est = ________________
19. satisfy + ing = ________________ satisfy + ed = ________________
20. annoy + ed = ________________ annoy + ance = ________________

RULE #4
Doubling rule

Double the final consonant of a word before adding an ending when all three of the following are present:

a The last three letters of the word are a consonant, a vowel, and a consonant (CVC).

b The word is only one syllable (for example, *stop*) or is accented on the last syllable (for example, *begin*).

c The ending being added begins with a vowel.

	One-syllable words that end in CVC	*Words accented on the last syllable that end in CVC*
Examples	stop + ed = stopped	begin + ing = beginning
	flat + er = flatter	control + er = controller
	red + est = reddest	occur + ence = occurrence

Practice 5

A. First note whether each one-syllable word ends in the CVC pattern or with another pattern (VVC, VCC, etc.), and write the pattern in the first column. Then add to each word the endings shown.

	Word	Pattern of Last Three Letters	*-ed*	*-ing*
Examples	trip	________	________	________
	growl	________	________	________
1.	jog	________	________	________
2.	learn	________	________	________
3.	slam	________	________	________
4.	wrap	________	________	________
5.	rain	________	________	________
6.	dot	________	________	________
7.	flood	________	________	________
8.	beg	________	________	________
9.	clip	________	________	________
10.	burn	________	________	________

B. First note whether each two-syllable word ends in the CVC pattern or with another pattern (VVC, VCC, etc.), and write the pattern in the first column. Then add to each word the endings shown. *If a word ends in CVC, remember to check to see if the final syllable is stressed or not.*

	Word	Pattern of Last Three Letters	-ed	-ing
Examples	admit	______	______	______
	recall	______	______	______
11.	expel	______	______	______
12.	perform	______	______	______
13.	enter	______	______	______
14.	omit	______	______	______
15.	murder	______	______	______
16.	prefer	______	______	______
17.	occur	______	______	______
18.	explain	______	______	______
19.	submit	______	______	______
20.	reason	______	______	______

RULE #5
Rules for adding *-es* to nouns and verbs that end in *s*, *sh*, *ch*, or *x*

Most plurals are formed by adding *-s* to the singular noun, but in some cases *-es* is added. For nouns that end in *s, sh, ch,* or *x,* form the plural by adding *-es.*

Examples

kiss + es = kisses
coach + es = coaches
wish + es = wishes
tax + es = taxes

Most third-person singular verbs end in *-s* (he runs, she sings, it grows). But for verbs that end in *s, sh, ch,* or *x,* form the third-person singular with *-es.*

Examples

miss + es = misses
catch + es = catches
wash + es = washes
mix + es = mixes

Practice 6

Add *-s* or *-es* as needed to each of the following words.

1. bush ____________________
2. mix ____________________
3. pitch ____________________
4. glass ____________________
5. carpet ____________________
6. crash ____________________
7. box ____________________
8. watch ____________________
9. shine ____________________
10. business ____________________

RULE #6
Rules for adding *-es* to nouns and verbs that end in a consonant plus *y*

For nouns that end in a consonant plus *y*, form the plural by changing the *y* to *i* and adding *-es.*

Examples fly + es = fl**ies** lady + es = lad**ies**
canary + es = canar**ies**

For verbs that end in a consonant plus *y*, form the third-person singular by changing the *y* to *i* and adding *-es.*

Examples pity + es =pit**ies** marry + es = marr**ies**
bully + es = bull**ies**

Practice 7

Add *-s* or *-es* as needed to each of the following words. Where appropriate, change a final *y* to *i* before adding *-es.*

1. army ____________________
2. try ____________________
3. tray ____________________
4. hurry ____________________
5. attorney ____________________
6. variety ____________________
7. chimney ____________________
8. baby ____________________
9. journey ____________________
10. sympathy ____________________

Final Practice 1

Use the spelling rules in the chapter to write out the words indicated.

A. Complete each word with either *ie* or *ei.*

1. gr_____f **3.** n_____ghbor **5.** rel_____ve

2. dec_____ve **4.** fr_____nd

B. Use the *silent e* rule to write out each word shown.

6. time + ed = __________ **9.** fame + ous = __________

7. time + ly = __________ **10.** change + ing = __________

8. hope + ful = __________

C. Use the *Y* rule to write out each word shown.

11. fry + ed = __________ **14.** duty + ful = __________

12. easy + ly = __________ **15.** lonely + ness = __________

13. stay + ed = __________

D. Use the *doubling* rule to write out each word shown.

16. drop + ing = __________ **19.** jump + er = __________

17. pad + ing = __________ **20.** sad + est = __________

18. prefer + ed = __________

E. Add *-s* or *-es* as needed to each of the following words. Where appropriate, change a final *y* to *i* before adding *-es.*

21. box __________ **24.** valley __________

22. enemy __________ **25.** porch __________

23. country __________

Final Practice 2

Use the spelling rules in the chapter to write out the words indicated.

A. Complete each word with either *ie* or *ei.*

1. conc_____ve **3.** sobr_____ty **5.** ch_____f

2. f_____ld **4.** v_____n

B. Use the *silent e* rule to write out each word shown.

6. come + ing = _______________ **9.** accurate + ly = _______________

7. care + less = _______________ **10.** choose + ing = _______________

8. desire + able = _______________

C. Use the *Y* rule to write out each word shown.

11. reply + ed = _______________ **14.** glory + ous = _______________

12. pray + ing = _______________ **15.** study + ed = _______________

13. carry + ed = _______________

D. Use the *doubling* rule to write out each word shown.

16. bark + ing = _______________ **19.** mop + ed = _______________

17. rob + er = _______________ **20.** refer + ing = _______________

18. commit + ed = _______________

E. Add *-s* or *-es* as needed to each of the following words. Where appropriate, change a final *y* to *i* before adding *-es.*

21. city _______________ **24.** dress _______________

22. branch _______________ **25.** puppy _______________

23. subway _______________

37 Dictionary Use

OWNING A GOOD DICTIONARY

It is a good idea to own two dictionaries. The first dictionary should be a paperback that you can carry with you. Any of the following would be an excellent choice:

The American Heritage Dictionary, paperback edition
The Random House Dictionary, paperback edition
Webster's New World Dictionary, paperback edition

Your second dictionary should be a full-sized, hardcover edition, which should be kept in the room where you study. All the above dictionaries come in hardbound versions, which contain a good deal more information than the paperback editions. You can also access dictionaries online.

UNDERSTANDING DICTIONARY ENTRIES

Each word listed alphabetically in a dictionary is called an **entry word**. Here is a typical dictionary entry word:

> **thun•der** (thŭn′dər) *n.* **1.** The sound that follows lightning and is caused by rapidly expanding air in the path of the electrical discharge. **2.** A loud sound like thunder. —*v.* **1.** To produce a sound resembling thunder. **2.** To express in a loud or threatening way. —**thun′der•ous** *adj.*

Spelling and Syllables

The dictionary first gives the correct spelling and syllable breakdown of a word. Dots separate the words into syllables. Each syllable is a separate sound, and each sound includes a vowel. In the entry shown above, *thunder* is divided into two syllables.

● Practice 1

Use your dictionary to separate the following words into syllables. Put a slash (/) between each syllable and the next. Then write the number of syllables in each word. The first one is done for you as an example.

1. g u a r / a n / t e e ___3___ syllables

2. m o l e c u l e ______ syllables

3. v o c a b u l a r y ______ syllables

4. c a u l i f l o w e r ______ syllables

Pronunciation Symbols and Accent Marks

Most dictionary entry words are followed first by a pronunciation guide in parentheses, as in the entry for thunder:

thun•der (thŭn′dər)

The information in parentheses includes two kinds of symbols: *pronunciation symbols* and *accent marks.* Following is an explanation of each.

Pronunciation Symbols

The pronunciation symbols tell the sounds of consonants and vowels in a word. The sounds of the consonants are probably familiar to you, but you may find it helpful to review the vowel sounds. Vowels are the letters *a, e, i, o, u,* and sometimes *y.* To know how to pronounce the vowel sounds, use the **pronunciation key** in your dictionary. Such a key typically appears at the front of a dictionary or at the bottom of every other page of the dictionary. Here is a pronunciation key for the vowels and a few other sounds that often confuse dictionary users.

Pronunciation Guide

ă h**a**t	ā s**ay**	â d**ar**e	ĕ t**e**n	ē sh**e**	ĭ s**i**t	ī t**ie**, m**y**
ŏ l**o**t	ō g**o**	ô **a**ll	oi **oi**l	o͝o l**oo**k	o͞o c**oo**l	
th **th**in	*th* **th**is	ŭ **u**p	ûr f**ur**	yo͞o **u**se	ə **a**go, eas**i**ly	

The key tells you, for instance, that the sound of ă (called "short a") is pronounced like the *a* in *hat,* the sound of ā (called "long a") is pronounced like the *ay* in *say,* and so on. All the vowels with a cup-shaped symbol above them are called **short vowels.** All the vowels with a horizontal line above them are called **long vowels.** Note that long vowels have the sound of their own name. For example, long *a* sounds like the name of the letter *a.*

To use the above key, first find the symbol of the sound you wish to pronounce. For example, suppose you want to pronounce the short *i* sound. Locate the short *i* in the key and note how the sound is pronounced in the short word (*sit*) that appears next to the short *i.* This tells you that the short *i* has the sound of the *i* in the word *sit.* The key also tells you, for instance, that the short *e* has the sound of the *e* in the word *ten,* that the short *o* has the sound of the *o* in the word *lot,* and so on.

Finally, note that the last pronunciation symbol in the key looks like an upside-down e: ə. This symbol is known as the **schwa.** As you can see by the words that follow it, the schwa has a very short sound that sounds much like "uh" (as in ***a**go*) or "ih" (as in *eas**i**ly*).

Practice 2

Refer to the pronunciation key to answer the questions about the following words. Circle the letter of each of your answers.

1. **hic•cup** (hĭk′ŭp)
   The *i* in *hiccup* sounds like the *i* in
   a. pit. **b.** pie.
2. **si•lent** (sī′lənt)
   The *i* in *silent* sounds like the *i* in
   a. pit. **b.** pie.
3. **na•tive** (nā′tĭv)
   The *a* in *native* sounds like the *a* in
   a. father. **b.** pay.
4. **lot•ter•y** (lŏt′ə-rē)
   The *o* in *lottery* sounds like the *o* in
   a. pot. **b.** for.

Practice 3

Use your dictionary to find and write in the pronunciation symbols for the following words. Make sure you can pronounce each word. The first word has been done for you as an example.

1. reluctant *rĭ-lŭk′tənt*
2. homicide ____________
3. extravagant ____________
4. unanimous ____________

Accent Marks

Notice the mark in the pronunciation guide for *thunder* that is similar to an apostrophe:

thun•der (thŭn′dər)

The dark mark (′) is a bold accent mark, and it shows which syllable has the stronger stress. That means the syllable it follows is pronounced a little louder than the others. Syllables without an accent mark are unstressed. Some syllables are in between, and they are marked with a lighter accent mark (′).

The word *recognize,* for example, is accented like this:

rec•og•nize (rĕk′əg-nīz′)

Say *recognize* to yourself. Can you hear that the strongest accent is on *rec,* the first syllable? Can you hear that the last syllable, *nize,* is also accented but not as strongly? If not, say the word to yourself again until you hear the differences in accent sounds.

Practice 4

Answer the questions following each of the words below.

1. **pep·per·mint** (pĕp′ər-mĭnt′)
   a. How many syllables are in *peppermint*? __________
   b. Which syllable is most strongly accented? __________
2. **in·ter·me·di·ate** (ĭn′tər-mē′dē-ĭt)
   a. How many syllables are in *intermediate*? __________
   b. Which syllable is most strongly accented? __________
3. **in·her·it** (ĭn-hĕr′ĭt)
   a. How many syllables are in *inherit*? __________
   b. Which syllable is accented? __________
4. **con·tra·dic·tion** (kŏn′trə-dĭk′shən)
   a. How many syllables are in *contradiction*? __________
   b. Which syllable is most strongly accented? __________

Parts of Speech

Every word in the dictionary is either a noun, a verb, an adjective, or another part of speech. In dictionary entries, the parts of speech are shown by abbreviations in italics. In the entry for *thunder*, for example, the abbreviations *n.* and *v.* tell us that thunder can be both a noun and a verb.

When a word is more than one part of speech, the dictionary gives the definitions for each part of speech separately. In the above entry for thunder, the abbreviation telling us that thunder is a noun comes right after the pronunciation symbols; the two noun definitions follow. When the noun meanings end, the abbreviation *v.* tells us that the verb definitions will follow.

Parts of speech are abbreviated in order to save space. Following are common abbreviations for parts of speech.

n.—noun	*v.*—verb
pron.—pronoun	*conj.*—conjunction
adj.—adjective	*prep.*—preposition
adv.—adverb	*interj.*—interjection

Irregular Verb Forms and Irregular Spellings

After the part of speech, special information is given in entries for irregular verbs, for adjectives with irregularly spelled forms, and for irregularly spelled plurals.

For **irregular verbs**, the dictionary gives the past tense, the past participle, and the present participle. For example, the entry for *blow* shows that *blew* is the past tense, *blown* is the past participle, and *blowing* is the present participle.

blow (blō) *v.* **blew** (bloo), **blown** (blōn), **blowing.**

For **adjectives with irregularly spelled forms**, the comparative (used when comparing two things) and the superlative (used when comparing three or more things) are shown after the part of speech. The entry for *skinny*, for instance, shows that the comparative form of that adjective is *skinnier* and the superlative form is *skinniest.*

skin•ny (skĭn'ē) *adj.* **-ni•er, -ni•est.**

Irregular plural spellings are also included in this spot in an entry. For example, after the part of speech, the entry for *party* tells us that this word's plural ends in *-ies.*

par•ty (pär'tē) *n., pl.* **-ties.**

Definitions

Words often have more than one meaning. When they do, their definitions may be numbered in the dictionary. You can tell which definition of a word fits a given sentence by the meaning of the sentence. For example, the following are dictionary definitions for the verb form of *surprise*:

1 To take unawares.
2 To attack suddenly and unexpectedly.
3 To astonish or amaze with the unexpected.

Which of these definitions best fits the sentence below?

The soldiers *surprised* the enemy troops, who had bedded down for the night.
The answer is definition 2: The soldiers *suddenly attacked* the enemy troops.

Practice 5

A. Use your dictionary to answer the questions below about *obstinate.*

1. Which syllable in *obstinate* is most strongly accented? __________
2. How many syllables are in the word *obstinate*? __________
3. How many *schwa* sounds are in the word *obstinate*? __________
4. Does the first syllable in *obstinate* have a long or short *o* sound? __________
5. Which definition of *obstinate* applies in the following sentence? (Write out the full definition from your dictionary.)

   Felicia stayed home all week with an *obstinate* case of the flu.

   Definition: ____

   ____

B. Use your dictionary to answer the questions below about *solitary.*

6. How many syllables are in the word *solitary*? __________
7. Which syllable in *solitary* is most strongly accented? __________
8. Does the first syllable in *solitary* have a long or short *o* sound? __________
9. Which definition of *solitary* applies in the following sentence? (Write out the full definition from your dictionary.)

   The box of cookies was bought yesterday, and today there's only a *solitary* cookie remaining.

   Definition: ____

   ____

10. Which definition of *solitary* applies in the following sentence? (Write out the full definition from your dictionary.)

    Some people like to study in groups, but Sarita prefers *solitary* study.

    Definition: ____

    ____

Index